COLLECTOR'S GUIDE TO
CHILDREN'S BOOKS
1850 TO 1950
IDENTIFICATION & VALUES

Diane McClure Jones & Rosemary Jones

COLLECTOR BOOKS

A Division of Schroeder Publishing Co., Inc.

Cover design: Beth Summers
Book design: Joyce Cherry

⸺ ✦⇒ Searching For A Publisher? ⇐✦ ⸺

We are always looking for knowledgeable people considered to be experts within their fields. If you feel that there is a real need for a book on your collectible subject and have a large comprehensive collection, contact Collector Books.

Additional copies of this book may be ordered from:

COLLECTOR BOOKS
P.O. Box 3009
Paducah, Kentucky 42002-3009

@$18.95. Add $2.00 for postage and handling.

Copyright: Diane McClure Jones & Rosemary Jones, 1997

Printed in the U.S.A. by Image Graphics

— ⋆⇛ Contents ⇚⋆ —

—— ✺ Acknowledgments ✺ ——

We would like to thank the many helpful dealers at the 1995 Seattle Antiquarian Book Fair who gave generously of their time and shared their knowledge with us, and special thanks to Kirk Stines, Al Worden at Seattle Book Center, Shorey Books, Westside Story Books, all located in Seattle, and thank you, Fortners Books of Bainbridge, and a big thanks to Suzanne and Truman Price of Monmouth, Oregon.

For generosity beyond the call of friendship, thanks to Sabrina Urquhart, Kris Walberg, Yvonne Walberg, and Lynn Beltz who loaned us books from their private collections to use for the illustrations.

Introduction

When we told our friends, relatives, and fellow book collectors that we'd taken on the assignment of writing a price guide to children's books, we received various reactions. Our friends and relatives, accustomed to navigating around our overflowing bookshelves, thought this was a natural extension of our interests. Book collectors and dealers said things like "good idea" or "what a job," and very generously allowed us to remove book after book from their shelves to check prices, dates, and other information. Then everybody asked, "But how do you decide what to put in and what to leave out?"

It's a very good question, and we have several answers. First, we tried to put in those books that we actually saw and touched, books from our own collections, the collections of friends, and books seen at various shops. This let us confirm with our own eyes not only the details but also the quality and probable value. When this wasn't possible, we relied on recent auction or dealers' catalogs.

Second, we tried to confine our listings to books that were written primarily for children's entertainment. We find that many collectors, including ourselves, still read and greatly enjoy the stories of Wonderland, Oz, and Honey Bears. The initial purchase of their collections is almost always a book that they loved as a child.

Finally, we chose to cover only 100 years of publishing for children, 1850 to 1950. Finding children's books printed prior to 1850 is difficult and often they are too expensive for the average collector. After 1950, the quality of printing dropped as children's books entered a rather dull era marked by good writing but little or no illustration. While certain post–1950 authors or illustrators are becoming collectible, the prices for these books still seem to be highly speculative and many books are just coming into the secondary market. In other words, for this post–1950 market,

you're just as likely to find a particular title for a quarter at a garage sale as for $100 at an antiques mall.

Having made these rules, we stretched them at times for no better reason than we couldn't bear to leave out certain titles. We spent hours on the phone (thank heavens we are in the same area code) arguing about whether a title belonged or not. We slipped in a few books, like *Tarzan and the Jewels* of *Opar* which was originally written for adults, because they had brightened our own childhood afternoons.

And some books we added because our friends said, "But you have to put this in! I loved this book as a kid."

Beyond placing a value on certain books, we wanted to help collectors learn a little more about their collections. Sections in the back of this book include short biographies of well-known and lesser known children's book illustrators, a few facts about some of the publishers, including help in identifying their first editions; and some other resources for research including our favorite Internet newsgroup and Web site.

In the course of doing this book, we added several new titles to our collections. We hope that you, too, will be inspired to pull out old friends from under the bed or in the attic trunk, stoop a little lower at the local bookstore to peer at the shelves marked "Children's," and discover some true treasures.

We'd love to hear your suggestions for future price guides. Please address your comments to Rosemary Jones, 600 W. McGraw #2, Seattle, WA 98119, e-mail: healingpgs@aol.com.

Rosemary Jones
Diane McClure Jones

Explanation of Pricing

Prices of collectible books vary dramatically, due to changes in popularity of items. The revival of interest in an old novel for any reason, such as the production of a film based on the story, can either create or increase demand.

We have based our prices on suggested prices received from a number of antiquarian book dealers.

All quoted prices are for books in good condition but *without* dust jackets.

Good condition means clean, sound cover and spine without breaks or furred edges, clean undamaged pages, all pages and illustrations tightly attached. Price adjustments should be made for fingerprints, small tears, loose pages. Large reductions are made for broken and seriously damaged covers, loose and missing pages, torn pages, water stains and mold. In the case of children's books, other common damage found includes pencil and crayon marks.

Dust jackets: The value of a dust jacket on a child's book is often in proportion to its possible availability. The older the book and the younger the reader, the more valuable the dust jacket. In other words, a dust jacket for a 1920s picture book is harder to find than a dust jacket for a 1940s picture book. And a 1920s series book, written for twelve-year-olds, is more apt to still have its dust jacket than a picture book of that same era, written for four-year-olds.

A dust jacket in good condition can double or triple the price of a picture book.

A dust jacket in good condition can add 50% to the price of a book for twelve-year-old readers.

First editions are noted. First state and other specific variations that dramatically alter the price of a particular volume have not been considered.

This type of information is so specific and detailed that it needs to be obtained by the collector from a source specializing in a particular collection, such as a dealer or a club for collectors of a specific category. An example of this type of source is the International Wizard of Oz Club which published the *Bibliographia Oziana*, which describes in detail the editions, states, and specific variations found in Oz books. It does not, however, include price information, and is not available to non-members.

Illustrations are a major factor in determining the price of a children's book. The illustrator is the major factor; the number and condition of the illustrations is the secondary factor.

Rare books are designated as such in the listings and not priced. A rare book is one that is extremely difficult to find, and the price is usually determined at the time of the sale. It will often depend solely on how much an individual collector wants the book. Auction prices can go into the thousands of dollars for a particular sale to a particular customer, but that price may never be paid again for an identical volume and is therefore not a reliable guide to pricing.

Investments: Because of the fragile nature of paper and the "well-handled" condition of most children's books, most collectors collect children's books for the joy of finding and owning them. Some of them may be excellent investments. Some may lose value. Since we cannot guess which books will increase in value and which will decrease, we have in our own collections books that we love and acquired for their content rather than their potential monetary value.

Prices are for books in good condition but without dust jackets. See page 6 for further information on pricing. Dates following titles refer to the date of publication of the particular edition described. (Dates in parentheses indicate year of first copyright or first publication.)

A

ABBOTT, Jacob, 1803 – 1879, see Series, "Rollo and Florence."

ABBOTT, Jane
Aprilly, 1921, Lippincott, impressed design on cloth cover, illustrations . $15.00
Polly Put the Kettle On, 1925. $15.00
Red Robin, 1922, Lippincott, b/w illustrations by Harriet Richards. $15.00

ADAMS, Eustace
Over the Polar Ice, An Andy Lane Story, 1928, Grosset. $10.00

ADAMS, Frank, illustrator (nursery rhyme picture book)
The Frog Who Would A-Wooing Go (first published in 1904 by Blackie, Scotland), ca. 1912 edition, Dodge, NY, oversize, color paste-on pictorial cover, color endpapers and illustrations by author. $45.00

ADAMS, Katherine
Midsummer, 1921, Macmillan, b/w illustrations by Caswell. $20.00

ADDINGTON, Sarah, 1891 – 1940
Great Adventure of Mrs. Santa Claus, 1923, Little Brown, color illustrations. $35.00
Round the Year in Pudding Lane, 1924, Little Brown, illustrations. $35.00

ADE, George
Slim Princess, 1907, Bobbs Merrill, color paste-on pictorial cover, color plate illustrations by George F. Kerr. $25.00

1913 Platt edition

AESOP, ca. 500 B.C., see Crane, Walter.
Aesop's Fables, printed in English (1484) by William Caxton, has been produced in numerous nineteenth and twentieth century editions. Value depends on binding, illustrator, translator.
Aesop's Fables, 1848 edition, Coates, illustrations by John Tenniel. $150.00
Aesop's Fables, 1912 edition, Doubleday, translat-

ed by Vernon Jones, illustrated by Arthur Rackham. $100.00

Aesop's Fables, 1913 edition, Platt & Peck, color plate illustrations by J. M. Conde. $45.00

Aesop's Fables, ca. 1947, Grosset Dunlap, full-color wraparound illustration paper-on-boards cover, color frontispiece, 8 color plates plus b/w illustrations by Fritz Kredel. $20.00

AKERS, Floyd (L. Frank Baum), see Series, "Boy Fortune Hunters."

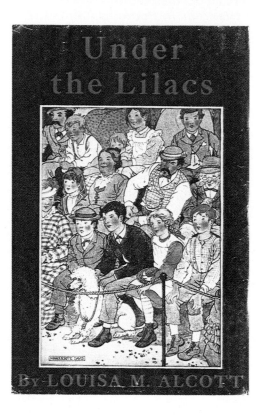

ALCOTT, Louisa May, b. Germantown, PA, 1832 – 1888

(Alcott's novels were written as individual books, but gained such wide popularity that they are often added as individual books to series or bundled into a series of their own, especially the books that contain the same characters. See series, "Little Women.")

Flower Fables, 1854, Briggs, 5 plate illustrations. $700.00

Eight Cousins, 1930 edition, Saalfield, b/w illustrations by Frances Brundage. $15.00

Jo's Boys, (1886) ca. 1947, Grosset Dunlap, full color wraparound illustration paper-on-boards cover, color frontispiece, 8 color plates plus b/w illustrations by Louis Jambor. $20.00

Little Men, 1871, Roberts. $95.00

Little Men, 1901, Little Brown, color plate illustra-

tions by Reginald Birch. $75.00

Little Men, undated ca. 1930 edition, Donohue, oversize, color illustrations. $30.00

Little Men, ca. 1947, Grosset Dunlap, full color wraparound illustration paper-on-boards cover, color frontispiece, 8 color plates plus b/w illustrations by D. W. Gorsline. $20.00

Little Men, 1933 edition, Blue Ribbon, illustrated by Erick Berry. $25.00

Little Women, 1869, Roberts, 2 volumes. Rare

Little Women, 1925 edition, Little Brown, illustrations by Jessie Wilcox Smith. $125.00. Later editions. $45.00

Little Women, undated ca. 1930 edition, Donohue, oversize, color cover and frontispiece illustrations. $30.00

Little Women, ca. 1947, Grosset Dunlap, full-color wraparound illustration paper-on-boards cover, color frontispiece, 8 color plates plus b/w illustrations by Louis Jambor. $20.00

Old Fashioned Girl, 1870, Boston, 1st edition. $150.00

Old Fashioned Girl, 1915 edition, Little Brown, color plate illustrations by Jessie Wilcox Smith. $75.00

Proverb Stories, 1886, Boston, illustrations. $80.00. Later editions $20.00

Rose in Bloom, (1876) 1927 edition, Little Brown, Orchard House endpapers, 6 color plate illustrations by Hattie Longstreet Price. $25.00

Spinning Wheel Stories, 1884, Boston. $80.00. Later editions $20.00

Under the Lilacs, (1877) 1928 edition, Little Brown, color plate illustrations by Marguerite Davis. $30.00

Under the Lilacs, (1877) 1950 edition, Little Brown, Orchard House endpapers, color plate illustrations by Marguerite Davis. $20.00

ALDIN, Cecil, see Illustrators.

ALDIS, Dorothy, b. Chicago, IL, 1896 – 1966

Everything and Anything, 1927, Minton Balch. $30.00

ALDRICH, Thomas Bailey, 1836 – 1907, editor of *Atlantic Monthly*

Story of a Bad Boy, (first published in 1870) 1895, Houghton, illustrations by Arthur Frost. $75.00

Story of a Bad Boy, 1937 edition, Saalfield, illustrated impressed cover, color frontispiece and b/w illustrations by Leslie Turner. $10.00

ALDRIDGE, Janet, see Series, "Meadowbrook Girls."

ALGER, Horatio Jr., 1834 – 1899, see Series, "Horatio Alger."
(Alger served as chaplain for a New York boys' home, and turned out more than one hundred novels on the theme of virtue rewarded. First editions can carry high prices, but are generally difficult to identify. The value of later editions usually is decided on the quality of the cover and on illustrations.)
Bertha's Christmas Vision, 1850, Boston, (probably Alger's first novel), 1st edition. Rare. Later editions $20.00
Helen Ford, 1866. Later editions $20.00
Jed the Poor-House Boy, 1890s edition, Winston. $10.00
Rupert's Ambition, 1890s edition, Winston. $10.00

ALLEE, Marjorie Hill, 1890 – 1945
Ann's Surprising Summer, 1933. $15.00
Little American Girl, 1938. $15.00
Off to Philadelphia, 1936, Houghton, 214 pages, color plates by David Hendrickson. $15.00

ALLINGHAM, William
In Fairy Land, 1870, Longmans, 16 color plate illustrations by Richard Doyle. $600.00
Fairy Shoemaker and Other Poems, 1928 edition, Macmillan, illustrations by Boris Artzybasheff. $40.00
Rhymes for the Young Folk, 1887, Cassell, standard size, illustrations by Helen Allingham, Kate Greenaway, Caroline Paterson, Harry Furniss. $65.00
Robin Redbreast and Other Verses, 1930 edition, Macmillan, illustrations by Greenaway, Allingham, Paterson, Furniss. $45.00

ALMOND, Linda
Peter Rabbit's Easter, 1921 Altemus, color plate illustrations (copy of Beatrix Potter character). $40.00

A.L.O.E., "A Lady of England," see Tucker, Charlotte.

ALTSHELER, Joseph, 1862 – 1919
Apache Gold, 1913, Appleton. $15.00
Guns of Bull Run, 1914, Appleton. $10.00
Hunters of the Guns of Bull Run, 1914, Appleton. $15.00
Lords of the Wild, 1919, Appleton. $10.00

AMES, Esther Merriam
Patsy for Keeps, 1932, Samuel Gabriel, oversize, 95 pages, cardboard cover with color illustra-tion, illustrated throughout. $35.00

ANDERSEN, Hans Christian, b. Denmark, 1805 – 1875
(There are numerous nineteenth and twentieth century editions of translations of his individual and collected works. Value depends on the illustrator, binding, rarity of edition. For example, rare editions include a limited edition that was signed by the illustrator Kay Nielsen.)
Andersen's Fairy Tales, translation by Lucas & Paull, 1945, Grosset Dunlap, hardbound cloth cover, illustrations by Arthur Szyk. $15.00
Andersen's Fairy Tales, ca. 1947, Grosset Dunlap, full color wraparound illustration paper-on-boards cover, color frontispiece, 8 color plates plus b/w illustrations by Arthur Szyk. $20.00
Complete Andersen, 1949, 6 boxed volumes, full color illustrations by Fritz Kredel. Each $20.00. Complete boxed set $200.00
Danish Fairy Legends and Tales, 1846, Pickering, translated by Caroline Peachey. $290.00
Danish Fairy Legends and Tales, 1897, Bliss Sands, illustrations by William Heath Robinson. $200.00
Fairy Tales, 1882, Sampson Low, translated by A. C. D. Ward, oversize, illustrations by E. V. B. $100.00
Fairy Tales, 1914, Tuck, illustrations by Mabel Lucie Attwell. $80.00
Fairy Tales, 1914, Doran, illustrations by Kay Nielsen. $250.00
Fairy Tales, 1924, Doran, illustrations by W. Heath Robinson. $175.00
Fairy Tales from Hans Christian Andersen, 1899 edition, London, illustrations by Charles Robinson. $150.00
Fairy Tales by Hans Andersen, 1911, trade edition, 28 color plate illustrations by Dulac. $250.00
Fairy Tales by Hans Andersen, 1916, London, illustrations by Harry Clarke. $200.00
Fairy Tales by Hans Andersen, 1932, Harrap, color plate illustrations by Arthur Rackham. $200.00
It's Perfectly True, translation by Paul Leysaac, 1938 Harcourt, b/w illustrations by Richard Bennett. $10.00
Little Mermaid, 1939 edition, Macmillan, illustrations by Dorothy Lathrop. $35.00
Stories from Hans Andersen, 1912, Hodder, illustrated by Edmund Dulac. $200.00
Stories and Fairy Tales, 1893, George Allen, 2 volume set, illustrations by Arthur Gaskin. $400.00
Wonderful Stories for Children, translated by

Mary Howitt, 1846 Chapman and Hall, London, thought to be the first English translation of Andersen's stories. Rare.

ANDERSON, Anne, illustrator
Anne Anderson's Fairy Book, 1928, London. $70.00

ANDERSON, Clarence W., b. Nebraska, 1891 – 1971, author-illustrator
Billy and Blaze, 1936, Macmillan, illustrated by author. $55.00
Black, Bay and Chestnut, 1939, illustrated by author. $55.00
Blaze and the Forest Fire, 1938, Macmillan, illustrated by author. $55.00
Blaze and the Gypsies, 1937 Macmillan, illustrated by author. $55.00

ANDERSON, Helen Foster
Cousins, 1946, Augustana, color endpapers and frontispiece, b/w illustrations by Laura Bannon. $10.00

ANDREWS, Jane, 1833 – 1887
Seven Little Sisters Who Live on the Round Ball That Floats in the Air, 1861, Boston, published with author listed as "anonymous." $75.00
Ten Boys Who Lived on the Road from Long Ago to Now, 1886, Boston. $75.00

APPLETON, Victor (Stratemeyer syndicate) see Series, "Tom Swift."

ARASON, Steingrimur, b. Iceland
Smoky Bay, 1942, Macmillan, illustrations by Gertrude Howe. $20.00

ARDIZZONE, Edward, illustrator-author
Little Tim and the Brave Sea Captain, 1936, Oxford. $200.00
Lucy Brown and Mr. Grimes, 1937, Oxford. $200.00
Tim and Lucy Go to Sea, 1938, Oxford. $175.00

ARMER, Laura Adams, b. California, 1874
Dark Circle of Branches, 1933, Longmans, illustrations by Sidney Armer. $15.00
Forest Pool, 1938, Longmans, illustrations by author. $15.00
Waterless Mountain, 1931, Longmans (1932 Newbery Medal), illustrated by author and Sidney Armer. $25.00

ARMOUR, R. C.
North American Fairy Tales, 1905, Lippincott, illustrations. $45.00

ARTZYBASHEFF, Boris, editor and illustrator, see Illustrators for additional information.
Aesop's Fables, 1933, Viking, 86 pages, b/w illustrations, wood engravings by author. $45.00
Poor Shaydullah, 1931, Viking, illustrations by author. $45.00
Seven Simeons, 1937, Viking, 31 pages, b/w illustrations, wood engravings by author. $45.00

ASQUITH, Cynthia
Treasure Ship, 1926, Scribner, oversize, color plates and b/w illustrations by several artists. $50.00

ATKINSON, Eleanor
Johnny Appleseed, 1915, Harper, 340 pages, b/w illustrations by Frank Merrill. $10.00

ATTWELL, Mabel Lucie, see Illustrators.

ATWATER, F. (Richard Tupper), b. Chicago 1892 – 1948
Doris and the Trolls, 1931, Rand, illustrations by John McGee $30.00
Mr. Popper's Penguins, 1938, Little Brown, written with Florence Atwater, illustrations by Robert Lawson. $45.00

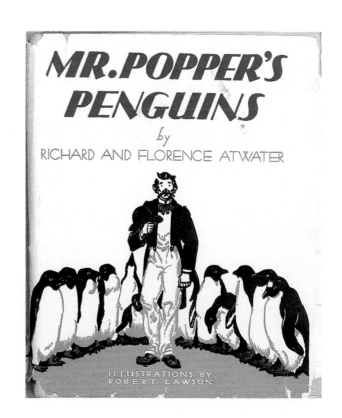

ATWATER, Montgomery
Government Hunter, 1940, Macmillan. $10.00

AUNT FANNY (Frances E. M. Barrow), 1822 – 1894
(Price is for individual titles and usually dou-
bles·per book for a complete set.)
Little Pet Books, 1860, 3 volumes. $20.00 ea.
Good Little Hearts, 1864, 4 volumes. $20.00 ea.

AUNT HATTIE (Harriette Newell Woods Baker),
1815 – 1893
Cora and the Doctor, 1855. $15.00
Tim, the Scissors Grinder, 1861. $10.00
Little Miss Fret, 1869. $20.00

AVERILL, Esther H.T., author-illustrator
Voyages of Jack Cartier, 1937. $15.00
Adventures of Jack Ninepins, 1944, Hale, 65
pages, color illustrations by author. $20.00
Jenny's First Party, 1948. $15.00
King Philip the Indian Chief, 1950. $15.00

AWDRY, Rev. W.
Thomas the Tank Engine (Part of *Railway Series,*
with illustrations by Gunvor Edwards), 1946,
London. $50.00

B

BACON, Peggy, author-illustrator
Ballad of Tangle Street, 1929. $20.00
Catcalls, 1935. $15.00
Lion-Hearted Kitten, 1927. $20.00
Mercy and the Mouse, 1928. $15.00
Mischief in Mayfield, 1933. $15.00
Terrible Nuisance, 1931, Harcourt Junior Literary
Guild edition, b/w illustrations by author.
$15.00

BAGNOLD, Enid
Alice and Thomas and Jane, 1931, Knopf. $35.00
National Velvet, 1935, Morrow. $50.00

BAILEY, Alice Cooper
Skating Gander, 1927, Volland, color illustrated
cardboard cover, 93 pages, color illustrations
throughout by Marie Honre Myers. $35.00

BAILEY, Arthur Scott, see Series, "Tuck-Me-In."
Tale of Cuffy Bear, 1915, Grosset, illustrations by
Harry Smith. $20.00

BAILEY, Carolyn Sherwin, b. NY, 1875 – 1961
Children of the Handcrafts, 1935, Viking, b/w litho-
graph illustrations by Grace Paull. $20.00
Little Rabbit Who Wanted Red Wings, 1931, Platt
Munk, color illustrations by Dorothy Grider.

$15.00
Merry Christmas Book, 1948, Whitman. $15.00
Miss Hickory, 1946, Viking (1947 Newbery Medal),
b/w illustrations, lithographs by Ruth Gannett.
$25.00

BAILEY, Margaret
Little Man With One Shoe, 1921, Little Brown,
impressed cover, b/w illustrations by Alice Preston.
$15.00

BAIN, Edward U.
S-O-S Helicopter, 1947, Whitman. $5.00

BAKER, Cornelia
Magic Image from India, 1909, Philadelphia, illustrations by Harry Lachman. $75.00

BAKER, Etta, see Series, "Fairmont Girls."

BAKER, Margaret
Peacock Eggs, 1932, Junior Literary Guild, cloth
cover, b/w silhouette illustrations by Mary
Baker. $20.00
Tomson's Halloween, 1929, Dodd Mead, silhou-
ette illustrations by Mary Baker. $20.00

BAKER, Nina Brown, 1888 – 1957
He Wouldn't Be King, 1941, Vanguard. $10.00
Juarez, Hero of Mexico, 1942, Vanguard. $10.00

BAKER, Rachel Mininberg
First Woman Doctor, 1944, Messner. $10.00

BAKER, Willard, see Series, "Bob Dexter, Boy
Rancher."

BALCH, Glenn
Christmas Horse, 1949, Crowell. $20.00
Tiger Roan, 1938, Crowell. $20.00

BALDWIN, Arthur J.
Sou'wester Goes North, 1938, Random, illustrated
by Gordon Grant. $30.00

BALDWIN, Faith, see Series, "Headline Books."

BALDWIN, James 1841 – 1925, see Series,
"Scribner."
Sampo, Wonder Tale of the Old North, 1912,
Scribner, color illustrations by N. C. Wyeth.
$85.00
Story of the Golden Age, 1887, Scribner, color
plates by Howard Pyle. $95.00
Story of Roland, 1883, Scribner, color plate illus-

trations by Reginald Birch. $95.00
Story of Siegfried, 1882, Scribner, color plate illustrations by Howard Pyle. $100.00
Story of Siegfried, 1931 edition, Scribner, 6 color plate illustrations by Peter Hurd. $35.00

BALL, Martha Jane
Timothy Crunchit, the Calico Bunny, 1930, Laidlaw, illustrations by Gay Woodring, oversize. $25.00

BALLANTYNE, Robert Michael
Coral Island, 1858, London, 1st edition. $150.00
Gorilla Hunters, 1861, London, 1st edition. $100.00

BANCROFT, Alberta
Goblins of Haubeck, 1925, Robert McBride, NY, b/w illustrations by Harold Sichel. $15.00

BANCROFT, Edith, see Series, "Jane Allen."
Jane Allen of the Sub Team, 1917, Cupples, b/w illustrations by Roy Williams. $10.00

BANCROFT, Laura (L. Frank Baum)
Babes in Birdland, 1911, reissue of *Policeman Bluejay,* paste-on-pictorial. $300.00
Mr. Woodchuck, 1906, Reilly Britton, small size. $95.00
Policeman Bluejay, 1907, Reilly Britton, illustrations by Wright. Rare
Sugar Loaf Mountain, 1906, Reilly Britton. $125.00
Twinkle Tales, 1906, 6 book series, illustrations by Maginel Wright Enright. $200.00 ea.
Twinkle and Chubbins, 1911, reissue of *Twinkle Tales* in one volume. $400.00

BANK, Clair. see Series, "Adventure Girls, Beverly Gray."

BANNERMAN, Helen, 1863 – 1946
(These stories were written in India to send to the author's children at school in Scotland, and originally illustrated by the author.)
Story of Little Black Sambo, 1899, Richards, small size, author illustrations. Rare
Story of Little Black Sambo, 1901, Stokes, author illustrated. $350.00
Story of Little Black Sambo, 1905, Chicago edition (introduction by L. Frank Baum). $125.00
Little Black Sambo, 1925, Platt & Munk, color illustrations by Eulalie. $75.00
Little Black Sambo, 1931, NY, oversize, full page color illustrations by Fern Peat. $70.00
New Little Black Sambo, 1939, Whitman, oversize,

color illustrations by Juanita Bennett. $30.00
Story of Little Black Mingo, 1901, London. Rare
Story of Little Black Mingo, 1902, London, illustrations by author. $85.00
Story of Little Black Quibba, 1902, London 1st edition, small size. $350.00
Story of Little Black Bobtail, 1909, London, 1st edition, James Nisbet Co. Rare

BANNON, Laura, illustrator
Manuela's Birthday, 1939, Whitman, color illustrations by author. $25.00

BARBOUR, Ralph Henry, 1870 – 1944
Captain of the Crew, 1906, Appleton, b/w illustrations by C. Relyea. $10.00
Crimson Sweater, 1906, Appleton. $10.00
Full-Back Foster, 1919, Dodd, b/w illustrations by E. Caswell. $10.00
Goal to Go, 1933, Appleton. $10.00
Good Manners for Boys, 1937, Appleton. $15 .00
Half-Back, 1899, Appleton. $15.00
Maid in Arcady, 1906, Lippincott, color paste-on-pictorial and gilt trim on cloth cover, tinted photograph illustrations by Frederic von Rapp. $25.00
Purple Pennant, 1916, Appleton, color paste-on-pictorial, gilt top edge of pages, 4 three-color plates by Norman Rockwell. $50.00

BARNES, Annie M.
Laurel Token, ca. 1900, Lee & Shepard, small size, cloth cover, illustrations by G. W. Picknell. $15.00

BARNETT, Grace and Olive
Homesteaders' Horses, 1941, Oxford, illustrations by authors. $20.00

BARNEY, Maginel Wright Enright, see Illustrators, Wright, Maginel.

BARRIE, James Matthew, b. Scotland, 1860 – 1937
Alice-sit-by-fire (first published in 1919 London), a play, 1922, Scribner American edition. $35.00
Peter and Wendy, 1911, Scribner, illustrations, 1st American edition. $60.00
Peter and Wendy, 1923, Scribner, 12 color plate illustrations by Mabel Lucie Attwell. $125.00
Peter Pan in Kensington Gardens, 1906, London, trade edition, 50 color plate illustrations by Arthur Rackham. $300.00
Peter Pan, Retold, 1916, Silver Burdett, small size, 72 pages, print illustration on cloth cover, illus-

trated endpapers, color and b/w illustrations by Alice Woodward. $30.00

BARRINGER, Marie
Martin the Goose Boy, 1932, Doubleday, 188 pages, color and b/w illustrations by Maude and Miska Petersham. $45.00
Four and Lena, 1938, Doubleday, color and b/w illustrations by Maude and Miska Petersham. $45.00

BARROWS, Marjorie
Johnny Giraffe, 1935, Grosset, color and b/w illustrations. $20.00
Muggins Mouse, 1932, Reilly, illustrated by Keith Ward. $50.00
Muggins Mouse, 1932, Whitman edition, illustrations by Keith Ward. $30.00
Pet Show, 1944, Samuel Lowe, color illustrations by Ilona. $30.00

BARTON, George
Bell Haven Nine, 1914, Winston, b/w illustrations by Charles Gray. $10.00

BARTON, May Hollis, see Series, "Barton Books."
Hazel Hood's Strange Discovery, 1928, Cupples, printed cover illustration, b/w frontispiece. $10.00

BARTON, Olive, see Series, "Nancy and Nick."

BARTUSEK, Libushka
Happy Times in Czechoslovakia, 1940, Knopf, color illustrations by Yarka Bures. $10.00

BARUCH, Dorothy
Day with Betsy Ann, 1927, Harper, b/w illustrations by Winifred Bromhall. $25.00
Sally Does It, 1940, Appleton, 73 pages, line drawing by Robb Beebe. $15.00

BASTERMAN, Catherine
Johnny Longfoot, 1947, Bobbs Merrill, color paste-on illustration on cover, color frontispiece, b/w illustrations by Warren Chappell. $25.00

BATES, Katherine Lee, editor
Once Upon a Time, 1921, Rand McNally, oversize, cover with color paste-on pictorial, color illustrations by Margaret Evans Price. $65.00
Jack and the Beanstalk, 1927, Rand McNally, small size, illustrations by M. E. Price. $30.00

BATES, Capt. Gordon, see Series, "Khaki Boys."

BAUM, L. Frank, b. Chittenango, NY, 1856 – 1919 (Pseudonyms: Floyd Akers, Laura Bancroft, John Estes Cook, Capt. Hugh Fitzgerald, Suzanne Metcalf, Schuyler Staunton, Edith Van Dyne), see Series, "Oz Books."
American Fairy Tales, 1901, Hill, b/w illustrations, standard size, cover illustrations by Seymour. $400.00
American Fairy Tales, 1908, Bobbs Merrill, revised edition, 16 color plate illustrations by George Kerr. $300.00
American Fairy Tales, later printings with 8 color plate illustrations $100.00
Army Alphabet, 1900, Hill, oversize, color illustrations by Kennedy. Rare
Dot and Tot of Merryland, 1901, Donohue, impressed illustration on cover, color illustrated endpapers and color illustrations throughout by W. W. Denslow. $300.00
Enchanted Island of Yew, 1903, Donohue, impressed illustration on cover, 8 color plate illustrations by Fanny Cory. $200.00
Father Goose: His Book, 1900, Donohue, oversize, color illustrations by Denslow. $600.00
Father Goose: His Book, 1903 edition, Bobbs-Merrill. $200.00
Father Goose: His Book, 1913 edition, Donohue. $150.00
John Dough and the Cherub, 1906, Reilly Britton, color plate illustrations by John Neill. $400.00
John Dough and the Cherub, later editions. $100.00
Life & Adventures of Santa Claus, 1902, Bowen-Merrill, color plate and b/w illustrations by Mary Cowles Clark. $400.00
Life & Adventures of Santa Claus, later editions with Clark illustrations. $85.00
Magical Monarch of Mo, 1903, Bobbs-Merrill, illustrations by Frank Verbeck. $200.00
Master Key, 1901, Bowen-Merrill, standard size, color plate illustrations by Fanny Cory. $100.00
Mother Goose in Prose, 1897, Way & Williams, oversize, 12 illustrations by Maxfield Parrish. Rare
Mother Goose in Prose, 1901 edition, George Hill. $300.00
Mother Goose in Prose, 1905 edition, Bobbs Merrill. $200.00
Queen Zixi of Ix, 1905 Century, 16 color plate illustrations by Richardson. $300.00
Queen Zixi of Ix, 1915 edition, Century. $150.00
Queen Zixi of Ix, 1919 edition, Century. $90.00
Sea Fairies, 1911, Reilly Britton, color paste-on pictorial cover, color plate illustrations by John Neill. $300.00
Sky Island, 1912, Reilly Britton, color paste-on pic-

torial cover, color plate illustrations by John Neill. $300.00

Snuggle Tales, 1916 – 17, 6 volume set, illustrations by Neill and others. $45.00 ea.

BAYLOR, Frances Courtenay
Juan and Juanita, (original copyright 1886) 1926 edition, Houghton, paste-on pictorial cover, illustrated endpapers, 4 color plates by Gustaf Tenggren. $20.00

BEACH, Stewart
Racing Start, 1941, Little Brown. $10.00

BEAMAN, S. G. Hulme
Stories from Toytown, 1938, London, illustrations by author. $40.00
Tales of Toytown, 1928, London, illustrations by author. $50.00
Seven Voyages of Sinbad the Sailor, retold by Beaman, 1926, McBride, oversize, 70 pages, 8 color plates. $45.00

BEATY, John Yocum
Baby Whale, Sharp Eyes, 1938, Lippincott, color illustrations by Helene Carter. $20.00

BECK, Ruth Everett
Little Buffalo Robe, 1914, Holt, 1st edition, 218 pages, b/w illustrations by Angel DeCora and Lone Star. $20.00

BECKER, Edna
900 Buckets of Paint, 1949, Abingdon, oblong, color illustrations by Margaret Bradfield. $15.00

BEERS, Ethel Lynn, 1827 – 1879
General Frankie: A Story for Little Folks, 1863. $15.00

BEIM, Jerrold and Lorraine Levey
Burro that Had a Name, 1939, Harcourt, illustrations by Howard Simon. $20.00
Two is a Team, 1945, Harcourt, illustrated by Ernest Crichlow. $15.00

BELL, Lilian
Runaway Equator, 1910, Stokes, 118 pages, color paste-on illustration on cloth cover, b/w illustrations by Peter Newell. $50.00

BELL, Margaret Elizabeth
Danger on Old Baldy, 1944, Morrow. $15.00
Enemies in Icy Strait, 1945, Morrow. $15.00
Watch for a Tall White Sail, 1948, Morrow. $10.00

BELL, Thelma Harrington
Mountain Boy, 1947, Doubleday, illustrated by Corydon Bell. $20.00
Black Face, 1931, Doubleday, 48 pages, illustrated by Corydon Bell. $25.00
Pawnee, 1950, Viking, oversize, b/w illustrations by Corydon Bell. $20.00

BELL, William
Sacred Scimitar, 1938 edition, Goldsmith. $10.00

BELLOC, Hillaire, b. France, 1870 – 1953
(Belloc was educated at Oxford and a member of the British parliament.)
Bad Child's Book of Beasts, 1896, London, illustrations by Basil Blackwood. $85.00
Bad Child's Book of Beasts, 1930, Knopf, illustrations, 1st American edition. $30.00
Cautionary Tales for Children, 1908, London, illustrations by Blackwood. $75.00
Moral Alphabet, 1899, London. $70.00
More Beasts for Worse Children, 1897, London. $75.00

BEMELMANS, Ludwig, author-illustrator
Castle Number Nine, 1937, Viking, oversize, color illustrations by author. $35.00
Hansi, (first published in 1934) 1942 edition, Viking, oversize, color illustrations by author. $30.00
Madeline, 1939, NY, oversize, color illustrations by author. $100.00
Madeline, later editions. $35.00

BENET, Rosemary Carr and Stephen Vincent
Book of Americans, 1933, Rinehart, illustrated by Charles Child. $65.00

BENNETT, Charles H.
Bennett's Fables: From Aesop and Others, 1857, color illustrations by author. Rare.

BENNETT, John
Master Skylark, 1897, Appleton, illustrated by Reginald Birch. $100.00
Master Skylark, 1922, Century, oversize, color paste-on pictorial on cover, color plates by Henry Pitz. $35.00

BENNETT, Richard
Shawneen and the Gander, 1937, Doubleday, illustrations by author. $25.00
Hannah Marie, 1939, Doubleday, illustrated endpapers, illustrations by author. $20.00

BENSON, Irene, see Series, "Campfire Girls."

BENSON, Sally
Stories of the Gods and Heroes, 1940, Dial, b/w illustrations by Steele Savage. $20.00

BERNARD, Florence
Through the Cloud Mountain, 1922, illustrations by Gertrude Kay. $65.00

BERRY, Erick
Honey of the Nile, 1938, Oxford, illustrations by author. $15.00
Seven Bear Skins, 1948, Winston, 275 pages, b/w illustrations by author. $15.00
Winged Girl of Knossos, 1933, Appleton, illustrations by author. $15.00

BESKOW, Elsa, author-illustrator
Aunt Green, Aunt Brown and Aunt Lavender, 1928, Harper, oversize oblong, color illustration on paper-covered boards, color illustrations by author. $65.00
Aunt Brown's Birthday, 1930, Harper, oversize oblong, color illustration on paper-covered boards, color illustrations by author. $65.00
Buddy's Adventure in the Blueberry Patch, 1931, Harper, oversize oblong, color illustration on paper-covered boards, color illustrations by author. $65.00
Olle's Ski Trip, 1928, Harper, oversize, color illustration on paper-covered boards, color illustrations by author. $45.00
Pelle's New Suit, 1929, Harper, oversize oblong, color illustration on paper-covered boards, color illustrations by author. $45.00
Pelle's New Suit, edition ca. 1930s, small size square, color illustrations by Eulalie. $35.00
Peter's Voyage, 1931, Knopf, oversize square, illustrated paper-covered boards, color illustratons by author. $45.00
Tale of the Wee Little Old Woman, 1930, Harper, oversize square, illustrated paper-covered boards, color illustratons by author. $45.00

BETTS, Ethel Franklin, illustrator, see Chapin, Anna, and Riley, James.
Complete Mother Goose, 1909, Stokes, color illustrations by Betts. $125.00
One Thousand Poems for Children, collected by Ingpen, 1923, Macrae, illustrations by Betts. $55.00

BETZ, Betty
Your Manners are Showing, 1946, Grosset. $10.00

BIANCO, Margery Williams, 1881 – 1944

Adventures of Andy, 1927, Doran, 227 pages, color and b/w illustrations by Leo Underwood. $25.00
Apple Tree, 1926, Doran, small b/w illustrations by Boris Artzybasheff. $35.00
Good Friends, 1934, Viking, 142 pages, b/w illustration lithographs by Grace Paull. $20.00
Hurdy Gurdy Man, 1933, Oxford, small square, paper-covered boards, b/w illustrations by Robert Lawson. $35.00
Little Wooden Doll, 1925, Macmillan, small size, color illustrations by Pamela Bianco. $35.00
Other People's Houses, 1939, Viking, 201 pages, color endpapers, frontispiece by Kate Seredy. $35.00
Penny and the White Horse, 1942, Messner, oversize with color illustrations. $25.00
Poor Cecco, 1925, Doran, b/w and color illustrations by Arthur Rackham. $100.00
Poor Cecco, 1944, edition Doubleday, color illustrations by Arthur Rackham. $25.00
Skin Horse, 1927, Doran, illustrations by Pamela Bianco. $30.00
Street of Little Shops, 1932, Hale, small size, 112 pages, b/w illustrations by Grace Paull. $20.00
Velveteen Rabbit (published under "Williams", 1922 NY, 1st editions rare), 1926 Doubleday edition, illustrated by William Nicholson. $200.00
Winterbound, 1936, Viking, 234 pages, decorations by Kate Seredy. $35.00

BIANCO, Pamela, b. London, 1906, author–illustrator, see Illustrator section for additional information.
Playtime in Cherry Street, 1948, Oxford, small size, 96 pages, b/w illustrations by author. $20.00
Joy and the Christmas Angel, 1949, Oxford, small size, two-color and b/w illustrations by author. $20.00

BIGHAM, Madge Alford, b. Georgia
Stories of Mother Goose Village, 1903, Rand, small size, two-color illustrations throughout. $40.00
Tales of Mother Goose Village, 1904, Rand, two-color illustrations throughout. $40.00

BIG LITTLE BOOKS, see Series, "Big Little Books."

BIRNEY, Hoffman
Pinto Pony, 1930, Penn, illustrations by Clyde Lee. $15.00

BISCHOFF, Ilse Marthe, author-illustrator, see Bontemps, Arna.

BISHOP, Claire Huchet
Five Chinese Brothers, 1938, Coward McCann, standard size oblong, b/w/yellow illustrations by Kurt Wiese. $50.00
Pancakes – Paris , 1947, Viking, 62 pages, illustrated by George Schreiber. $30.00
Man Who Lost His Head, 1942, Viking, 55 pages, b/w illustrations by Robert McCloskey. $30.00
King's Day, 1940, Coward, b/w illustrations by Doris Spiegel. $20.00

BLACK, Irma Simonton
Cocker Spaniel, 1938, Holiday $15.00

BLACKWOOD, Basil, illustrator, see Belloc, Hillaire.

BLAIR, Walter
Tall Tale America, 1944, Coward, illustrated by Glen Rounds. $35.00

BLAISDELL, Mary F.
Bunny Rabbit's Diary, (1915) 1931 Little, Brown school edition, easy reader, small size, printed illustration on cover, color and b/w illustrations by George Kerr. $30.00
Mother Goose Children, 1916, Little Brown, small square, color illustrations, easy read book. $30.00
Twilight Town, (1913) 1922 edition, Little Brown, color illustrations by Henrietta Adams. $30.00

BLAKE, William b. London, 1757 – 1827
Songs of Innocence, (1789) 1927 edition, Medici Society, illustrated by Jacynth Parsons. $15.00

BLANCHARD, Amy, see Series, "Dear Little Girl."
Four Corners, 1906 Jacobs, impressed cover illustration with gilt, 5 b/w illustrations. $15.00

BLOUGH, Glenn
Monkey with a Notion, 1946, Holt, 88 pages, b/w illustrations by John DeCuir. $15.00

BLUMBERG, Fannie Burgheim
Rowena Teena Tot and the Blackberries, 1934 Whitman, 32 pages, paste-on pictorial cover, color endpapers, color illustrations by Mary Grosjean. $60.00
Rowena Teena Tot and the Runaway Turkey, 1936, Whitman, 32 pages, paste-on pictorial cover, color endpapers, color illustrations by Mary Grosjean. $60.00

BLUNT, Betty Bacon
Double Trouble, 1945, Crowell, ring-bound boards, illustrations by author $25.00

BLYTON, Enid, see Series, "Famous Five."
Mary Mouse and the Doll's House, 1942, Leicester. $35.00
Noddy Goes to Toyland, Sampson London, small size, color illustrations by Beek. $35.00
Noddy in Toytown, 1949, Sampson London, small size, color illustrations by Beek. $35.00

BOLTON, Ivy May
Shadow of the Crown, 1931, Longmans, 268 pages, printed illustration on cover, b/w illustrations by Henry Pitz. $20.00

BONEHILL, Capt. Ralph, see Series, "Boy Hunter."

BONNER, Mary Graham, b. NY
Daddy's Bedtime Stories, 1916 – 17, 4 volumes. $20.00 ea.
Hidden Village Mystery, 1948, Knopf, b/w illustrations by Bob Meyers. $10.00
Mysterious Caboose, 1949, Knopf. $20.00
Mrs. Cucumber Green, 1927, Milton Bradley, color plates by Janet Laura Scott. $30.00

BONTEMPS, Arna
Fast Sooner Hound, 1942, Mifflin, illustrated by Virginia Lee Burton. $45.00
Sad-Faced Boy, 1937, Houghton, illustrations by

Virginia Burton. $50.00
You Can't Pet A Possum, 1934, Morrow 1st edition, color and b/w illustrations by Ilse Bischoff. $75.00

BOSHER, Kate Langley
Mary Cary, 1910, Harper, impressed cover illustration. $25.00
Mary Cary, ca. 1940 edition, Grosset. $5.00

BOSSCHERE, Jean de
Weird Islands, 1922, McBride, 210 pages, illustrated cover, color frontispiece, b/w illustrations by author. $30.00

BOTHWELL, Jean
Little Boat Boy, 1945, Harcourt, b/w illustrations by Margaret Ayer. $20.00

BOURGEOIS, Florence
Beachcomber Bobbie, 1935, Doubleday, small oblong, color illustrated cover, color illustrations by author. $20.00
Molly and Michael, 1936, Doubleday, color illustrations by author $20.00
Peter, Peter, Pumpkin Grower, 1937, Doubleday, color illustrations by author. $20.00

BOUVET, Marguerite
Prince Tip-Top, (1892), 1899 edition, McClurg, b/w illustrations by Helen Armstrong. $20.00

BOWMAN, Anne
(Wrote numerous adventure stories for boys, most firsts by George Routledge & Sons, GB.)
Among the Tartar Tents, 1861, Routledge, small size, gilt on cover, b/w illustrations $30.00
The Boy Voyagers, 1859 Routledge, small size, gilt on cover, b/w illustrations. $30.00
Kangaroo Hunters, 1859, Routledge, small size, gilt on cover, b/w illustrations. $30.00
Bear Hunters, 1960, Routledge, small size, gilt on cover, b/w illustrations. $30.00

BOWMAN, James, 1880 – 1961
Pecos Bill, 1937, Whitman, color illustrated by Laura Bannon. $25.00
Tales from a Finnish Stupa, 1936, Whitman, color illustrated by Laura Bannon. $25.00

BOYLAN, Grace Duffie, 1862 – 1935
Kids of Many Colors, 1901, Chicago, illustrations by Ike Morgan. $100.00
Steps to Nowhere, 1910, NY, color paste-on pictorial cover, illustrations by Ike Morgan. $50.00
Yama Yama Land, 1909, Reilly Britton, b/w and two-color

and full color, including 2 double-page color plate illustrations by Edgar Keller. $100.00

BOYLSTON, Helen Dore, see Series, "Sue Barton."

BRADLEY, Milton, 1836 – 1911, publisher
Paradise of Childhood, 1869, the first American kindergarten manual. Rare

BRANDEIS, Madeline, film producer
(Set of books with printed illustration on cover, b/w documentary-type photo illustrations from Pathe films, ca. 1930s Grosset Dunlap.)
Little Dutch Tulip Girl. $15.00
Little Indian Weaver. $15.00
Little Spanish Dancer. $15.00
Little Swiss Wood Carver. $15.00
Wee Scotch Piper. $15.00

BRANN, Esther
Lupe Goes to School, 1930, Macmillan, b/w illustrations by author. $15.00
Nanette and the Wooden Shoes, 1929, Macmillan, illustrated endpapers, color frontispiece, color plate illustrations by author. $25.00
Yann and His Island, 1932, Macmillan, color frontispiece, b/w illustrations by author. $15.00
Another New Year, 1936, Macmillan, small size, easy read, color illustrations by author. $20.00

BRAZIL, Angela, 1868 – 1947.
Wrote over 60 novels about school girls including:
Fortunes of Phillippa, 1907, London. $10.00
Madcap of the School, 1917, London. $10.00

BRENDA (Mrs. G. Castle Smith)
Froggy's Little Brother, 1875 London, 1st editions rare. Later editions $15.00

BRENT-DYER, Elinor
Jo of the Chalet School, 1926, London. $15.00

BRETT, Edna Payson
Merry Scout, 1922, Rand McNally, b/w and color plate illustrations by Garada Clark Riley. $20.00

BREWSTER, John
Under the Tent of the Sky, 1937, Macmillan, 205 pages, poetry collection, b/w drawings by Robert Lawson. $20.00

BRICE, Tony, illustrator
Little Hippo and his Red Bicycle, 1943, Rand

McNally , illustrations. $25.00
Three Little Kittens, 1938, Rand McNally, small size, b/w/red illustrations. $15.00

BRILL, Ethel C. (also used the pseudonym Edwin Burritt)
Madeleine Takes Command, 1946, McGraw, b/w illustrations by Bruce Adams. $10.00
Secret Cache, 1932, Cupples, b/w frontispiece. $10.00
When Lighthouses Are Dark, 1921, Holt. $10.00
White Brother, 1932, Holt. $10.00

BRINE, Mary
How a Dear Little Couple Went Abroad, 1903, Altemus, lithograph and gilt decorated cover, b/w illustrations. $25.00

BRINK, Carol, b. Idaho, 1895
All Over Town, 1939, Macmillan. $20.00
Anything Can Happen on a River, 1934 Macmillan. $20.00
Baby Island, 1937. $15.00
Caddie Woodlawn, 1935, Macmillan (1936 Newbery Medal), illustrations by Kate Seredy $35.00
Magical Melons, 1944, Macmillan. $15.00

BROCK, Charles E, see Illustrators.

BROCK, Emma Lillian illustrator-author
Beppo, 1936, Whitman, oversize, color illustrations by author. $35.00

BROCK, Henry Matthew, illustrator (brother of Charles Brock)
Book of Fairy Tales, ca. 1900, Warne, gilt decoration on cover, illustrated by Brock. $100.00

BROMHALL, Winifred
Mrs. Polly's Party, 1949, Knopf, oversize, paste-on pictorial cover, color illustrations by author. $20.00
Johanna Arrives, 1941, Knopf, color illustrations by author. $20.00

BRONSON, Wilfrid
Coyotes, 1946, Harcourt. $25.00
Pinto's Journey, 1948, Messner, b/w and color illustrations by author. $25.00
Water People, 1935, Wise Co., oversize nature picture book with color illustrations by the author. $25.00

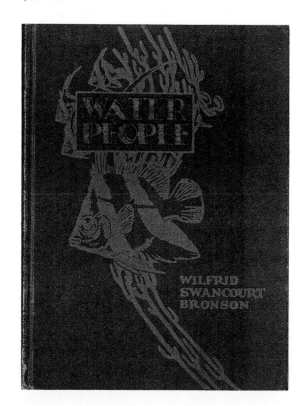

BROOKE, L. Leslie, 1862 – 1940, illustrator
Golden Goose Book, 1906, Warne, illustrations by Brooke. $55.00
Johnny Crow's Garden, 1903, Warne, picture book, color illustrations by author. $65.00
Johnny Crow's Garden, 1932 edition, Warne, color illustrations. $35.00
Johnny Crow's Party, 1907, Warne, picture book,

color illustrations by author. $65.00

Johnny Crow's Party, 1930 edition, Warne, oversize. $40.00

Johnny Crow's New Garden, 1935, Warne, color illustrations by author. $55.00

Nursery Rhyme, undated, Warne, oversize, paste-on color cover illustration of Bo Peep, 16 color plates and b/w illustrations by author. $65.00

Ring o' Roses, a Nursery Rhyme Picture Book, undated Warne, illustrated by Brooke. $65.00

Tailor and the Crow, an Old Rhyme with New Drawings, 1911, Warne small size, about 50 pages, color paste-on pictorial, color plates and b/w illustrations by Brooke. $55.00

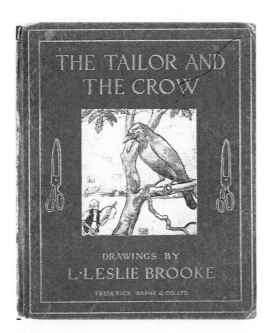

BROOKS, Amy b. Boston, d. 1916, author-illustrator, see Series, "Princess Polly," "Prue," "Randy Books."

Dorothy Dainty at Foam Ridge, 1918, Boston. $20.00

At the Sign of the Three Birches, 1916. $10.00

BROOKS, Edna, see Series, "Khaki Girls."

BROOKS, Gwendolyn
Street in Bronzeville, 1945, Harper. $100.00

BROOKS, John
Jimmy Makes the Varsity, 1928, Grosset, b/w illustrations by George Avison. $10.00

BROOKS, Walter R., 1886 – 1958
Ernestine Takes Over, 1935. $15.00

Freddy the Detective, 1932, Knopf, 263 pages, illustrated by Kurt Weise. $25.00

Wiggins for President, 1939. $15.00
Freddy Goes to Florida, 1949, Knopf. $15.00

BROWN, Abbie Farwell
In the Days of Giants, 1902, Houghton, b/w illustrations by E. B. Smith. $20.00

BROWN, Helen Dawes
Her Sixteenth Year, 1901. $10.00
How Phoebe Found Herself, 1912. $10.00
Little Jean, 1918. $10.00

BROWN, Margaret Wise
Golden Egg Book, 1944, Doubleday, illustrations by Leonard Weisgard. $35.00

Indoor Noisy Book, 1942, Scott. $20.00

Little Island, 1946, Doubleday, illustrations by Leonard Weisgard (1947 Caldecott art). $55.00

Runaway Bunny, 1942, Harper, illustrations by Clement Hurd. $45.00

Winter Noisy Book, 1947, Scott, illustrations by Charles Shaw. $55.00

BROWN, Paul
Crazy Quilt, 1934, Scribner, illustrations by author. $35.00

No Trouble at All, 1940, Scribner, illustrations by author. $30.00

Piper's Pony, 1935, Scribner, illustrations by author. $35.00

BROWNE, Frances
Granny's Wonderful Chair, 1916, Dutton, illustrations by Katherine Pyle. $80.00

Granny's Wonderful Chair, 1928 edition, Saalfield, b/w illustrations by Florence Williams. $10.00

Granny's Wonderful Chair, undated Grosset, color frontispiece and endpapers by Pelagie Doane. $15.00

BROWNING, Robert, b. London, 1812 – 1889
Pied Piper of Hamelin, 1888, Routledge, 35 color illustrations by Kate Greenaway. $300.00

Pied Piper of Hamelin, 1910 edition, Chicago, illustrations by Hope Dunlap. $45.00

Pied Piper of Hamelin, 1931 edition, McLoughlin, illustrated by Jack Perkins. $20.00

Pied Piper of Hamelin, 1934 London, limited edition, signed by Rackham, illustrations by Arthur Rackham, slipcase.   To $1000.00

BRUCE, Dorita Fairlie
Dimsie Moves Up, 1921, London. $15.00
Dimsie Moves Up Again, 1922, London. $15.00
Dimsie Goes Back, 1927, London. $15.00

BRUCE, Mary Grant,
Billabong novels, ca. 1911. $15.00 ea.

BRUNDAGE, Frances, author-illustrator
What Happened to Tommy, 1920s, NY. $40.00

BRYANT, Sara Cone
Best Stories to Tell Children (first published 1905)
   1912 edition, Houghton Mifflin, 16 color plate
   illustrations by Patten Wilson. $35.00
Epaminondas and His Auntie, 1938, Houghton
   Mifflin, illustrations. $20.00
Stories to Tell to Children, 1924 edition, Houghton,
   illustrated by R. L. Field. $35.00

BUCK, Pearl b. West Virginia, 1892 – 1973
Dragon Fish, 1944, NY. $15.00
Water Buffalo Children, 1934, Day, illustrations by
   William A Smith. $25.00

BUGBEE, Emma
Peggy Goes Overseas, 1945, Dodd. $10.00

BULLER, Marguerite
Story of Woofin-Poofin, 1929, McBride, oversize,
   18 pages, color plate illustrations by author.
   $35.00

BUNNY (Carl Schultze, 1866 – 1939), cartoonist
Latest Larks of Foxy Grandpa, 1902 Donohue, folio
   oblong of cartoon series in color. $85.00

BUNYAN, John, b. England, 1628 – 88, minister
Pilgrim's Progress, retold by Mary Godolphin,
   1939 Stokes, illustrated by Robert Lawson.
   $35.00

BURGESS, Gelett, 1866 – 1951, author-illustrator
   (There are several later editions of most of the
   Goop books, generally priced about $30.00)
Burgess Nonsense Book, 1901 Stokes. $150.00
Goop Directory of Juvenile Offenders, 1913
   Stokes, oversize, illustrations. $200.00
Goops and How to Be Them, 1900, Stokes, over-
   size, illustrations. $200.00
Goops and How to Be Them, 1928 edition, Lippin-
   cott, oversize. $40.00
More Goops and How Not to Be Them, 1903
   Stokes, oversize, illustrations. $200.00
Goop Tales Alphabetically Told, 1904, Stokes,
   oversize, illustrations. $200.00
Why Be a Goop?, 1924, Stokes, illustrations.
   $200.00

BURGESS, Thornton Waldo, see Series, "Bedtime Story-Books," "Green Forest," "Smiling

Pool", "Mother West Wind."
Burgess Animal Book for Children, ca. 1920, Little
   Brown, full-page color and b/w illustrations by
   Louis Fuertes. $50.00
Burgess Animal Book for Children 1950 edition,
   Little Brown, color paste-on pictorial cover,
   full-page color and b/w illustrations by Louis
   Fuertes. $15.00
Burgess Bird Book for Children, 1919, Little Brown
   1st edition, color plate illustrations by Fuertes.
   $100.00
Burgess Flower Book for Children, Little Brown,
   color and b/w illustrations. $50.00
Burgess Seashore Book for Children, Little Brown,
   color and b/w illustrations. $45.00
Tales from the Storyteller's House, 1937, Little
   Brown, color illustrations by Lemuel Palmer.
   $55.00
While the Story Log Burns, 1938, Little Brown. $45.00
Woe Begone Little Bear, 1929, Little Brown. $45.00

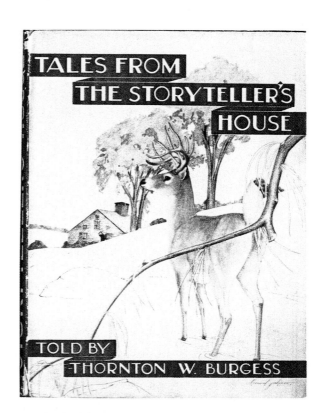

BURLINGAME, Eugene Watson
Grateful Elephant, 1923, New Haven, illustrations
   by Dorothy Lathrop. $100.00

BURNETT, Alice, see Series, "Merryvale Girls."

BURNETT, Emma
Missionary Twig, 1890, American Tract Society,

small size, impressed and gilt decorated cover, b/w illustrations by Whitney. $10.00

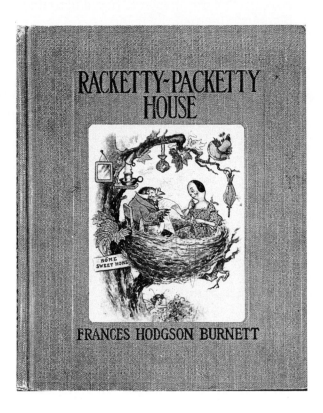

BURNETT, Frances Hodgson, b. England 1849 – 1924, moved to America in the 1860s

Giovanni and the Other, 1892, NY, illustrations by Reginald Birch. $65.00

Little Princess, 1905, Scribner's, illustrations by Ethel Franklin Betts, (see *Sara Crewe*). $100.00

Little Lord Fauntleroy, 1886, NY, illustrations by Reginald Birch. $300.00

Little Lord Fauntleroy, 1888 edition, Warne, red cloth covered boards with gold impressed design, illustrations by Reginald Birch. $100.00

Little Lord Fauntleroy, 1889, Scribner, oversize, paper-covered-boards with color and gilt decoration, 26 b/w illustrations by Reginald Birch. $45.00

Little Lord Fauntleroy, 1906 edition, small size, impressed green/red/gilt cover design, 24 b/w illustrations by Reginald Birch. $20.00

Little Lord Fauntleroy, 1911 edition with color plate illustrations by Reginald Birch. $75.00

Little Lord Fauntleroy, 1925, Warne, illustrations by Charles Brock. $45.00

The One I Knew the Best of All, 1893, Warne, autobiography, illustrations by Reginald Birch. $55.00

Racketty-Packetty House, 1906, Century, small size, color paste-on pictorial cover, color plate illustrations by Harrison Cady. $75.00

Sara Crewe, 1888, Scribners (reprinted as *Little Princess* in 1905), illustrated by Reginald Birch. $95.00

Sara Crewe, 1897 edition, small size, impressed green/red/gilt cover design, 18 b/w illustrations by Reginald Birch. $20.00

Secret Garden, 1911, Stokes, paste-on pictorial cover, color plate illustrations by Maria Kirk. $100.00

Secret Garden, 1911, Heinemann, illustrated by Charles Robinson. $125.00

Shuttle, 1907, Stokes, oval paste-on illustration on cover. $20.00

BURNHAM, Clara Louise

Dr. Latimer, ca. 1907 edition Grosset Dunlap, advertised as "Dr. Latimer is a lovable character and his entry into the lives of the Ivison girls is fraught with blessed consequences to them and the greedy reader." $15.00

Jewel's Story Book, 1904 Houghton, b/w illustrations by Robert Schmitt. $15.00

Right Princess, (1902) 1904 edition Houghton. $10.00

BURNHAM, Margaret, see Series, "Girl Aviator."

BURROUGHS, Edgar Rice, see Series, "Tarzan."

Tarzan Twins, 1927, Volland, 126 pages, color illustrations throughout by Douglas Grant. $40.00

BURTON, Virginia Lee, illustrator-author, picture books

Calico, the Wonder Horse, 1941, Houghton, small oblong, printed illustrated cover, black drawings by author printed on series of different colors of pages. $50.00

Choo Choo, 1937, Houghton, oversize, b/w illustrations by author. $55.00

Katy and the Big Snow, 1943, Houghton Mifflin, oversize oblong, color illustrations by author. $75.00

Katy and the Big Snow, 1943, Weekly Reader edition. $20.00

Little House, 1942, Houghton Mifflin, 1st edition (1943 Caldecott), oversize, color illustrations by author. $100.00

Mike Mulligan and His Steam Shovel, 1939, Houghton Mifflin, oversize, color illustrations by author. $100.00

Mike Mulligan and His Steam Shovel, 1939, Weekly Reader Edition. $15.00

BUSH, Bertha E.
Prairie Rose, (1910) 1927, Little Brown, color paste-on pictorial cover, 5 color plates by Henry Pitz. $20.00

BUTLER, Ellis
Jibby Jones, 1923, Houghton, b/w illustrations by Arthur Dorr. $10.00
Jibby Jones, and the Alligator, 1924, Houghton, b/w illustrations by Arthur Dorr. $10.00
Jo Ann, Tomboy, 1933, Houghton, b/w illustrations by Ruth King. $10.00
Pups and Pies, short story collection, 1938, Sun Dial. $5.00

CADY, Harrison, b. Massachusetts, 1877, illustrator, see Series, "Bedtime Storybooks," "Smiling Pool," "Wishing Stone."

CALDECOTT, Randolph, 1846 – 1886, illustrator
House That Jack Built, 1879, Warne. $75.00
Queen of Hearts, (1881 Warne, illustrations rare,) undated ca. 1920s, Warne, color illustrations $55.00
R. Caldecott's Picture Book No. 1, first published in 1879 by Warner. Rare
R. Caldecott's Picture Book No. 1, undated edition ca. 1920s, Warne, 9" x 8", impressed illustration on cloth-covered boards, color illustrations throughout. $55.00
Some of Aesop's Fables, 1883, NY, color illustrations. $95.00

CALHOUN, Frances
Miss Minerva and William Green Hill, 1909, Reilly. $40.00

CAMPBELL, Ruth
Cat Whose Whiskers Slipped, 1925, Volland, color illustrations throughout by Ve Elizabeth Cadie. $55.00
Cat Whose Whisker Slipped, 1938 edition, Wise-Parslow, Ve Elizabeth Cadie color illustrations. $30.00

CANFIELD, Dorothy
Understood Betsy, 1916, Holt, color illustration on cover, b/w illustrations by Ada Williams. $20.00
Made-to-Order Stories, 1925, Harcourt, color frontipiece and b/w illustrations by Dorothy Lathrop. $20.00

CANIFF, Milton
Terry and the Pirates, 1946, NY, illustrations by author. $35.00

CAPUANA, Luigi
Golden Feather, 1930, Dutton 1st edition, 205 pages, color frontispiece, b/w illustrations by Margaret Freeman. $15.00
Italian Fairy Tales, translated by Dorothy Emmrich, 1929, Dutton, illustrated by Margaret Freeman. $15.00

CARPENTER, Frances, b.1890 (daughter of Frank O. Carpenter), see Series "Our Little Friends."
Tales of a Chinese Grandmother, ca. 1940, Doubleday. $25.00
Tales of a Russian Grandmother, 1933, Doubleday, 292 pages, illustrated by I. Bilibine. $30.00
Tales of a Basque Grandmother, 1930, Junior Literary Guild, 271 pages, illustrated by Pedro Garmendia. $35.00

CARPENTER, Frank O.
Around the World With Children, 1917, American Book, photo illustrations. $25.00

CARR, Mary Jane
Peggy and Paul and Laddy, 1936, Crowell, color endpapers, b/w illustrations by Kathleen Voute. $18.00

CARR, Sarah Pratt, see Series, "Billy To-Morrow."

CARR, Warner
Little Lost Lammie, 1916, Whitman, color paste-on cover, illustrated in color and b/w by author. $25.00

CARRIGHAR, Sally
One Day on Beetle Rock, 1945, Knopf, b/w illustrations by Henry Kane. $15.00

CARROLL, Lewis (Rev. C. L. Dodgson, 1832 – 1898)
Alice's Adventures in Wonderland, 1865, London, illustrations by Sir John Tenniel. Rare
Alice's Adventures in Wonderland, 1870 edition, Lee & Shepard, Boston, small size, red cloth-over-boards, gilt edged pages, Tenniel illustrations. $85.00
Alice's Adventures in Wonderland, 1897 edition, Altemus, paste-on cover illustration, 4 color and over 40 b/w illustrations. $85.00
Alice's Adventures in Wonderland, 1901, Harper, full-page illustrations by Peter Newell. $85.00
Alice's Adventures in Wonderland, 1907, Heinemann, London, illustrations by Arthur Rackham. $250.00
Alice's Adventures in Wonderland, 1907, color

plate illustrations by Bessie Pease Gutmann. $225.00

Alice's Adventures in Wonderland, 1912, Blackie, illustrations by Frank Adams. $35.00

Alice's Adventures in Wonderland, 1919, NY, color plate illustrations by Maria Kirk. $55.00

Alice's Adventures in Wonderland, 1923, Philadelphia, color and b/w illustrations by Gertrude Kay. $60.00

Alice's Adventures in Wonderland and Through the Looking Glass, ca. 1917, Grosset Dunlap, illustrations are full-page photos from "moving picture" by Nonpareil Feature Film Co, starring Viola Savoy. $45.00

Alice's Adventures in Wonderland, 1928, Whitman, Tenniel illustrations. $45.00

Alice's Adventures Under Ground, 1886, Macmillan, red cover with gilt lettering and decoration, 37 illustrations by the author. $700.00

Alice in Wonderland, 1910, Raphael Tuck, illustrations by Mabel Lucie Attwell. $100.00

Alice in Wonderland, ca. 1947, Grosset Dunlap, full-color wraparound illustration on paper-covered boards, color frontispiece, 8 color plates plus b/w Tenniel illustrations. $20.00

Nursery Alice, 1890, white cover with color illustration by E. G. Thomson, color-tinted Tenniel illustrations. $350.00

Rhyme? And Reason? 1883, Macmillan, cloth cover with gilt, illustrations by Arthur B. Frost and Henry Holiday. $250.00

Sylvie and Bruno, 1889, Macmillan, red cover with gilt, illustrations by Harry Furniss.   Rare

Sylvie and Bruno Concluded, 1893, Macmillan, gilt-decorated cover, illustrations by Harry Furniss.   Rare

Through the Looking Glass, 1872, illustrations by Tenniel. Rare

CARSON, Captain James, see Series, "Saddle Boys," "Speedwell Boys."

CARTER, Russell Gordon, 1892 – 1957, see Series, "Bob Hanson", "Patriot Lad."
Teen-Age Historical Stories, 1948. $10.00
Teen-Age Animal Stories, 1948. $10.00
White Plume of Navarre, 1928, Volland, deluxe edition with heavily impressed cover design, color illustrations by Beatrice Stevens. $50.00
White Plume of Navarre, 1928, Volland, color paste-on pictorial, color illustrations by Beatrice Stevens. $40.00

CAUDILL, Rebecca
Barry and Daughter, 1943. $15.00
Happy Little Family, 1947. $15.00

Tree of Freedom, 1949. $15.00

CAVANNA, Betty
Going on Sixteen, 1946, Westminster. $15.00

CHADWICK, Lester, see Series, "Baseball Joe," "College Sports."

CHALMERS, Margaret, see Series, "Peter Loomis."

CHAMBERLAIN, Ethel
Minnie the Fish Who Lived in a Shoe, 1928, Graham. $25.00

CHAMBERS, Maria
Water Carrier's Secrets, 1942, Oxford, two-color illustrations by Leonard Weisgard. $10.00

CHAMBERS, Robert W.
River-Land, A Story for Children, 1904, Harper, oversize, color and b/w illustrations by Elizabeth Shippen Green. $95.00

CHAMOUD, Simone
Picture Tales from the French, 1933, Stokes, small size oblong, b/w illustrations by Grace Gilkison. $15.00

CHAPIN, Anna Alice
Now-A-Days Fairy Book, 1911, Dodd, oversize, color plates by Jessie Willcox Smith. $200.00
True Story of Humpty Dumpty, 1905, Dodd, illustrations by Ethel Betts. $125.00
Babes in Toyland, 1924, Dodd, color illustrations by Ethel Betts. $200.00

CHAPIN, Frederic
Pinky and the Plumed Knight, 1909, Saalfield, illustrated cover, color and b/w illustrations by Merle Johnson. $35.00

CHAPMAN, Allen, see Series, "Radio Boys," "Railroad Stories."

CHAPMAN, Maristan (John and Mary Ilsley)
Mountain Mystery, 1941, Appleton. $15.00

CHELEY, Frank Howard, 1889 – 1941
Boy Riders of the Rockies, 1928. $15.00
Buffalo Roost, 1909. $15.00
By Emberglow, 1937. $15.00
Told by the Campfire, 1911. $15.00

CHENEY, Edna D. L., 1824 – 1904
Child of the Tide, 1875. $10.00

Sally Williams, the Mountain Girl, 1873. $15.00

CHIPMAN, Charles P.
Page and the Prince, 1908. $15.00
Two Boys and a Dog, 1903. $15.00

CHISHOLM, Louey, edited stories for *Young Folks* periodical
Enchanted Land, undated Nelson, cloth-over-boards,16 color plate illustrations by Katharine Cameron . $45.00

CHRISMAN, Arthur, b. Virginia, 1889 – 1953
Shen of the Sea, 1925, Dutton (1926 Newbery Medal). $30.00
Treasures Long Hidden, 1941, Dutton, 1st edition, 302 pages, b/w illustrations by Weda Yap. $15.00

CHURCH, Alfred John, 1829 – 1912
Odyssey for Boys and Girls, 1906 edition, Macmillan. $20.00
Stories from the Greek Tragedians, 1879, Dodd. $30.00

CLARK, Ann Nolan
In My Mother's House, 1941, Viking, illustrations by Velino Herrera. $20.00
Little Navajo Bluebird, 1943, Viking, 143 pages, illustrated by Paul Lantz. $20.00

CLARK, Margery (Mary Clark and Margery Quigley)
Poppy Seed Cakes, 1929, Doubleday, illustrated by Maud and Miska Petersham. $30.00

CLARKE, Covington
Sky Caravan, 1931, Reilly Lee. $10.00

CLARKE, Sarah, see Series, "Boy Donald," "Little Miss Weezy."
Merry Five, 1897. $20.00

CLAUDY, Carl Harry
Girl Reporter, 1930. $15.00
Tell Me Why Stories, 1912 – 16, 4 books. $10.00 ea.
Thousand Years a Minute, 1933, Grosset, 216 pages, color endpaper illustration, two-color frontispiece. $10.00

CLEARY, Beverly
Henry Huggins, 1950, Morrow, 155 pages, illustrations by Louis Darling, 1st edition. $35.00

COATSWORTH, Elizabeth, b. New York, 1893
Away Goes Sally, 1934, Macmillan, illustrated by Helen Sewell. $25.00
Cat and the Captain, 1927, Macmillan, illustrations by Gertrude Kaye. $25.00
Cat Who Went to Heaven, 1930, Macmillan (1931 Newbery Medal). $50.00
Fair American, 1940, Macmillan, illustrated by Helen Sewell. $25.00
Five Bushel Farm, 1939, Macmillan, illustrated by Helen Sewell. $25.00
Golden Horseshoe, 1935, Macmillan, illustrated by Robert Lawson. $35.00
Houseboat Summer, 1942, Macmillan, illustrated by Marguerite Davis. $15.00

COE, Fanny
First Book of Stories for the Story Teller, 1910, Houghton, 222 pages. $10.00

COLLIER, Virginia
Roland the Warrior, 1934, Harcourt, 237 pages, two-color illustrations by Frank Schoonover. $20.00

COLLINGS, Ellsworth
Adventures on a Dude Ranch, 1940, Bobbs. $10.00

COLLODI, Carlo (Carlo Lorenzini)
Adventures of Pinocchio , (1883 Italy) translated by M. A. Murray, 1892, Cassell, 1st American edition.   Rare
Adventures of Pinocchio, 1916 edition, Whitman, color illustrations by Alice Carsey. $35.00
Adventures of Pinocchio, 1932 edition, Doubleday, illustrations by Maud and Miska Petersham. $35.00
Adventures of Pinocchio, 1940 edition, illustrations by Tony Sarg. $35.00
Pinocchio, 1920 edition, Philadelphia, illustrations by Maria Kirk. $50.00
Pinocchio, ca. 1947, Grosset Dunlap, full-color wraparound illustration on paper-on-boards cover, color frontispiece, 8 color plates plus b/w illustrations by Fritz Kredel. $20.00
Pinocchio, 1946 edition, Random House, oversize, color illustrations by Lois Lenski. $25.00

COLT, Terry Strickland
Knights, Goats and Battleships, 1930 Doubleday Junior Books, b/w/orange endpapers and illustrations by Marjorie Flack. $10.00

COLUM, Padraic
Adventures of Odysseus and the Tale of Troy,

1918, Macmillan, color and b/w illustrations by Willy Pogany. $40.00

At the Gateways of Day, 1924, Yale, 217 pages, b/w Juliette May Fraser. $20.00

Big Tree of Bunlahy, 1933, Macmillan 1st edition, 166 pages, color frontispiece, b/w illustrations by Jack Yeats. $20.00

Children of Odin, 1920, Macmillan, illustrated by Willy Pogany. $30.00

Children Who Followed the Piper (1922 Macmillan), 1938, Macmillan, small size, blue cloth-covered boards with printed illustration, 152 pages, b/w illustrations by Dugald Stewart Walker. $25.00

Forge in the Forest, 1925, Macmillan, illustrations by Boris Artzybasheff. $35.00

Girl Who Sat by the Ashes, The, 1919, MacMillan, illustrations by Dugald Stewart Walker. $25.00

Golden Fleece and the Heroes Who Lived Before Achilles, 1921, Macmillan, illustrations by Willy Pogany. $30.00

King of Ireland's Son, 1921, Macmillan, 4 color plates plus b/w illustrations by Willy Pogany. $35.00

Orpheus, Myths of the World, 1930, Macmillan, illustrated by Boris Artzybasheff. $25.00

Peep Show Man, 1924, Macmillan, illustrations by Lois Lenski. $20.00

COOLIDGE, Susan (Sarah Chauncey Woolsey, 1835 – 1905), see Series, "Katy Did ."

COOK, M. E.
Blackie and His Family, 1949, Harcourt, small size,

b/w illustrations by Michael Bevans. $15.00

COOKE, Donald E.
Firebird, 1939, Winston, 144 pages, color plates and b/w illustrations by the author. $25.00

COOPER, James Fenimore
Deerslayer, 1925, Scribner, illustrations by N. C. Wyeth. $75.00

Last of the Mohicans, 1919, Scribner, illustrations by N. C. Wyeth. $75.00

COPELAND, Walter
Babes and Blossoms, undated edition ca. 1900, Caldwell, 16 arts and crafts style color plates by Charles Robinson. $185.00

CORE, Sue
Christmas on the Isthmus, 1935, Claremont Press, b/w illustrations by Anne Cordts McKeown. $15.00

CORY, David, see Series, "Billy Bunny," "Little Journeys."

CORY, Fanny Y., illustrator, see Baum.

CORYELL, Hubert V.
Klondike Gold, 1938, Macmillan. $10.00

Indian Brother, 1935, Harcourt, b/w illustrations by Henry Pitz. $20.00

Scalp Hunters (copyright 1936) 1941 edition, Harcourt, b/w illustrations by Wilfred Jones. $15.00

COTHRAN, Jean
Magic Bells, 1949, Aladdin, 1st edition, small size, 142 pages, b/w illustrations by Peter Burchard. $15.00

COUSSENS, Penryhn
Child's Book of Stories, ca. 1911, Dodd Mead, illustrations by Jessie Willcox Smith. $125.00

COX-McCORMACK, Nancy
Peeps, Volland, small size, color illustrations. $35.00

COX, Palmer, b. Canada, 1840 – 1924, author-illustrator
Bomba the Merry Old King, (1897) 1902 edition, Hurst, color illustrated cardboard cover, b/w illustrations on newsprint by author. $30.00

Brownies at Home, 1893, Century, illustrations by author. $150.00

Brownies Round the World, 1894, Unwin, illustrations by author. $100.00
Brownies: Their Book, 1887, Century, illustrations by author. $100.00
Brownie Year Book, 1895, Century, illustrations by author. $100.00
Jolly Chinee, 1900, NY, illustrations by author. $50.00
Palmer Cox's Queer People, 1888, Century, illustrations by author. $100.00
Queerie Queers with Hands, Wings and Claws, 1887, Larkin, illustrations by author. $100.00

CRANE, Alan
Gloucester Joe, 1943, Nelson, oversize, 4 color illustrations by author. $15.00

CRANE, Laura, see Series, "Automobile Girls."

CRANE, Lucy, translator from German
Household Stories, 1923 edition, Macmillan, pen-and-ink illustrations by Walter Crane. $55.00

CRANE, Walter, author-illustrator (illustrated numerous books by other authors)
Baby's Own Aesop, 1887, Edmond Evans, square, color illustrations. $150.00
Flora's Feast, a Masque of Flowers, 1899, Cassell. $150.00
Walter Crane's Picture Books: Volume 1, undated, ca. 1895 edition, Lane, oversize, color engravings by Edmund Evans, plus designs and drawings by Crane. $250.00

CREEKMORE, Raymond, author-illustrator
Little Fu, 1947, Macmillan, oversize picture book, b/w illustrations. $15.00

CRESSWELL, Beatrice F.
Royal Progress of King Pepito, 1889, Young, illustrations by Kate Greenaway. $95.00

CRESWICK
Robin Hood, 1917, McKay, illustrations by N. C. Wyeth. $70.00

CREW, Helen
Trojan Boy (copyright 1928 Century) 1936, Appleton, b/w illustrations by Richard Rodgers. $15.00

CROCKETT, Lucy Herndon
Lucio and His Nuong, 1939, Holt, oversize picture book, three-color illustrations by author. $20.00

CROCKETT, S. R.
Sweetheart Travelers, 1895, Stokes, b/w illustrations by Gordon Browne. $25.00

CROSBY, Percy, b. Brooklyn, 1891, author-illustrator
Skippy: A Novel, 1929, Grosset, cartoon illustrations. $45.00

CROWLEY, Maude
Azor and the Blue Eyed Cow, 1941, Oxford, illustrations by Helen Sewell. $20.00
Azor and the Haddock, 1949, Oxford, illustrations by Helen Sewell. $20.00

CRUIKSHANK, George, 1792 – 1878, illustrator
Fairy Library, 4 volumes (*Cinderella and the Glass Slipper, History of Jack and the Beanstalk, Hop-o-My-Thumb and the Seven League Boots, Puss in Boots*), 1853 Bogue, full set rare. $200.00 ea.

CULBERTSON, Polly
Bear Facts, 1948, Winston. $15.00

CUNNINGHAM, Caroline
Talking Stone, 1939, Knopf, 116 pages, brown print on cream paper with wood block illustrations by Richard Floethe. $25.00

CURTIS, Alice Bertha, see Series "Grandpa's Little Girl," "Frontier Girls," "Little Maid," "Little Runaways," "Yankee Girl."
Little Maid of Quebec, 1936, Penn. $15.00
Winter on the Prairie, 1945, Crowell. $15.00

CURWOOD, James Oliver
Valley of Silent Men (copyright 1920), undated ca. 1940s edition, Grosset. $10.00

CUTLER, Mary McCrae
Girl Who Kept Up, ca. 1900, Lee & Shepard, small size, cloth-covered boards, illustrations by Louise Williams. $15.00

D

DALGLIESH, Alice
America Travels, 1933, Macmillan, illustrations by Hildegarde Woodward. $20.00
Blue Teapot, 1931, Macmillan, color and b/w illustrations by Hildegarde Woodward. $25.00
Book for Jennifer, 1940, Scribner, illustrations by Katherine Milhous. $15.00

Enchanted Book, 1947, Scribner, 246 pages, color plate illustrations by Concetta Cacciola. $25.00

Hollyberries, 1939, Scribner, small size, color illustrations by Pru Herric. $25.00

Little Angel, 1943, Scribner, illustrations by Katherine Milhous. $10.00

Relief's Rocker, 1932, Macmillan, b/w illustrations by Hildegarde Woodward. $15.00

Roundabout, 1934, Macmillan, illustrations by Hildegarde Woodward. $15.00

Smiths and Rusty, 1936, Scribner, illustrations by Berta and Elmer Hader. $25.00

Wings for the Smiths, 1937, Scribner, color illustrations by Berta and Elmer Hader. $25.00

Young Aunts, 1939, Scribner, color and b/w illustrations by Charlotte Becker. $15.00

West Indian Play Days, 1926, Rand McNally, small size, impressed cover illustration, color frontispiece, b/w illustrations by Margaret E. Price. $20.00

DALLAS, Dorin
Dandelion Down and Small Flowerpot, 1923, Stratford, color illustrations. $50.00

DALY, Maureen
Seventeenth Summer, 1942, Dodd 1st edition. $35.00
Smarter and Smoother, 1944. $10.00

DALZIEL, Brothers, illustrators
Dalziel's Arabian Nights, 1865 Ward Lock, 2 volume set. Rare
National Nursery Rhymes, 1870, Novello Ewer. Rare.

DANA, Charles A.
German Fairy Tales, translated by Dana, undated ca. 1900, Conkey, red cloth-covered boards, b/w illustrations throughout. $20.00

DANE, George Ezra and Beatrice J.
Once There Was and Was Not, 1938, Doubleday, small size, 270 pages, color frontispiece, b/w illustrations by Rheo Wells. $10.00

DANIEL, Hawthorne
Shuttle and Sword, 1932, Macmillan, 169 pages, b/w illustrations by Thomas Voter. $15.00
Dorothy Stanhope, Virginian, 1931, Coward McCann, color frontispiece and b/w illustrations by Richard Holberg. $15.00

DARBY, Ada Claire, 1883 – 1953, see Series, "Scally Alden."

Keturah Came Round the Horn, 1935, Stokes, b/w illustrations by Grace Gilkinson. $15.00

Peace Pipes at Portage, 1938, Stokes, map endpapers, b/w illustrations by Grace Gilkinson. $15.00

DARINGER, Helen F.
Adopted Jane, 1947, Harcourt, 225 pages, illustrations by Kate Seredy. $10.00
Pilgrim Kate, 1949, Harcourt, illustrations by Kate Seredy. $10.00

DARLING, Mary Greenleaf, b. Massachusetts, 1848, see Series, "American Girls."
Girl of the Century, 1902, Lee & Shepard. $15.00
Gladys, A Romance, 1887, Lee & Shepard. $15.00

DAUDET, Alphonse
Pope's Mule (copyright 1925), 1942 edition, Macmillan, small size, 78 pages, color frontispiece, b/w illustrations by Heronard. $15.00

DAUGHERTY, James Henry, b. North Carolina, 1889
Abraham Lincoln, 1943, Viking (Newbery Award). $35.00
Andy and the Lion, 1938, Viking, illustrated by the author. $50.00
Daniel Boone, 1939, Viking (Newbery Award), 1st edition, author illustrated. $40.00

DAUGHERTY, Sonia
Vanka's Donkey, 1940, Stokes, small size, 62 pages, easy reader, illustrations by James Daugherty. $20.00

D'AULAIRE, Ingri and Edgar author-illustrators (specialized in oversize picture books with full-page color illustrations by the authors.)
Abraham Lincoln, 1939, Doubleday (1940 Caldecott Award). $60.00
East of the Sun and West of the Moon, 1938, Viking. $75.00
George Washington, 1936, Doubleday 1st edition, oversize, color illustrated paper-covered boards, full color lithography illustrations throughout by authors. $45.00
Wings for Per, 1944, Doubleday. $100.00

D'AULNEY, Mme. La Contesse
White Cat, 1928, Macmillan 1st edition, oversize, color illustrations by E. Mackinstrey. $25.00

DAVENPORT, Emma
Happy Holidays, 1880s, Griffith, impressed with

gold and silver gilt on red cover, small size, b/w frontispiece by F. Gilbert. $20.00

DAVIDSON, Edith
Blowing Away of Mr. Bushy Tail, The, 1910 Duffield, NY, small size, picture book, color illustrations by Clara Atwood. $25.00
Bunnikias Bunnies in Camp, 1909. $25.00
Nibbles Poppelty Poppett, 1911. $25.00

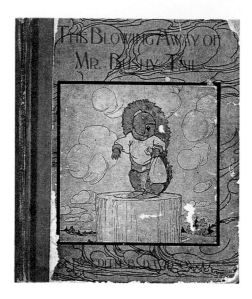

DAVIES, E. Chivers
Tales of Serbian Life, 1919, Harrap, 8 color plates. $20.00

DAVIS, Lavinia, b. New York, 1909
Fish Hook Island Mystery, 1945, Doubleday. $10.00
Hobby Horse, 1939, Doubleday, b/w Paul Brown. $15.00

DAVIS, Mary Gould
Three Golden Oranges, 1936, Longmans, written with Ralph Boggs, illustrations by Emma Brock. $30.00
With Cap and Bells, 1927. $5.00

DAVIS, Richard Harding
Boy Scout and Other Stories (1891), 1923 edition, Scribner, gilt and color paste-on pictorial, 4 color plates. $20.00
Stories for Boys (1891), 1916 edition, Scribner, gilt and color paste-on pictorial, 4 color plates. $20.00

DAVIS, Robert
Padre Porko, the Gentlemanly Pig, 1939, Holiday, small size, 165 pages, pen-and-ink illustrations

by Fritz Eichenberg. $15.00

DAWSON, Elmer, see Series, "Gary Grayson."

DAWSON, Lucy
Lucy Dawson's Dogs, 1938, Whitman. $20.00

DAWSON, Mitchell
Magic Firecrackers, 1949, Viking, b/w illustrations by Kurt Wiese. $10.00

DEAN, Graham
Treasure Hunt of the S18, 1934, Goldsmith, color illustrated boards. $15.00

DE ANGELI, Marguerite
Bright April, 1946, Doubleday, square, color illustrations by author. $25.00
Door in the Wall, 1949, Doubleday (1950 Newbery Medal), color and b/w illustrations by author. $35.00
Henner's Lydia, 1936, Doubleday, author illustrations. $25.00
Skippack School, 1939, Doubleday, author illustrations. $25.00
Ted and Nina Have a Happy Rainy Day, 1936, Doubleday. $30.00
Thee, Hannah, 1941, Doubleday. $25.00
Up the Hill, 1942, Doubleday, illustrated by author $20.00
Yonie Wondernose, 1944, Doubleday, author illustrations. $30.00

DEARBORN, Blanche, see Series, "Dearborn."

DEFOE, Daniel, see Series, "Scribner Classics."
Robinson Crusoe, 1920 edition, Cosmopolitan, oversize, illustrations by N. C. Wyeth. $100.00
Robinson Crusoe, ca. 1947 Grosset Dunlap, full-color wraparound illustration on paper-on-boards, color frontispiece, 8 color plates plus b/w illustrations by Lynd Ward. $20.00

DE HUFF, Elizabeth Willis
Taytay's Tales, 1922, Harcourt, small size, 212 pages, color frontispiece and b/w illustrations by Fred Kabotie and Otis Polelonema. $20.00

DE JONG, Meindert
Dirk's Dog Bello, 1939, Harper, illustrations by Kurt Wiese. $10.00
Bells of the Harbor, 1941, Harper, b/w illustrations by Kurt Wiese. $10.00

DELAFIELD, Clelia
Mrs. Mallard's Ducklings, 1946, Lothrop, picture

book, illustrations by Leonard Weisgard. $20.00

DE LA MARE, Walter, 1873 – 1956
Animal Stories, 1939, Scribner, 418 pages, b/w illustrations. $25.00
Come Hither, 1923, Knopf, illustrations by Alec Buckels. $40.00
Crossings: A Fairy Play, 1923, Knopf, 1st edition, music by C. Armstrong Gibbs, color frontispiece and b/w illustrations by Dorothy Lathrop. $25.00
Down a Down Derry, 1922, Constable, color plate illustrations by Dorothy Lathrop. $65.00
Peacock Pie, 1913, Constable. $75.00
Peacock Pie, 1924, Holt, 16 color plate illustrations by C. L. Fraser. $75.00
Peacock Pie, 1925, Holt, gilt impressed design on cover, illustrations by Heath Robinson. $50.00
Three Mulla-Mulgars, 1910, London. $100.00
Three Mulla-Mulgars, 1919 edition, Knopf, color plates and b/w illustrations by Dorothy Lathrop. $45.00

DENISON, Muriel
Susannah at Boarding School, 1938, NY. $10.00
Susannah of the Mounties, 1936. $15.00
Susannah Rides Again, 1940. $10.00
Susannah of the Yukon, 1936. $15.00

DENNIS, Morgan, 1893 – 1960
Burlap, 1945, Viking, 42 pages, ink wash and crayon illustrations by author. $20.00
Flip, 1941, Viking, 63 pages, illustrations by author. $30.00
Flip and the Cows, 1942, Viking, 63 pages, illustrations by author. $20.00
Holiday, 1946, Viking, 61 pages, illustrations by author. $20.00
Pup Himself, 1943, Viking, 42 pages, ink wash and crayon illustrations by author. $25.00

DENNIS, Wesley, illustrator, see author, Henry, Marguerite.

DENSLOW, W. W., 1856 – 1915 illustrator, see Baum, L. Frank, and Series, "Oz."
Billy Bounce, 1906, written with Dudley A. Bragdon, impressed color illustration on cover, color plate illustrations by Denslow. $200.00
Denslow's Animal Fair, 1904, NY, picture book, color illustrations. $200.00
Denslow's Mother Goose, 1901, NY, picture book, color illustrations. $250.00
Night Before Christmas, The, (Clement Moore), 1902, Dillingham, picture book, color illustrations. $200.00

DETMOLD, E. J. (Edward Julius), illustrator
Aesop's Fables, 1909, 25 color plates. $400.00
Book of Baby Pets, 1913, Stoughton, color plate illustrations by author. $250.00
Pictures from Birdland, 1899, Dutton, oversize, color plate illustrations by author and his brother, Charles Maurice Detmold. $400.00

DE VRIES, Julianne, see Series, "Banner Campfire Girls."

DIAZ, Abby Morton
Polly Cologne, 1881, Lothrop, b/w illustrations by Morgan Sweeney. $45.00

1915 Reilly edition

DICKENS, Charles, b. England, 1812 – 1870
Captain Boldheart, 1930 edition, Macmillan, small size, color plate illustrations by Beatrice Pearse. $35.00
Child's History of England, 1852, London, red cloth-over-boards, 3 volume set. $900.00 Individual volumes $125.00 ea.
Christmas Books, 1854, Chapman, illustrated by John Leach. Rare
Christmas Carol, A, (1843) 1911 edition, London, illustrated by A. C. Michael. $60.00
Christmas Carol, A, 1913 edition, Dutton, small size, white and gilt cover, color plate illustrations by C. E. Brock. $20.00

Christmas Carol, A, 1915 limited edition, Lippincott, signed by Rackham, tissue-protected 12 color plate illustrations by Arthur Rackham. $800.00

Christmas Carol, A, 1915 trade edition, Lippincott, tissue-protected 12 color plate illustrations by Arthur Rackham. $150.00

Christmas Carol, A, 1915 edition, Reilly, small size with color illustrations (addition to Reilly's *Children's Red Book* series but listed inside as *Children's Own Book* series). $45.00

Little Dorrit (written 1855 – 57), undated edition, ca. 1865, Chapman,cover with gilt, illustrations by H. K. Browne. $300.00

Oliver Twist, 1894, Chapman, color illustrations by George Cruikshank. $250.00

Tale of Two Cities, ca. 1947 edition, Grosset Dunlap, full-color wraparound illustration on paper-on-boards, color frontispiece, 8 color plates plus b/w illustrations by Rafaello Busoni $20.00

DILLINGHAM, Frances
Proud Little Baxter, 1898. $10.00
Christmas Tree Scholar and Other Stories, 1900. $15.00

DIONNE QUINTUPLETS Books
(The quintuplets were born in 1934, and numerous books were published using photographs and drawings of them, including picture books, story books, paper doll books.)
Dionne Quintuplets Picture Album, 1936, Dell, no author credit, 36 pages, photo illustrations. $65.00

DISNEY, WALT, STUDIO PRODUCTIONS
Three Little Pigs, 1933, Blue Ribbon Books NY, oversize picture book, color illustrations. $75.00
Clarabelle Cow, 1938, Whitman, small size, color cover, b/w illustrations $25.00

DOANE, Pelagie, illustrator
Mother Goose, 1940, Random House, full-color illustrations. $35.00
Favorite Nursery Songs, music arrangements by Inez Bertail, 1941, Random House, color illustrations. $35.00

DODGE, Mary Mapes, 1831 – 1905, editor *St. Nichlas Magazine,* 1873 – 1905
Donald and Dorothy, (1883), 1906 edition, Century, with original b/w illustrations. $15.00
Hans Brinker, 1866, O'Kane, illustrations by Thomas Nast and F. O. C. Darley. $275.00
Hans Brinker, 1915, Scribner, illustrated by George Wharton Edwards. $50.00
Hans Brinker, 1931 edition, color illustrations by Alice Carsey. $45.00
Hans Brinker, 1933 edition, illustrated by George Wharton Edwards, see Series "Scribner Classics."
Hans Brinker, ca. 1947, Grosset Dunlap, full-color wraparound illustration on paper-on-boards, color frontispiece, 8 color plates plus b/w illustrations by C. L. Baldridge. $20.00

DONAHEY, Mary, b. NY, 1876
Apple Pie Inn, 1942, Crowell, b/w illustrations by Henrietta Jones . $20.00
Peter and Prue, 1924. $95.00

DONAHEY, William
Teenie Weenie Land, 1923, Beckley. $50.00
Teenie Weenie Neighbors, 1945. $35.00
Teenie Weenie Town, 1942, Whittlesey. $35.00

DONNELL, Annie Hamilton
Rebecca Mary, ca. 1910 edition, Grosset Dunlap, illustrations by Elizabeth Shipman Green. $15.00

DOOTSON, Lily Lee
Who Am I?, 1935, Rand McNally, small size, b/w silhouette illustrations by Clarence Biers. $20.00

DOPP, Kathrine E., b. Wisconsin, 1863, see Series, "Bobby and Betty."

DOUGLAS, Amanda, see Series, "Helen Grant," "Little Girl," "Little Red House," Sherburne."
Almost as Good as a Boy, ca. 1900 edition Lee & Shepard. $15.00
Helen Grant's School Days, ca. 1900 edition, Lee & Shepard. $10.00

DOYLE, Arthur Conan
White Company, 1928, Harper, illustrations by James Daugherty. $50.00

DOYLE, Richard, illustrator, see author Allingham, William.

DU BOIS, William Pene, illustrator-author
Twenty-One Balloons, 1947, Viking (1948 Newbery Medal). $35.00
Twenty-One Balloons, later printings. $15.00

DULAC, Edmund, illustrator
Edmund Dulac's Fairy Book, 1916, NY, 15 color plates, trade edition. $200.00
Edmund Dulac's Fairy Book, 1916 trade edition, NY. $85.00
Fairy Book: Fairy Tales of Allied Nations, 1916, London, 18 color plate illustrations. $150.00
Sinbad, the Sailor, 1911, London, color plate illustrations, trade edition. $150.00

DUMAS, Alexandre, b. France, 1802 – 1870
Three Musketeers (1844), ca. 1947 edition, Grosset Dunlap, full-color wraparound illustration on paper-on-boards, color frontispiece, 8 color plates plus b/w illustrations by E. C. Van Swearingen. $20.00

DUNCAN, Julia, see Series, "Doris Force."

DUNCAN, Norman
Suitable Child, 1909, Reyell, paper-over-boards cover with gilt, tipped in plates, illustrations by Elizabeth Green. $75.00

DUNHAM, Curtis
Golden Goblin, 1906, Bobbs Merrill, gilt design on cover, color plate illustrations by George F. Kerr. $65.00
Two in a Zoo, 1904, Bobbs Merrill, illustrated by Oliver Herford. $85.00

DUNNE
St. George and the Witches, 1939, Holt, b/w illustrations by Lloyd Coe. $20.00

DURSTON, George
Boy Scouts to the Rescue, 1921, Saalfield. $8.00

DUVOISIN, Roger
Petunia, 1950, Knopf, Weekly Reader edition, oversize, author illustrations. $10.00

 ❖❀ E ❀❖

EAMES, Genevieve
Pat Rides the Trail, 1946, Messner. $10.00

EASTWICK, Ivy
Fairies and Suchlike, 1946, Dutton, 1st edition, poetry, small size, 64 pages, b/w/tan illustra-

tions by Decie Merwin. $10.00

EATON, Seymour
More About the Roosevelt Bears, 1907, oversize, color paste-on pictorial, 15 full-color illustrations by Floyd Campbell. $200.00
Teddy B and Teddy G, The Bear Detectives, 1909, Stern, illustrations by Floyd Campbell. $200.00
Roosevelt Bears Abroad, ca. 1900, Stern, illustrations by Floyd Campbell. $200.00
Roosevelt Bears, Their Travels and Adventures, 1906 Stern, 16 color plates by Floyd Campbell. $200.00

ECHOLS, William Waterhouse
Knights of Charlemagne, (first listed copyright 1928), 1938, Longmans, 362 pages, b/w illustrations by Henry Pitz. $20.00

EDMONDS, Walter, b. NY, 1903
Matchlock Gun, 1941, Dodd 1st edition (1942 Newbery Medal), illustrations by Paul Lantz. $100.00
Tom Whipple, 1942, Dodd, illustrations by Paul Lantz. $50.00
Wilderness Clearing, 1944, Dodd. $50.00

EDWARDS, Florence Dunn
Menino, 1940, Grosset and Dunlap, color illustrations by Mary Hellmuth. $15.00

EDWARDS, George, illustrator, see series, "Scribner Classics."

EDWARDS, Leo, see Series, "Jerry Todd," "Poppy Ott."

EELLS, Elsie Spicer
Fairy Tales from Brazil (copyright 1917 Dodd), 1937 edition, Dodd, small size, 210 pages, b/w illustrations by Helen Barton. $15.00

EGGLESTON, Edward
Hoosier School Boy, 1883, New York, 1st edition, illustrated. $200.00
Hoosier School-Master (originally published 1871 Orange Judd), 1899 edition, Grosset Dunlap, illustrations by Frank Beard. $20.00

EHA (E. H. Aiken)
Tribes on My Frontier, 1909, London, cover with gilt, line drawings by F. C. MacRae. $45.00

ELIOT, Ethel Cook
House on the Edge of Things, 1923, Beacon Press, color paste-on pictorial and gilt decoration on

cover, color plates by Frances Eliot Fremont-Smith. $30.00

ELIOT, T. S., 1888 – 1965
Old Possum's Book of Practical Cats, 1939, Faber 1st edition, London, oversize.   Rare

ELLIS, Edward S, see Series, "Boy Pioneer," "Deerfoot," "Log Cabin," "Forest And Prairie," "New Deerfoot," "Northwest."
Four Boys, 1896, Winston, illustrations by W. C. Jackson. $15.00
Iron Heart, War Chief of the Iroquois, 1890s, Winston, illustrated. $15.00

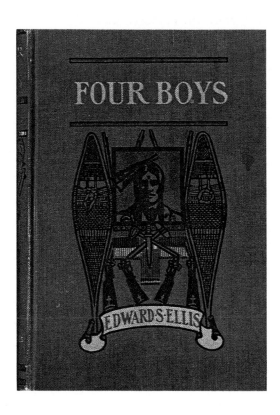

EMERSON, Alice, see Series, "Ruth Fielding."

EMERY, Carlyle
Twinkle Town Tales, 1932, Whitman, oversize, pictorial cover, color illustrations by Arthur Henderson. $35.00

ENRIGHT, Elizabeth, b. Chicago, 1909 – 1968, author-illustrator
Four-Storey Mistake, 1942, Rinehart. $20.00
Kintu, 1935, Rinehart. $25.00
Saturdays, 1941, Rinehart. $20.00
Then There Were Five, 1944, Rinehart. $20.00
Thimble Summer, 1938, (1939 Newbery Medal). $35.00

ENRIQUEZ, Major C. M.
Khyberie, 1939, Black, London, 178 pages, b/w illustrations by K. F. Barker. $5.00

ESTES, Eleanor
Hundred Dresses, 1944, Harcourt, illustrations by Louis Slobodkin. $15.00
Middle Moffat, 1942, Harcourt, illustrations by Louis Slobodkin. $15.00
Moffatts, 1941, NY, illustrations by Louis Slobodkin. $15.00
Rufus M, 1943, Harcourt, illustrated by Louis Slobodkin. $15.00

ETS, Marie Hall, author-illustrator
Mister Penny, 1935, Viking. $35.00

EULALIE, illustrator
Little Black Sambo, see authors Bannerman, Helen, and Piper, Watty.

EVANS, C. S.
Cinderella, 1919, London, color frontispiece, silhouette illustrations by Arthur Rackham, limited artist-signed first edition rare, trade first edition. $400.00

EVANS, E.
To Sweep the Spanish Main, 1932, Harrap, oversize, color and b/w illustrations. $25.00

EVANS, Eva Knox
Araminta, 1935, Putnam, illustrations by Erick Berry. $35.00
Araminta's Goat, 1938, Putnam, illustrations by Erick Berry. $30.00
Jerome Anthony, 1936, Putnam, illustrations by Erick Berry. $30.00

EVANS, Florence
Woodland Elf, 1906, Saalfield, impressed cover illustration, b/w illustrations by Carll Williams. $20.00

E. V. B. (Mrs. E. V. Boyle), author-illustrator
Child's Play, 1852, 1st edition.   Rare
New Child's Play, 1877, 1st edition.   Rare

EVERSON, Florence and Howard
Secret Cave, 1930, Dutton, illustrated by Lucinda Smith. $10.00

EWING, Juliana Horatia, 1841 –1885
("Aunt Judy" of *Aunt Judy's Magazine,* founded 1866 by Ewing's mother, Margaret Gatty. Ewing's novels were often serialized in *AJM* before book publication.)

Brownies and Other Tales (1870), undated, London, color plate and b/w illustrations by E. H. Shepard. $55.00

Jackanapes (1884), 1903 edition, Altemus, cover illustration, b/w illustrations by Caldecott. $20.00

Jackanapes, 1948 edition, illustrations by Tasha Tudor. $35.00

Stories by Juliana Horatia Ewing, 1920, Duffield, oversize, 426 pages, color paste-on illustration and gilt lettering on cloth cover, 8 color plate illustrations by Edna Cooke. $45.00

Three Christmas Trees, 1930 edition, Macmillan, small size, b/w illustrations by Pamela Bianco. $15.00

─────── ⇥⇒ **F** ⇒⇤ ───────

FAIRFAX, Virginia, see Series, "Girl Scout Mystery."

FALLS, Charles
ABC Book, 1925, Doubleday, oversize picture book, 30 pages, three–color woodcut illustrations by author. $100.00

FARJEON, Eleanor
One Foot in Fairyland, 1938 Stokes, illustrated by Robert Lawson. $35.00

Sing for Your Supper, 1938 Stokes 1st edition, small size, 137 pages, b/w illustrations by Isobel and J. M. Sale. $20.00

FARLEY, Walter, see Series, "Black Stallion" and series, "Island Stallion."

FARMER SMITH, see Smith, George Henry.

FARROW, G. E.
Adventures in Wallypug Land, 1898. $100.00
Wallypug in Fogland, 1903. $80.00
Wallypug in London, 1898. $80.00
Wallypug of Why, 1895, illustrations by Harry Furniss. $100.00

FAUCETT, T. Benjamin
Venturous Vegetables at the Frolic Grounds, 1924, Burt, paste-on pictorial cover, color frontispiece, green ink on green paper tipped-in plates. $45.00

FAULKNER, Georgene
Melindy's Medal, 1945, Messner, illustrations by C. E. Fox. $10.00
White Elephant and Other Tales From India, The, "retold" by author, 1929, Volland, cover color

illustration, color endpapers and color illustrations throughout by Frederick Richardson $50.00.

FENNER, Phyllis
Adventure Rare and Magical, 1945, Knopf, 1st edition, b/w illustrations by Henry Pitz. $15.00
Demons and Dervishes, 1946, Knopf, 1st edition, 184 pages, b/w illustrations by Henry Pitz. $15.00
Princesses and Peasant Boys, 1944, Knopf, 1st edition, b/w illustrations by Henry Pitz. $15.00
There Was a Horse, 1941, Knopf, 1st edition, 280 pages, b/w illustrations by Henry Pitz. $15.00

FIELD, Eugene
Lullabye Land, undated, ca. 1897, Scribner, b/w illustrations by Charles Robinson. $45.00
Poems of Childhood, 1904, Scribner, 8 color plate illustrations by Maxfield Parrish. $100.00
Sugar Plum Tree and Other Verses, 1930 edition Saalfield picture book, oversize,12 full-page color illustrations by Fern Bisel Peat. $45.00
Wynken, Blynken and Nod and Other Verses, 1930 edition, Saalfield picture book, oversize, 12 full-page color illustrations by Fern Bisel Peat. $45.00

FIELD, Rachel
American Folk and Fairy Tales, 1929, Scribner,

illustrations by Margaret Freeman. $25.00

Calico Bush, 1931, Macmillan, illustrations by Allen Lewis. $25.00

Hitty, 1929 Macmillan, 1st edition (1930 Newbery Medal), illustrations by Dorothy Lathrop. $100.00 later editions. $20.00

Little Book of Days, 1927, Doubleday, illustrations by author. $20.00

Little Dog Toby, 1928, Macmillan, small size, 116 pages, b/w illustrations by author. $25.00

FIELDING, Jane, see Series, "Furry Folk Stories"

FIELDS, Joseph
Junior Miss, 1941. $15.00

FILLMORE, Parker
Hickory Limb, The, 1910, John Lane, small size, b/w paste-on illustration on cover, b/w illustrations by Rose O'Neill. $25.00

Laughing Prince, 1921, Harcourt, b/w illustrations by Jay Van Everen. $15.00

Mighty Mikko, a Book of Finnish Fairy Tales, 1922, Harcourt, illustrations by Jay Van Everen. $15.00

THE HICKORY LIMB

FINGER, Charles J., born in England 1871 – 1941
Golden Tales from Faraway, 1940, Winston, 233 pages, color frontispiece, b/w illustrations by Helen Finger. $15.00

Tales from Silver Lands, 1924, Doubleday (1925 Newbery Medal). $45.00

FINLEY, Martha, see Series, "Elsie Dinsmore" and "Mildred."

FINST, Rudy
Dancing Queen, 1946, Herfin, oblong, 95 pages, illustrated cover boards, color and b/w illustrations. $20.00

FINTA, Alexander
Herdboy of Hungary, 1932, Harper, 1st edition, oversize, 166 pages, illustrated endpapers, b/w illustrations by author. $35.00

FITZGERALD, Capt. Hugh (L. Frank Baum)
Sam Steele's Adventures on Land and Sea, 1906, Reilly, 1st edition, color paste-on pictorial and gilt cover decorations. $300.00 Later editions, $120.00

Sam Steele's Adventures in Panama, 1907, Reilly, paste-on pictorial, gilt lettering. $300.00

FITZHUGH, Percy, see Series, "Pee-Wee Harris," "Roy Blakely," "Tom Slade," "Westy Martin."

FITZPATRICK, Sir Percy
Jock of the Bushveld, 1907, London. $15.00

FLACK, Marjorie
All Around Town, 1929, Doubleday, illustrations by author. $45.00

Angus and the Cat, 1931, Doubleday, 32 pages, illustrations by author. $40.00

Angus and the Ducks, 1930, Doubleday, color illustrations by author. $45.00

Angus Lost, 1932, Doubleday, 32 pages, illustrations by author. $40.00

Ask Mr. Bear, 1932, Macmillan, illustrations by author. $35.00

Boats on the River, 1946, Viking, oversize oblong, color illustrations by Jay Hyde Barnum. $35.00

Christopher, 1935, Scribner, easy read, color illustrated cover, color endpapers and illustrations by author. $25.00

Humphrey, 1934, Doubleday, oversize, color illustrated paper-covered boards, color endpapers, color illustrations by author. $35.00

Story about Ping, 1933, NY, 32 pages, easy read, color illustrated paper-covered boards, color illustrations by Kurt Weise. $45.00

Tim Tadpole and the Great Bullfrog, 1934, Doubleday, illustrations by author. $30.00

Topsy, 1935, Doubleday, oblong, easy read, color illustrations by author. $35.00

Walter the Lazy Mouse, 1941, Doubleday, oversize, color illustrations by author. $30.00

William and His Lost Kitten, 1938, Houghton, oblong, color illustrations. $25.00

FLEMING, Patricia Crew
Rico the Young Rancher, 1942, Heath, small 64 pages, color paste-on-pictorial, color and b/w illustrations by Weda Yap. $10.00

FLOWER, Jessie Graham, see Series, "Grace Harlowe."

FORBES, Esther
Johnny Tremain, 1943, Houghton (1944 Newbery Medal), illustrations by Lynd Ward. $20.00

FORD, Paul Leicester
Checkered Love Affair, 1903, Dodd, impressed cover with gilt, cover and page frame designs by George Wharton Edwards, tissue over 5 b/w photogravures by Harrison Fisher. $50.00

FORESTER, C. S.
Poo-Poo and the Dragons, 1942, Little Brown, illustrations by Robert Lawson, hard-to-find. $125.00

FOSTER, Elizabeth
GiGi in America, 1946, Houghton, b/w illustrations by Phyllis Cote. $10.00

FOX, Fontaine, cartoonist
Toonerville Trolley and Other Cartoons, 1921, Cupples, 52 pages, blw cartoons. $60.00

FOX, Frances Margaret
Adventures of Sonny Bear (first published 1916 Rand McNally), 1935 edition Book-Elf Rand McNally small size, color illustrations by Warner Carr. $35.00

FRANCIS, Laurence
Through Thick and Thin, 1890, Estes, Boston, 225 pages, b/w full-page illustrations. $25.00

FRANCIS, Sally
Scat Scat, 1929, Platt, small, easy read, color illustrations by Elizabeth Collison. $10.00

FRANKLIN, Laurence B.
Story Book of Knowledge, 1918, Whitman, oversize, 235 pages, gilt impressed cover, b/w illustrations by Alice Carsey. $20.00

FRASER, Chelsea Curtis, 1876 – 1954
Boy Hikers, 1918. $10.00
Boys' Book of Sea Fights, 1920. $10.00
Good Old Chums, 1911. $10.00

FREES, Harry Whittier
Circus Day at Catnip Center, 1932, Manning. $15.00

FRENCH, Allen
Story of Rolf (1904), 1924 edition, Beacon Hill Bookshelf Series, 5 color plate illustrations by Henry Pitz. $20.00
Story of Grettir the Strong, 1908, Dutton, illustrations by F. I. Bennett. $25.00

SLOWLY KANANA RAISED THE LANCE—*Page 159*

Photo is frontispiece of book

FRENCH, Harry W.
Lance of Kanana (originally published 1892), 1932 edition, Junior Literary Guild, 3 color wood block illustrations by Wilfred Jones. $15.00

FREY, Hildegarde, see Series, "Camp Fire Girls."

FRIEDLANDER, Gerald
Jewish Fairy Book, 1920, Stokes, 8 color plate illustrations by George Hood. $45.00

FRISKEY, Margaret
Annie and the Wooden Skates, 1942, Oxford, 62 pages, illustrations by Lucia Patton. $20.00
Goat Afloat, 1942, Whitman. $25.00
House That Ran Away, 1944, Whitman, easy read, color paste-on pictorial cover, color and b/w illustrations by Lucia Patton. $25.00

Wings Over the Wood Shed 1941, Whitman, easy read, color paste-on pictorial cover, color and b/w illustrations by Lucia Patton. $25.00

FRITH, Henry
King Arthur and His Knights, 1932, Garden City reprint, illustrations by Frank E. Schoonover. $30.00

FROST, Frances
Windy Foot at the County Fair, 1947, Whittlesey, b/w illustrations by Lee Townsend. $15.00

FRYER, Jane Eayer
Mary Frances First Aid Book, 1916, Winston, color illustrations. $135.00
Mary Frances Garden Book, 1916, Winston, color paste-on pictorial cover, illustrations by Zwirner $65.00
Mary Frances Sewing Book, 1913, Winston, color illustrations by Jane A. Boyer. $95.00
Mary Frances Storybook, 1921, Winston, illustrated by Edwin Prittie. $50.00

FULLER, Eunice
Book of Friendly Giants, 1914, Century, 325 pages, b/w illustrations by Pamela Coleman Smith. $15.00

FULTON, Reed
Davy Jones's Locker. $10.00
Powder Dock Mystery, 1927, Doubleday. $15.00
Powder Dock Mystery, 1936, Doubleday, Young Moderns edition. $10.00
Tide's Secret. $10.00

FYLEMAN, Rose
Gay Go Up, 1930, Doubleday, small size, 106 pages, b/w illustrations by Decie Merwin. $15.00
Katy Kruse Dolly Book, 1927, Doran, color illustrated paper-on-board cover, oversize oblong, 12 color photo illustrations of Kathy Kruse dolls in scenes. $65.00
Rose Fyleman Fairy Book, 1923, Doran, 12 color plate illustrations by Hilda Miller. $40.00
Rainbow Cat, 1923, Doran, color plate illustrations by T. C. Grosvenor. $25.00
Strange Adventures of Captain Marwhopple, 1932, Doubleday, color frontispiece and b/w illustrations by Lindsay. $20.00
Tea Time Tales (1929), 1939, Doran, 246 pages, color plate illustrations by Erick Berry. $25.00

↠ **G** ↞

GAG, Wanda, b. Minnesota 1893 – 1946, author-illustrator
Funny Thing, 1929, Coward McCann, illustrations by author. $75.00
Gone is Gone, 1935, Coward McCann, small, b/w illustrations by author. $35.00
Millions of Cats, 1928, Coward McCann, tan cloth cover with large illustration, oblong picture book with b/w illustrations $95.00
Millions of Cats, 1928, Coward McCann, orange library weight cover with small silhouette illustration of cats, oblong picture book with b/w illustrations. $45.00

GAGGIN, Eva R.
An Ear for Uncle Emil, 1939, Viking, illustrations by Kate Seredy. $20.00

GALE, Leah
Hurdy Gurdy Holiday, 1942, Harper, oversize, color lithographs by Barbara Latham. $25.00

GALL, Alice and CREW, Fleming
Wagtail, 1932, Oxford, illustrations by Kurt Wiese. $25.00
Royal Mimkin, 1934, Oxford, illustrations by Camille Masline. $20.00

GALSWORTHY, John
Awakening, 1920, Scribner, oversize, gilt impressed cover, two-color illustrations by R. H. Sauter. $25.00

GALT, Katherine, See series, "Girl Scout."

GANNETT, Ruth Stiles

My Father's Dragon, 1948, Random, illustrated by author. $20.00

GARDNER, Elsie, see Series, "Mayflower."

GARIS, Cleo, see Series, "Garis," "Arden Blake Mystery."

GARIS, Howard R. b. New York, 1873 – 1962, see Series, "Garis," "Buddy Books," "Daddy," "Uncle Wiggily," "Happy Home," "Rick And Ruddy." (Under pseudonyms, Garis wrote Stratemeyer syndicate series books, often two dozen or more novels a year. Garis became famous as the author of the Uncle Wiggily stories, syndicated in newspapers, read over radio, collected in book form. He also created the Uncle Wiggily board game. Under his own name, he wrote numerous juveniles, including:)
From Office Boy to Reporter. $20.00
Larry Dexter, the Young Reporter. $20.00

GARIS, Lilian, 1872 – 1954, see Series, "Garis," "Barbara Hale," "Girl Scout," "Joan, Let's Make Believe," "Melody Lane Mystery", "Nancy Brandon," "Sally."
Two Little Girls, 1901 $15.00

GARIS, Roger, see Series, "Garis."
(Son of Howard and Lilian, also wrote books for the Stratemeyer series. In his biography of his family, *My Father Was Uncle Wiggily*, 1966 McGraw-Hill, Roger Garis estimated that the four Garises wrote over a thousand juveniles between 1905 and 1935.)

GARNETT, Eve
Family from One End Street, 1937, Vanguard, 207 pages, b/w illustrations by author. $20.00

GARNETT, Louie Ayers
Muffin Shop, 1910, McNally, oversize picture book, color illustrations by Hope Dunlap. $95.00

GARRARD, Phillis
Banana Tree House, 1938, Coward McCann, watercolor illustrations by Berta and Elmer Hader. $45.00

GARST, Shannon
Buffalo Bill, 1948, Messner, b/w illustrations by Elton Fox. $10.00
Jack London, Magnet for Adventure, 1944, Messner, 216 pages, color endpapers, b/w illustrations by Hamilton Greene. $10.00
Silver Spurs for Cowboy Boots, 1949, Abingdon, b/w illustrations by Charles Hargens. $10.00

GATES, Doris

Blue Willow, 1940, Viking, (Newbery Award) illustrated by Paul Lantz. $35.00
Sarah's Idea, 1938, Viking, illustrated by Marjorie Torrey. $20.00
Sensible Kate, 1943, Viking, illustrated by Marjorie Torrey. $15.00

GATES, Josephine Scribner, 1859 – 1930, see Series, "Live Dolls."

GAY, Romney, author-illustrator of picture books
Bonny's Wish, 1938, Grosset, small size, illustrations. $15.00
Tommy Grows Wise, 1939, G&D, small size, color illustrations by author. $25.00

GAY, Zhenya and Pachila Crespi
Fish Story, 1939, Garden City, oversize square, illustrated boards. $15.00

GIBSON, Katherine
Bow Bells, 1943, Longmans 1st edition, 125 pages, wood block b/w illustrations by Vera Bock. $15.00
Golden Bird, 1927 Macmillan, 1st edition, color frontispiece, b/w full-page illustrations by Edwin Sommer. $20.00
Jock's Castle, 1940, Longmans, illustrations by Vera Bock. $15.00
Oak Tree House, 1936, Longmans, illustrations by Vera Bock. $15.00

GILBERT, Paul T.
Bertram and His Funny Animals, 1934, Rand McNally, color endpaper illustrations, b/w illustrations by Minnie H. Rousseff $35.00

GILLHAM, Charles Edward
Beyond the Clapping Mountains, 1943, Macmillan, illustrations by an unnamed Eskimo girl. $20.00

GILSON, Roy Rolfe
In the Morning Glow, 1902, Grosset, b/w illustrations. $10.00

GINTHER, Mrs. Pemberton, see Series, "Hilda of Greycot," "Miss Pat."
Secret Stair, 1928. $15.00
Jade Necklace, 1929. $15.00
Thirteenth Spoon, 1930. $15.00

GIRVAN, Helen
Blue Treasure, 1937, Farrar, map endpapers, b/w illustrations by Harriet O'Brien. $15.00
Felicity Way, 1942, Farrar, printed cover illustration, 275 pages, b/w illustrations by Gertrude Howe. $10.00

Phantom on Skis, 1939, Rinehart, printed cover illustration, 275 pages, b/w illustrations by Alan Haemer. $10.00

GLASPELL, Susan
Cherished and Shared of Old, 1940, Messner, small, two-color cover, endpaper and two-color illustrations by Alice Harvey. $5.00

GLEIT, Maria
Pierre Keeps Watch, 1944, Scribner, b/w illustrations by Helene Carter. $10.00

GODFREY, Vincent
John Holmes at Annapolis, 1927, Houghton, 4 b/w illustrations signed CM. $15.00

GOETZ, Delia
Panchita, 1941, Harcourt, 180 pages, illustrated two-color endpapers, illustrations by Charlotte Chase. $20.00

GOLDING, Harry
Willie Winkie, 1920, small size, paste-on pictorial on cover with impressed design, 85 pages, color endpapers, color plate illustrations by Margaret Tarrant. $35.00

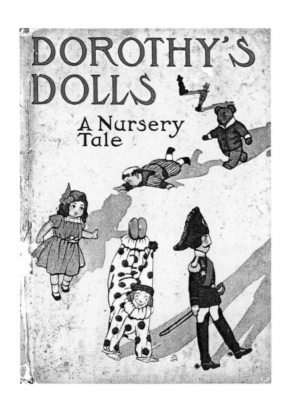

GOLDSMITH, Milton
Dorothy's Dolls, 1908, Cupples, Leon NY, small size, color plate illustrations by H. Harmony. $35.00

GOLLUMB, Joseph
That Year at Lincoln High, 1934, Macmillan, b/w illustrations by Edward Caswell. $15.00
Tuning in at Lincoln High School, 1925, Macmillan 1st edition, gilt imprinted black cover, 4 b/w illustrations. $15.00
Up at the High School, 1945, Harcourt, 217 pages, 4 b/w illustrations. $10.00
Working Through Lincoln High School, 1936, Macmillan, printed illustration on cover. $10.00

GOMME, George
Queen's Story Book, 1898, Longmans, gilt decorated cover, 445 pages, b/w plate illustrations by W. Heath Robinson. $30.00

GORDON, Elizabeth, see Series "Dolly And Molly," "Patsy Carroll."
Billy Bunny's Fortune, 1919, Volland, small size, illustrations by Maginel Wright Enright. $45.00
Bird Children, 1912, Volland, color illustrations by M. T. Ross. $85.00
Flower Children, 1910, Volland, color illustrations by M. T. Ross. $85.00
Flower Children, 1939 edition, Wise-Parslow. $25.00
Happy Home Children, 1924, Volland, small size, color illustrations by Marion Foster. $45.00
Lorraine and the Little People, (became first of a four book series) 1915, NY, small size, color illustrations by Penny Ross. $35.00
Really So Stories (1924), 1937 edition, Wise-Parslow, color plate illustrations by John Rae. $15.00
Tale of Johnny Mouse, Volland, small size, color illustrations. $45.00
Turned-Into's, 1920, Volland, color illustrations by Janet Laura Scott $45.00
Watermelon Pete and Other Stories, 1924, Rand, small size, illustrated. $35.00

GORDON, Patricia
Boy Jones, 1943, Viking, two-color endpapers, b/w illustrations by Adrienne Adams. $10.00

GOSS, Charles
Little Saint Sunshine, 1902, Bowen Merrill, gilt impressed design on cover, b/w illustrations by Virginia Keep. $30.00

GOSS, Warren Lee
In the Navy, or, Father Against Son, 1898, Crowell, printed illustration with gilt on cover, b/w illustrations by Burns. $15.00

Jack Allen, 1895, Crowell, b/w illustrations by Frank Merrill. $15.00

Jack Gregory, 1923, Crowell, 4 color plates by Howard Hastings. $20.00

Tom Clifton, 1892, Crowell, small size, b/w illustrations by W. H. Shelton. $15.00

GOUDGE, Elizabeth
Blue Hills, 1942, Coward McCann, 288 pages, two-color illustrations by Aldren Watson. $15.00

Little White Horse, 1946, Coward McCann, b/w frontispiece by Walter Hodges. $10.00

Pilgrim's Inn, 1948, Coward McCann, 346 pages. $10.00

Smoky House, 1940, Coward McCann, 286 pages, illustrations by Richard Floethe. $10.00

Well of the Star, 1941, Coward McCann, 42 pages. $5.00

GOULD, Elizabeth, see Series, "Felicia," "Polly Prentiss."

GOVAN, Christine Noble
Narcissus and de Chillun, 1938, Houghton, b/w illustrations by Alice Caddy. $20.00

Those Plummer Children, 1934, Houghton, b/w illustrations by Alice Caddy. $20.00

String and the No-Tail Cat, 1939, Houghton, 39 pages, two-color illustrations by Susanne Suba. $15.00

Sweet Possum Valley, 1940, Houghton, b/w illustrations by Manning Lee. $15.00

GRABO, Carl
Cat in Grandfather's House, 1929, Laidlaw, b/w illustrations by M. F. Iserman. $15.00

Peter and the Princess, Reilly Lee, color endpapers and 8 color plates by John Neill. $225.00

GRAHAM, Lorenz
Tales of Momolu, 1946, Reynal, 169 pages, b/w illustrations by Letterio Calapai. $10.00

GRAHAM, Tom (Sinclair Lewis)
Hike and the Aeroplane, 1912, NY. $150.00

GRAHAME, Kenneth 1859 – 1932, see Series, "Limited Edition Club."
Dream Days, ca. 1902, Dodd Mead, 10 color plate illustrations by Maxfield Parrish. $125.00

Dream Days, 1930 edition, Dodd Mead, b/w illustrations by E. H . Shepard. $35.00

Golden Age, 1900, NY, illustrations by Maxfield Parrish. $125.00

Golden Age, 1915, edition, London, oversize, 19 color plate illustrations by J. Enright-Moony. $50.00

Wind in the Willows, 1908, Methuen London, frontispiece by Graham Robertson. Rare

Wind in the Willows, 1908, edition Scribners, illustrations by Ernest Shepard. $80.00

Wind in the Willows, 1913 edition, NY, illustrations by Paul Bransom. $175.00

Wind in the Willows, 1915 edition, Scribners, 340 pages, illustrated endpapers, 12 color plate illustrations by Nancy Barnhart. $35.00

GRAMATKY, Hardie, author-illustrator
Creepers Jeep, 1948. $30.00

Hercules, 1940, Putman. $30.00

Little Toot, 1939, Putnam. $50.00

Loopy, 1941. $40.00

GRANICK, Harry
Run, Run!, 1941, Simon Schuster, printed cover illustration, b/w illustrations by Gregor Duncan. $10.00

GRANT, Capt. George
Heels of the Gale, 1937, Little Brown, b/w illustrations by Paul Quinn. $15.00

GRAY, Elizabeth Janet b. Philadelphia, 1902
Adam of the Road, 1942, Viking 1st edition (1943 Newbery Medal), illustrated by Robert Lawson. $65.00 later printings $35.00

Fair Adventure, 1940, Viking, illustrated by A. K. Reischer. $35.00

GRAY, Harold, see Series, "Little Orphan Annie."

GRAYHAM, Mary
Margaret Ellison, 1889, Bradley, impressed cover design with gilt, b/w frontispiece. $10.00

Nellie West, 1889, Bradley, impressed cover design with gilt, b/w frontispiece. $10.00

Whole Armor, 1889, Bradley, impressed cover design with gilt, b/w frontispiece. $10.00

GREEN, Elizabeth Shippen, illustrator
May Day Revels and Plays Given by the Scholars of Bryn Mawr College May 6 and 7, 1932, 1932 Bryn Mawr, oversize, full-page illustrations by Green. $150.00

May Day Revels and Plays Given by the Scholars of Bryn Mawr College May 8 and 9, 1936, 1936, Bryn Mawr, oversize, full-page illustrations by Green. $125.00

GREENAWAY, Kate, 1846 – 1901, author-illustrator. See Allingham, Browning, Harte. All of her own books are author-illustrated.
A, Apple Pie, 1886, Routledge. $150.00

Almanacks for 1883, 1884, 1885, 1886, 1887, 1888,

1889, 1890, 1891, 1892, 1893, 1894, 1895, Routledge, small size. $130.00 ea.

Almanack and Diary for 1897, Dent, small size. $150.00

Day in A Child's Life, poems set to music by Myles B. Foster "late organist of the Foundling Hospital," 1881, Routledge. $200.00

Kate Greenaway's Alphabet, ca. 1885, Routledge, small size. $150.00

Kate Greenaway's Birthday Book for Children, 1880, Routledge, verses by Mrs. Sale Barker, small size. $100.00

Marigold Garden, 1885, Routledge, oversize. $150.00

Marigold Garden, undated ca. l900, Warne, oversize, engraved by Evans, color illustrations by Greenaway. $150.00

Mother Goose, traditional rhymes, 1881, Routledge, small size. $145.00

Mother Goose, undated early Warne edition, small size, engraved by Evans, color illustrations by Greenaway. $135.00

Painting Book, 1884, Routledge, b/w outlines of earlier illustrations to color. Uncolored. $125.00.

Under the Window, 1878, Routledge, standard size. $150.00.

GREENE, Frances Nimmo
With Spurs of Gold, 1926, Little Brown, 290 pages. $10.00

GREENE, Graham, b. England, 1904
Little Train, 1946, London, illustrations by Dorothy Craigie. $45.00

GREENE, Homer
Lincoln Conscript, 1909, Houghton, 281 pages, b/w illustrations by T. de Thulstrup. $10.00

Pickett's Gap, 1906, Macmillan, b/w illustrations. $10.00

GREENE, Kathleen C.
Small, 1936, Lippincott, 265 pages, printed illustration on cover, color frontispiece, b/w illustrations by C. B. Falls. $10.00

GREGOR, Elmer Russell
Mason and His Rangers, 1926, Appleton, printed cover illustration, b/w frontispiece. $15.00

Medicine Buffalo, 1925, Appleton, printed cover illustration, color frontispiece. $15.00

Red Arrow, 1915, Harper, printed cover illustration, 4 illustrations. $15.00

Running Fox, 1918, Appleton, printed cover illustration. $15.00

Spotted Deer, 1922, Appleton, printed cover illustration. $15.00

GREY, Katherine
Hills of Gold, 1933, Little Brown, b/w illustrations by Franz Geritz. $10.00

Hills of Gold, 1941, Beacon Hill Bookshelf edition, color paste-on pictorial cover, color plate illustrations by Tom Lea. $15.00

Rolling Wheels, 1932, Little Brown, b/w illustrations by Franz Geritz. $10.00

GREY OWL
Sajo and Her Beaver People, 1936, Scribner, 182 pages, sketches by author. $20.00

GRIERSON, Elizabeth
Scottish Fairy Book, undated, Stokes, author's foreword dated 1910, 306 pages, color frontispiece, b/w illustrations by Morris Meredith Williams. $20.00

GRIFFIN, George H.
Legends of the Evergreen Coast, 1934, Clark Stuart, Canada, 1st edition, 142 pages, b/w illustrations by Probus-Pleming. $20.00

GRIFFITH, Helen, see Series, "Louie Maude."

GRIMM, The Brothers (Jakob, 1785 – 1863 and Wilhelm, 1786 – 1859)
(The Grimm brothers were scholars and lecturers who collected folk stories. When these stories were translated into English, they became favorites for illustrators. The value of these books for the collector generally depends on the illustrator and quality of print, paper and binding.)

Fairy Ring, 1846, London, illustrations by Richard Doyle. Rare

German Popular Stories, English translations,1820s edition, London, full-page illustrations by George Cruikshank. Rare

Grimm's Fairy Tales, 1888, London, illustrations by Walter Crane. $100.00

Grimm's Fairy Tales, 1900 trade edition, London, Arthur Rackham illustrations. $550.00

Grimm's Fairy Tales, 1914, Platt & Peck, color frontispiece, two-color illustrations. 20.00

Grimm's Fairy Tales, 1914, Cupples & Leon, 12 color plate illustrations by Johnny Gruelle. $95.00

Grimm's Fairy Stories, 1922 edition, Cupples, b/w illustrations by R. E. Owen, 3 color plates from the 1914 Cupples edition by Johnny Gruelle. $45.00

Grimm's Fairy Tales, 1945 edition, Grosset & Dunlap, cloth covered boards, color plate illustrations by Fritz Kredel, boxed. $25.00

Grimm's Fairy Tales, ca. 1947 edition, Grosset Dunlap, full-color wraparound illustration on paper-on-boards cover, color frontispiece, 8 color plates plus b/w illustrations by Fritz Kredel. $20.00

Snow White, 1938, Coward, illustrations by Wanda Gag. $50.00

Tales from Grimm, 1936, Coward, illustrated by Wanda Gag. $55.00

Three Gay Tales from Grimm, 1943, Coward, illustrated by Wanda Gag. $40.00

GRINNELL, George Bird
Blackfoot Lodge Tales, 1892, Scribner. $15.00
Pawnee Hero Stories, 1904, Scribner. $15.00

GRISHINA, N. G.
Gresha and His Clay Pig, 1930, Stokes, color and b/w illustrations by author. $25.00

Magic Squirrel, 1934, Lippincott, color and b/w illustrations by author. $25.00

Peter Pea, 1926, Stokes, color illustrations by author. $30.00

GRISWALD, Lotta
Deering of Deal, 1912, Macmillan, printed illustration on cover, full-page illustrations by George Harper. $15.00

Winds of Deal, 1914, Macmillan, 320 pages, b/w illustrations by George Harper. $15.00

GROSS, Milt, 1895 – 1953, cartoonist
Nize Baby, 1926, Doran, 1st edition, 207 pages, orange cloth cover with pictorial, cartoon-style illustrations by author. $95.00

GROSVENOR, Johnston
Boy Pioneer or Strange Stories of the Great Valley, 1917, Harper, 4 b/w full-page illustrations by Frank Merritt. $15.00

Strange Stories of the Great River, 1918, Harper, illustrations by Louderback. $15.00

GROSVENOR, Abbie J. G.
Winged Moccasins, 1933, Appleton, b/w illustrations. $15.00

GROTH, Eleanor
Adventures in a Dishpan, 1936, Grosset, oversize, 28 pages, color boards, endpapers and color illustrations by Milt Groth. $20.00

GROVE, Harriet Pyne, see Series, "Adventurous Allens," "Ann Sterling," "Girls Mystery," "Greycliff Girls."

GROVER, Eulalie Osgood, b.1873
Overall Boys, 1905, Rand McNally, illustrated. $65.00

Overall Boys, 1924 edition, Rand McNally, color illustrations by Bertha Corbett. $35.00

Sunbonnet Babies Book, 1902, Rand McNally, illustrated by author. $65.00

Sunbonnet Babies Book, 1902, Chicago, color illustrations by Bertha Corbett. $100.00

1924 edition

GRUELLE, Johnny, b. Illinois 1880 – 1938, author-illustrator, see Series, "All About," "Raggedy Ann."
(First editions of Gruelle's books are becoming highly collectible and expensive. However, his books are still reprinted regularly, and later editions are numerous.)

Beloved Belindy, 1926, Volland, color boards, color illustrations by author. $100.00

Beloved Belindy, 1946 edition, Donahue. $40.00

Cheery Scarecrow, 1929, Volland, small size, color illustrations by author. $55.00

Eddie Elephant, 1921, Volland, small size, color illustrations by author. $55.00

Cruise of Rickety Robin, 1931, Manning, oversize, paper cover, illustrated, collection of stories previously published in *Woman's World* magazine, a Manning publication. $65.00

Funny Little Book, 1918, Volland, small size, color illustrations by author. $45.00

Johnny Mouse and the Wishing Stick, 1922, Bobbs-Merrill, color illustrations, with presentation box. $200.00. Without box $85.00

Little Brown Bear, 1920, Volland, small size, color illustrations by author. $45.00

Little Sunny Stories, 1919, Volland, small size, color illustrations by author. $45.00

Magical Land of Noom, 1922, Volland, color plates and b/w illustrations. $125.00

Orphant Annie Story Book, adaptation of James Whitcomb Riley poem, 1921, Bobbs-Merrill, color illustrations. $85.00

Travels of Timmy Toodles, 1916, John Martin Book, 30 pages, orange cardboard cover, collection of stories printed earlier, illustrated throughout. $50.00

Wooden Willie, 1927, Volland, color illustrations, in box. $150.00. Without box $75.00

GUERBER, Helene
Myths of Northern Lands, 1895, American. $15.00

GUNNARSON, Gunnar
Good Shepard, 1940, Bobbs Merrill, 84 pages, b/w illustrations by Masha Simkovitch. $20.00

GURY, Jeremy
Round and Round Horse, 1943, Holt, oblong, b/w illustrations by Reginald Marsh. $15.00

GUTMANN, Bessie Pease, illustrator, see Carroll, Stevenson.

GUYOL, Louise
Funny House, 1922, Brimmer, 1 color plate, b/w illustrations by Emily Freret. $10.00

H

HABBERTON, John
Helen's Babies, (1876 Loring), 1908 edition, Grosset, impressed cover illustration, b/w illustrations by Tod Druggins. $20.00

HADALL, Arnold
Felicity Dances, 1938, Lippincott, photo illustrations. $15.00

HADER, Berta and Elmer, author-illustrators of picture books
Big Snow, 1948, Macmillan (1949 Caldecott art) color and b/w illustrations by authors. $50.00

Billy Butter, 1936, Macmillan, color and b/w illustrations by authors. $35.00

Cat and the Kitten, 1940, Macmillan, color and b/w illustrations by authors. $30.00

Farmer in the Dell, 1931, Macmillan, oversize, color and b/w illustrations by authors. $45.00

Little Stone House, 1944, NY, illustrated by authors. $20.00

HADOTH, Gunby
Mystery of Black Pearl Island, 1932, Stokes, b/w illustrations by George Mabie. $10.00

HAGGARD, H. Rider
King Solomon's Mines, 1885, Cassell 1st edition. $125.00.

King Solomon's Mines, later editions. $15.00

HALE, Lucretia P., b. Boston, 1820 – 1900
(The Peterkin Papers were short magazine stories by Hale, published 1866 – 1880, and then collected into books.)

Peterkin Papers, The, 1880, James Osgood, illustrations by F. G. Attwood. $225.00

Peterkin Papers, The, 1924 edition, Houghton Mifflin, standard size, b/w line & 4 color plate illustrations by Harold Brett. $45.00

HALE, Sarah
Good Little Boy's Book, ca. 1848, illustrated. $100.00

HANDFORTH, Thomas Schofield, b. Washington, 1897 – 1948, illustrator-author
Mei Li, 1938, Doubleday (1939 Caldecott). $45.00

HANKINS, Maude McGehee
Daddy Dander, 1928, Volland, small, color illustrations throughout by Ve Elizabeth Cady. $25.00

HANSHAW, Hazel Phillips
My Book of Best Stories from History, undated (ca. 1930), Cassell, 12 color plate illustrations by A. C. Michael. $35.00

HARDY, Alice Dale. See series, "Flyaway Stories," "Riddle Club."

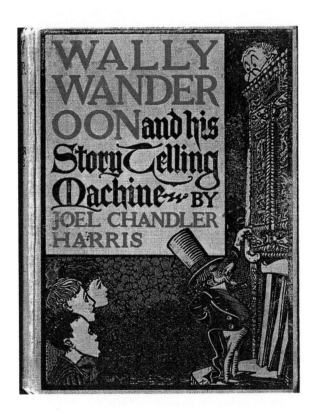

HARRIS, Joel Chandler, 1848 – 1908, see Series, "Uncle Remus."
Daddy Jake the Runaway (1889), 1896 edition, Century, gilt impressed cover, b/w illustrations by Karl Mosely. $25.00
Wally Wanderoon and His Story Telling Machine, 1908 McClure, impressed cover illustration, b/w illustrations by Karl Mosely. $65.00

HARRIS, Leila and Kilroy
Lost Hole of Bingoola, 1942, Bobbs Merrill, 1st edition, 207 pages, b/w illustrations by Will Forrest. $15.00

HARRIS, May V.
Carnival Time, 1938, Whitman, 62 pages, color paste-on pictorial, color endpapers and color illustrations by Kurt Wiese. $25.00

HARRISON, Herbert
Lad of Kent, 1927, Macmillan, b/w illustrations. $10.00

HART, Elizabeth Anne
The Runaway, 1872, London. $15.00

HARTE, Bret, b. New York, 1836 – 1902
Queen of Pirate Isle, 1886, Chatto, illustrations by Kate Greenaway, 1st edition. Rare

HARTLEY, George Inness
Boy Hunters in Demerara, 1921, Century, printed illustration on cover, illustrations by J. Clinton Shepard. $15.00

HASKELL, Helen Eggleston, see Series, "Katrinka."
Katrinka, (1915) 1929 edition, Dutton, gilt impressed cover, color frontispiece, b/w illustrations. $15.00

HAUMAN, George and Doris
Happy Harbor, 1938, Macmillan, 60 pages, map endpapers, two-color illustrations by author. $15.00

HAVARD, Aline, see Series, "Lucy Gordon."

HAWES, Charles, b. New York, 1889 – 1923
Dark Frigate, 1923, Little Brown (1924 Newbery Award), color plate illustrations by Anton Otto Fischer. $45.00
Mutineers, 1919, Torbell, color plate illustrations by Anton Otto Fischer. $35.00

HAWKINS, Sheila
Appleby John the Miller's Lad, 1939, Harper, oversize, 92 pages, b/w/orange illustrations by author. $30.00
Bruzzy Bear and the Cabin Boy, 1940, Harper, oversize, color illustrated paper-covered boards, color endpapers, color and b/w illustrations by author. $25.00

HAWKS, Ellison
Boys' Book of Remarkable Machinery, 1928, Dodd, color paste-on pictorial cover, b/w photograph illustrations. $15.00

HAWLEY, Mabel (Stratemeyer Syndicate pseudonym), see Series, "Four Little Blossoms."

HAWTHORNE, Nathaniel, 1804 – 1864, see Series, "Scribner Classics," "Windermere."
Tanglewood Tales, 1918, color plate illustrations by Dulac. $375.00
Tanglewood Tales for Boys and Girls, 1887, Houghton, illustrations by George Wharton Edwards. $50.00
Wonder Book for Boys and Girls, 1851, Houghton, illustrations by Walter Crane.   Rare
Wonder Book, 1910 edition, Houghton, 60 color designs including 18 color plate illustrations by Walter Crane. $45.00
Wonder Book for Boys and Girls, 1892 edition, Houghton, 60 color lithograph illustrations by Walter Crane. $200.00
Wonder Book and Tanglewood Tales, (copyright 1910 Dodd Mead), 1938 edition, Dodd Mead, 10 color plate illustrations by Maxfield Parrish. $60.00

HAYES, Marjorie
Alice-Albert Elephant, 1938, Little Brown, b/w illustrations by Kurt Wiese. $15.00

HAYNES, Louise Marshall
Over the Rainbow Bridge, ca.1920s, Volland, color illustrations. $45.00

HEAL, Edith
Mr. Pink and the House on the Roof, 1941, Messner, oversize, 58 pages, color and b/w illustrations by Cay Ferry. $20.00

HEARN, Lafcadio
Japanese Fairy Tales, ca. 1900, Tokyo, 5 volume set. $600.00
Japanese Fairy Tales, 1918, Boni, 1st American edition. $35.00

HECHT, Ben
Cat That Jumped Out of the Story, 1947, Winston, illustrated by Peggy Bacon. $35.00

HEINLEIN, Robert
Space Cadet, 1948, Scribner, 1st edition. $45.00

HEISENFELT, Kathryn
Children of Holland, 1934, Grosset, oversize, color illustrated paper covered boards, color endpapers, color illustrations by Charlotte Stone. $35.00

HELLIS, Nellie
Little King Davie, 1905, Page, small, impressed color illustration on cover, b/w illustrations. $10.00

HENRY, Marguerite, b. Wisconsin, 1902
Auno and Tauno, 1940, Whitman, oversize, color illustrations by Gladys Rourke Blackwood. $35.00
Geraldine Belinda, 1942, Platt, small size, picture book, color illustrations by Gladys Rourke Blackwood. $15.00
Justin Morgan Had a Horse, 1945, Wilcox, illustrated by Wesley Dennis. $35.00
King of the Wind, 1948, Rand McNally (1949 Newbery Medal) illustrations by Wesley Dennis. $45.00
Misty of Chincoteague, 1947, Rand McNally, illustrations by Wesley Dennis. $35.00

HENRY, Robert S.
On the Railroad, 1936, Saalfield, picture book, oversize, color illustrations by Otto Kuhler. $35.00

HENTY, G. A.
(Henty was England's Horatio Alger and wrote numerous didactic novels for school boys. His books bring a higher price in England.)
Beric the Briton, 1893, London. $10.00

HERBERT, Mrs. S. A. F.
Dick Langdon's Career, 1885, American Tract, impressed cover illustration. $10.00

HERBERTSON, Agnes Grozier
Teddy and Trots in Wonderland, ca. 1890, NY, illustrations by Thomas Maybank. $75.00
Cap-O-Yellow, 1908, Hodder, small size, color paste-on pictorial with gilt cover, color plate illustrations by F. V. Poole. $40.00

HEWARD, Constance, see Series, "Ameliaranne."
Twins and Tabiffa, 1923, Jacobs, small size, 122 pages, color paste-on pictorial cover, color endpapers and color plate illustrations by Susan Beatrice Pearse. $40.00

HEWES, Agnes Danforth
Boy of the Lost Crusade, 1923, Houghton, color plates by Gustaf Tenggren. $20.00
Codfish Musket, 1936, Doubleday, b/w illustrations by Armstrong Perry. $10.00
Glory of the Sea, 1933, Knopf 1st edition, color title page by N. C. Wyeth. $20.00
Sword of Roland Arnot, 1939, Houghton, color plates by Paul Strayer. $20.00

Swords on the Sea, 1928, Knopf, illustrations by Lon Block. $20.00

HEYWARD, DuBose, b. Charleston, SC, 1885 – 1940
Country Bunny and the Little Gold Shoes, 1939, Houghton, illustrations by Marjorie Flack. $35.00

HIGGINS, Aileen, see Series, "Little Princess."

HILL, Mabel Betsy author-illustrator, see Series "Apple Market Street."
Along Comes Judy-Jo, 1943, Stokes, color paste-on pictorial cover, b/w illustrations by author. $20.00
Big, Little, Smaller and Least, 1936, Lippincott, easy read, color paste-on pictorial cover, b/w illustrations by author. $20.00
Down Along Apple Market Street, 1934, Lippincott, small oblong, color illustrations by author. $25.00
Surprise for Judy-Jo, 1939, Stokes, small oblong, color endpapers and color illustrations by author. $25.00

HILL, William L.
Jackieboy in Rainbowland, 1911, Chicago, paste-on pictorial cover, illustrations by Fanny Cory $60.00

HINKLE, Thomas C.
Black Storm, 1929, Morrow, b/w illustrations. $10.00
King, Story of a Sheep Dog, 1936, Morrow. $10.00
Shag, 1931, Morrow, b/w illustrations. $10.00
Tawny, 1927, Morrow, b/w illustrations. $10.00

HOFFMANN, Heinrich
Slovenly Peter, translated by Mark Twain, 1935, Limited Edition Club, illustrated, in box. $125.00

HOFMAN, Caroline
Little Red Balloon, Volland, small size, color illustrations. $35.00
Wise Gray Cat, Volland, small size, color illustrations. $35.00

HOGAN, Inez
Bear Twins, 1936, Dutton, illustrations by author. $10.00
Kangaroo Twins, 1938, Dutton, illustrations by author. $10.00

HOLLAND, Rupert Sargent
Knight of the Golden Spur, 1922, Century, standard size, b/w full page illustrations by Reginald Birch. $30.00
All Round Our House, 1919, Jacobs, poetry collection, b/w endpapers and illustrations by Samuel Palmer. $15.00

HOLLING, Holling Clancy
Book of Cowboys, 1936, illustrations by author $15.00
Book of Indians, 1935, illustrations by author $20.00
Paddle-to-the-Sea, 1941, Boston. $15.00
Tree in the Trail, 1942, Houghton, color illustrations by author. $20.00

HOPE, Laura Lee, Stratemeyer syndicate pseudonym, see Series, "Bobbsey Twins," "Blythe Girls," "Bunny Brown," "Make Believe Stories," "Outdoor Girls," "Six Little Bunkers."

HORN, Madeline D.
Farm on the Hill, 1936, Scribner, three-color illustrations by Grant Wood. $50.00

HORNIBROOKE, Isabel
Anne of Seacrest High, 1924. $10.00
Camp and Trail, 1897. $10.00
Camp Fire Girls and Mount Greylock, 1917. $15.00
Keel to Kite, 1908. $10.00

HUBBELL, Rose Strong
Quacky Doodles' and Danny Daddles' Book, 1916, Volland, full-color illustrations by Johnny Gruelle. $85.00

HUDSON, W. H. 1841 – 1922
Green Mansions, 1904, Duckworth. $100.00
Little Boy Lost, 1920, Knopf, oversize, color plate illustrations by Dorothy Lathrop. $85.00

HUGHES, Thomas, 1822 – 96
Tom Brown's School Days, by an Old Boy, 1857, Macmillan, leather cover with gilt edges. $300.00
Tom Brown's School Days, by an Old Boy, 1869 Macmillan, illustrated by Arthur Hughes. Rare
Tom Brown's School Days, by an Old Boy, 1878 edition, Arthur Hughes illustrations. $50.00

HULE, Blanche
Father Goosey Gander, 1898, Donohue, color illustrations. $45.00

HUMPHREY, Grace, see Series, "Father Takes."

HUMPHREY, Maud, illustrator, famous for her paintings of nursery children costumed in elaborate hats and dresses, she often used her young son, Humphrey Bogart, as a model, see Tucker, E. S.

Children of the Revolution, 1900, Stokes, oversize, color illustrations $200.00

Favorite Rhymes from Mother Goose, 1891, NY, oversize, illustrated cover, color illustrations. $300.00

Maud Humphrey's Book of Fairy Tales, 1892, Stokes, color illustrations. $220.00

Make-Believe Men and Women, 1897, Stokes, oversize, line illustrations by Elizabeth Tucker, cover and color plate illustrations by Maud Humphrey. $250.00

HUNT, Blanche
Little Brown Koko, oversize, color boards, illustrated. $75.00
Stories of Little Brown Koko, 1940 edition, illustrations by Dorothy Wagstaff. $40.00

HUNT, Francis, see Series, "Mary and Jerry Mystery."

HUTCHINSON, Veronica S.
Chimney Story Fairy Tales, 1926, Minton Balch, NY, standard size, b/w illustrations by Lois Lenski. $25.00
Fireside Stories, 1925, Minton Balch, b/w illustrations by Lois Lenski. $25.00

HUTCHINSON, W. M. L.
Golden Porch (1st edition 1925), 1937, Longmans, small, two-color frontispiece, 10 b/w illustrations by Dugald Stewart Walker. $20.00
Orpheus with his Lute (1st edition 1926), 1931, Longmans, small, two-color frontispiece, 10 b/w illustrations by Dugald Stewart Walker. $20.00

HYDE, Elizabeth
Little Brothers to the Scouts, 1917. $10.00
Little Sisters to the Camp Fire Girls, 1918. $10.00

INGELOW, Jean
Mopsa the Fairy, 1869, London. $200.00

IRVING, Washington 1783 – 1859
("Rip Van Winkle" first appeared as a short story in Irving's *Sketchbook,* 1820.)
Bold Dragoon, edited by Anne Moore, 1930, Knopf, b/w illustrations by James Daugherty. $20.00
Child's Rip Van Winkle, 1908, illustrations by Maria Kirk. $55.00
Legend of Sleepy Hollow, 1926 edition, Saalfield, John Newbery Series, color frontispiece and 3 b/w full page illustrations by Frances Brundage. $20.00
Rip Van Winkle , 1897 edition, Russell, color illustrations by Will Bradley. $100.00
Rip Van Winkle , 1921 edition, McKay, 8 color plates plus b/w illustrations by N. C. Wyeth. $65.00
Tales from Washington Irving's Traveller, 1913, Philadelphia, paste-on pictorial cover, color illustrations by George Hood. $55.00

IRWIN, Inez, see Series, "Maida."

JACKSON, Helen Hunt (author of *Ramona*)
Nelly's Silver Mines, (1878 Roberts) 1932 edition, Little Brown, color paste-on illustration on cover, 4 color plate illustrations by Harriet Roosevelt Richards. $15.00

JACKSON, Leroy F.
Peter Patter Book, 1918, Rand McNally, oversize, color illustrations by Blanche Wright. $65.00
Peter Patter Book, 1919 edition, Rand McNally, oversize, color illustrations by Milo Winter. $65.00

Rimskittle Book, 1926, Rand McNally, oversize, color illustrations by Ruth Caroline Eger. $65.00

Jolly Jingle Picture Book, 1937 edition of *Rimskittle Book.* $65.00

JACOBS-BOND, Carrie
Tales of Little Dogs, 1921, Volland, small size, color illustrations by Katharine Sturges Dodge. $35.00

Tales of Little Cats, 1918, Volland, small size, color illustrations. $35.00

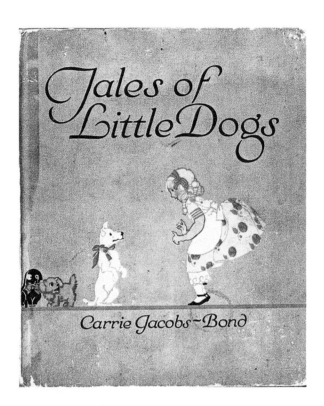

JAGENDORF, M.
New England Bean Pot, 1948, Vanguard, 272 pages, b/w illustrations by Donald McKay. $15.00

JAMES, Grace
Green Willow and Other Japanese Fairy Tales, 1910, Macmillan, 40 color plate illustrations by Warwick Goble. $400.00

JAMES, Will, b. Montana, 1892 – 1942
Smoky the Cowhorse, 1926, Scribner, 1st edition (1927 Newbery Medal). $60.00, later printings $20.00

JEFFERIES, Richard
Bevis, Story of a Boy, 1882, London 1st edition, 3 volumes. $250.00 set

JOHANSEN, Margaret, and Alice Lide
Secret of the Circle, 1937, Longmans, b/w illustra-

tions by Vera Bock. $10.00

JOHNS, Captain W. E. see Series, "Biggles."

JOHNSON, Burges, b. Vermont, 1877
Little Book of Nonsense, 1929, Harper, poetry collection, small size, 82 pages, b/w illustratons by Elizabeth MacKinstry. $20.00

JOHNSON, Constance Fuller Wheeler
Mary in California, 1922. $10.00
Mary in New Mexico, 1921. $10.00
When Mother Lets Us, 1908 – 12, 4 book series. $10.00 ea., complete set $60.00

JOHNSTON, Annie Fellows, see Series, "Little Colonel."
Georgina of the Rainbows, 1916, Britton. $25.00
Giant Scissors, 1898, L C Page. $25.00
Little Colonel, 1895, L. C. Page, 1st edition. $65.00
Little Colonel, 1935 Shirley Temple edition, A. L. Burt Chicago, photos from film. $45.00
Little Colonel's Good Time Book, 1924 edition L. C. Page, three-color arts and crafts borders on each page by P. Verburg. $25.00

JONES, Viola M.
Peter and Gretchen of old Nuremberg, 1935, Whitman, Junior Literary Guild edition, oversize, three-color illustrations throughout by Helen Sewell. $25.00

JORDAN, David Starr
Eric's Book of Beasts, 1912, Paul Elder, 1st edition, oversize, 114 pages, poems, illustrations by Shimada Sekko. $45.00

JUDD, Frances (Stratemeyer syndicate pseudonym) see Series, "Kay Tracey Mystery."

JUDD, Mary Catherine
Wigwam Stories (copyright 1901), 1929 edition, Ginn, small size, 275 pages, b/w photo illustrations by Angel de Cora. $20.00

JUDSON, Clara Ingram, 1879 – 1960, see series, "Mary Jane."
Green Ginger Jar, 1949, Houghton, printed cover illustration, b/w illustrations by Paul Brown. $15.00
Jerry and Jean Detectors, 1923, Rand, color plate illustrations by Dorothy Lake Gregory. $15.00
People Who Work Near Our House, 1942. $10.00
Sod House Winter, 1942, Houghton, b/w illustrations by Edward Caswell. $15.00

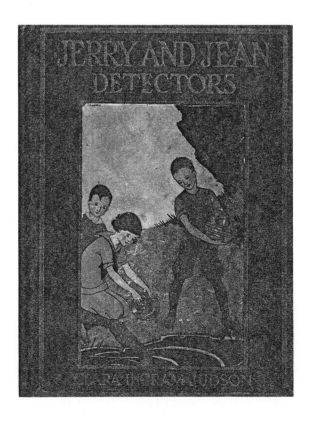

JUSTUS, May
Betty Lou of Big Log Mountain, 1928, Doubleday. $15.00
Betty Lou of Big Log Mountain, ca. 1938 edition,

Sun Dial Press, Young Moderns, illustrated by Starr Gephart. $10.00
Cabin on Kettle Creek, 1941. $5.00
Gabby Gaffer, 1929. $10.00
Honey Jane, 1935. $10.00
House in No-End Hollow, 1936. $10.00
Peter Pocket, 1927, Longmans, color frontispiece and map endpapers, b/w illustrations by Mabel Pugh. $10.00

K

KALIBALA, E. B. and DAVIS, Mary Gould
Wakaima and the Clay Man, 1946, Longmans, 145 pages, b/w illustrations by Avery Johnson. $15.00

KAUFFMAN, Reginald Wright
Seventy-Six!, color paste-on pictorial cover, b/w illustrations by Clyde DeLand. $20.00

KAY, Gertrude Alice, author-illustrator
Friends of Jimmy, 1926, Volland, oversize, color illustrations by author. $65.00
Jolly Old Shadow Man, Volland, small size, color illustrations. $65.00
When the Sandman Comes, 1914, Chicago, illustrations by author. $60.00

KEARY, A. and E.
Heroes of Asgard (1870 Macmillan), 1930, children's edition, Macmillan, small size, 16 color plates by C. E. Brock. $35.00

KEENE, Carolyn (Stratemeyer syndicate pseudonym) see Series, "Nancy Drew," "Dana Girls Mystery."

KELLY, Eric, b. Massachusetts, 1884
Blacksmith of Vilno, 1930, Macmillan, illustrations by Angelo Pruszynska. $20.00
Treasure Mountain, 1937, Macmillan, illustrations by Raymond Lufkin. $15.00
Trumpeter of Krakow, 1928, Macmillan, (1929 Newbery Medal), illustrations by Raymond Lufkin. $35.00

KENT, Rockwell illustrator, see Shepard, Esther.

KERR, George F., illustrator, see Ade, Baum and Dunham.

KILBOURNE, Charles, see Series, "Army Boy," "Baby Animals Books."

KILMER, Colleen Browne

La-La Man in Music Land, 1927, Lothrop, b/w/orange illustrations by Carmen Browne. $35.00

KING, Marian
Boy of Poland, 1934, Whitman, color paste-on pictorial, three-color plate illustrations by Eleanor Wilson. $20.00

KING, Mona Reid
Patsy Ann, Her Happy Times, 1935, Rand McNally, small size, cardboard cover with photo of Effanbee Patsy Ann doll, 64 pages, b/w photo illustrations. $35.00

KINGSLEY, Charles, 1819 – 1875
Heroes, Greek Fairy Tales for My Children, 1856, 8 illustrations by author. $400.00
Water Babies (first published 1863), 1908 edition, Dutton, color plate illustrations by Margaret Tarrant. $60.00
Water Babies, 1909, London, 42 color plate illustrations with tissue overlay by Warwick Goble. $500.00
Water Babies, 1915 edition, Houghton, 8 color plates plus b/w illustrations by W. Heath Robinson. $200.00
Water Babies, 1916, Tuck, illustrations by Mabel Lucie Attwell. $85.00
Water Babies, 1916 edition, Dodd Mead, color plate illustrations by Jessie Willcox Smith. $200.00
Water Babies, 1930 edition, London, illustrations by Anne Anderson. $75.00
Westward Ho!, 1856, see Series, "Scribner Classics."

KIPLING, Rudyard, 1865 – 1936, see Series, "Just So Stories."
All the Mowgli Stories, 1936 edition, Doubleday, illustrations by Kurt Wiese. $25.00
Captains Courageous, 1897, Macmillan, illustrated by I. W. Taber. $150.00
Jungle Book, 1894, Century. $65.00
Jungle Book, 1908 edition, London, color plate illustrations by M. and E. Detmold. $120.00
Jungle Book, 1913 edition, Century, color plate illustrations by M. and E. Detmold. $85.00
Jungle Book, 1932 edition, Doubleday, illustrations by Kurt Wiese. $40.00
Jungle Book, ca. 1947 edition, Grosset Dunlap, full-color wraparound illustration on paper-on-boards cover, color frontispiece, 8 color plates plus b/w illustrations by Fritz Eichenberg. $20.00
Just So Stories for Little Children, 1902, Macmillan, illustrations and cover design by author. $200.00
Kim, 1901, Macmillan, London, 1st edition, illustrations by J. Lockwood Kipling. $100.00
Kim, 1901, Doubleday, 1st American edition. $65.00
Puck of Pook's Hill, 1906, Macmillan. $50.00
Puck of Pook's Hill, 1906, Doubleday, color plate illustrations by Arthur Rackham. $150.00
Two Jungle Books, The, 1950 edition, Garden City, color paste-on pictorial on red cover. $20.00
Wee Willie Winkie (1888), 1938 edition, Whitman, small square, b/w/red illustrations by Veva Storey. $15.00

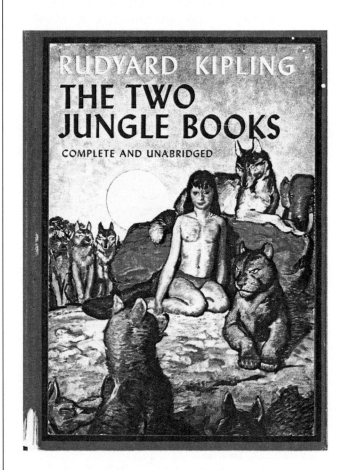

KIRBY, Mary and Elizabeth
Aunt Martha's Corner Cupboard (1928), 1936 edition, Whitman, color paste-on pictorial, color illustrations by Matilda Breuer. $15.00

KIRK, Maria
Favorite Rhymes of Mother Goose, 1910, NY, color illustrations by Kirk. $50.00

KJELGAARD, Jim
Kalak of the Ice, 1949, Holiday, illustrated by Bob Kuhn. $10.00
Snow Dog, 1948, Holiday, illustrated by Jacob Landau. $15.00

KNIGHT, Eric
Lassie Come Home, 1940, Winston, illustrated by Marguerite Kirmse. $20.00

KNOX, Kathleen
Fairy Gifts, 1874, Dutton, illustrations by Kate Greenaway. Rare

KNOX, Rose, see Series, "Riverboat."

KNOX, Thomas
John Boyd's Adventures, 1893, Appleton, gilt trimmed cover, b/w illustrations by Stacey. $10.00

KRAUSS, Ruth
Bears, 1948, Harper, two-color illustrations by Phyllis Rowland. $30.00

KREYMBORG, Alfred
Funnybone Alley, 1927, Macmillan, limited edition, oversize, color plate illustrations by Boris Artzybasheff. $100.00

LABOULAYE
Laboulaye's Fairy Book, translated, (1866), 1874 edition, Harper, b/w engraving illustrations. $40.00
Laboulaye's Fairy Book, translated by Mary Booth, (1866), 1920 edition, Harper, color paste-on illustration on cover, 12 color plates by Edward McCandlish. $50.00

LA FARGE, Oliver
Laughing Boy, 1929, Houghton. $20.00

LAGERFELD, Selma
Wonderful Adventures of Nils, (1907 Doubleday), undated edition, Grosset, b/w illustrations by Harold Heartt. $10.00

LAMB, Charles, 1775 – 1834
Adventures of Ulysses, 1928 edition, Platt Munk, oversize, 117 pages, gilt design on cover, two-color plate illustrations by M. H. Squire and E. Mars. $20.00
Tales from Shakespeare (1807), 1909 edition, London, color plate illustrations by Arthur Rackham. $200.00, later printings $45.00
Tales from Shakespeare, 1924 edition, Winston, color frontispiece, 11 b/w plate illustrations by Frank Godwin. $20.00

LAMBERT, Janet
Glory Be!, 1943, Dutton, b/w illustrations by Woody Ishmael. $10.00
Practically Perfect, 1947, Grosset. $5.00

LANG, Andrew b. Scotland 1844 – 1912, see series, "Lang Fairy Books."
Prince Prigio, 1889, Arrowsmith, small size, b/w illustrations by Gordon Browne. $40.00
Prince Prigio, 1942, Little Brown, illustrations by Robert Lawson. $40.00
Prince Ricardo of Pantouflia, 1893, Arrowsmith, b/w illustrations by Gordon Browne. $40.00
Princess Nobody, 1884, Longmans, color illustrations by Richard Doyle. Rare

LANG, Mrs. Andrew
Red Book of Heroes (1909), 1929 edition, Longmans, 8 color plates by H. J. Ford and Lancelot Speed. $25.00

LANGE, Dietrich, 1863 – 1940
Lost in the Fur Country, 1914. $10.00
Lure of the Black Hills, 1916. $10.00
On the Trail of the Sioux, 1912. $10.00

LANGER, Susanne
Cruise of the Little Dipper, 1923, 1st edition, color plates and b/w illustrations by Helen Sewell. $40.00

LANGWORTHY, John, see Series, "Aeroplane."

LANIER, Sydney
Boy's King Arthur, 1917, Scribner, 17 color plates by N. C. Wyeth. $95.00
Boy's King Arthur, later edition, see Series, "Scribner Classics."
King Arthur and his Knights of the Round Table, ca. 1947 edition, Grosset Dunlap, full color wraparound illustration on paper-on-boards cover, color frontispiece, 8 color plates plus b/w illustrations by Florian. $20.00

LASKEY, Muriel
Curious Chipmunk, 1946, Pied Piper, oversize, color illustrations by Georgi Helms. $15.00

LATHROP, Dorothy, b. New York, 1891, author-illustrator
Angel in the Woods, 1947, Macmillan, 1st edition, small size, b/w illustrations by author. $25.00
Animals of the Bible, 1937, Stokes, 1st edition (1938

Caldecott), illustrations by author. $50.00, later editions $20.00

Colt from Moon Mountain, 1941, NY , illustrations by author. $80.00

Fairy Circus, 1931, illustrations by author. $55.00

Hide and Go Seek, 1938, Macmillan. $75.00

Little White Goat, 1933, illustrations by author. $40.00

Lost Merry-Go-Round, 1934, color frontispiece, b/w illustrations by author. $30.00

Who Goes There?, 1935, Macmillan, illustrations by author. $30.00

LATHROP, Gilbert
Mystery Rides the Trail, 1937, Goldsmith. $10.00

LATTIMORE, Eleanor F., b. Shanghai, 1904
Jeremy's Isle, 1947, Morrow, b/w illustrations by author. $15.00

Jerry and the Pusa, 1932, Harcourt, b/w illustrations by author. $15.00

Junior, 1938, Harcourt, b/w illustrations by author. $15.00

Little Pear, 1931, Harcourt, illustrated by author. $25.00

Little Pear and His Friends, 1934, Harcourt, illustrated by author. $20.00

Seven Crowns, 1933, Harcourt, illustrated by author. $20.00

LAUGHLIN, Clara
Everybody's Lonesome, 1910, Revell, b/w illustrations by A. I. Keller. $10.00

LAWRENCE, Josephine, see Series, "Brother and Sister," "Elizabeth Ann."
Brothers and Sisters Holiday, 1921, Cupples, illustrations by Julia Greene. $20.00

Gingerbread Man, 1930, Whitman, b/w Johnny Gruelle illustrations from "Man in the Moon" used here and tinted by Robert Bezucha. $45.00

Man in the Moon Stories Told Over the Radio Phone, 1922, Cupples, orange cover with paste-on pictorial, 9 full-page color plate plus b/w illustrations by Johnny Gruelle. $150.00

Man in the Moon Stories Told Over the Radio Phone, 1930 edition, Whitman. $45.00

LAWSON, Robert, b. New York, 1892-1957, author-illustrator
Ben and Me, 1939, Little Brown, illustrated by author. $30.00

Just for Fun, 1940, Rand McNally, oversize, b/w illustrations by author. $35.00

Rabbit Hill, 1944, NY, (1945 Newbery Medal), illustrations by author. $45.00

Robbut, a Tale of Tails, 1948, Viking, b/w illustrations by author. $30.00

They Were Strong and Good, 1940, Viking (1941 Caldecott for art), illustrations by author. $50.00

LEAF, Munro
Munro Leaf's Fun Book, 1934, Stokes, b/w/red illustrations by author. $35.00

Story of Ferdinand, 1936, Viking, b/w illustrations by Robert Lawson. $150.00, later editions $35.00

Story of Ferdinand, 1938, Whitman, color illustrations from Disney. $20.00

Watchbirds, 1939, Stokes, oversize, line drawings by author. $25.00

Wee Gillis, 1938, Viking, oversize, tartan paper-over-board cover with corner illustration, illustrations by Robert Lawson. $50.00

Wee Gillis, 1943, Viking, oversize plain cover with corner illustration, illustrations by Robert Lawson. $25.00

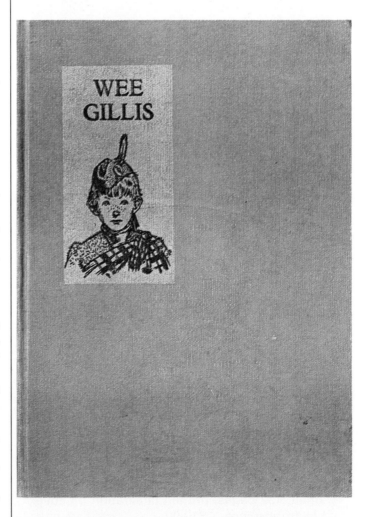

LEAR, Edward, author-illustrator
Book of Nonsense, 1855, London, oblong, 72 plate

illustrations. Rare
Laughable Lyrics, 1877, London. $450.00
Nonsense Songs, Stories, Botany and Alphabets, 1871,
Osgood, Boston, 1st American edition. $700.00

LE BLANC, Georgette
Blue Bird for Children, The, abridged school edition, 1914, Silver Burdett, printed cover illustration, color frontispiece and b/w illustrations by
Frederick Perrins. $20.00

LEE, Melicent Humason
Marcos, 1937, Whitman, oversize, color paste-on
pictorial, color endpapers, color illustrations by
Berta and Elmer Hader. $30.00
Saltwater Boy, 1941, Caxton, printed illustration
on cover, color frontispiece, b/w illustrations
by Leslie Lee. $20.00

LEET, Frank R.
Purr and Miew, 1931, Saalfield, oversize picture
book, 60 pages, color plate illustrations by Fern
Bisel Peat. $55.00

LE FEUVRE, Amy
Probable Sons, ca. 1900, London, religious tract,
small, 132 pages, printed illustration on cover,
b/w frontispiece. $10.00

LEFEVRE, Felicite
Little Grey Goose, 1925, MacRae, small, 98 pages,
color illustrations by Freda Derrick. $35.00

LEFROY, Ella
By the Gail Water, 1890, London, impressed cover
design with gilt, small size, 124 pages, b/w
frontispiece. $10.00

LEIGHTON, Clare
Musical Box, 1932, Longmans, 1st edition, oblong,
printed illustration on cover, b/w illustrations
by author. $30.00

LEIGHTON, Margaret
Singing Cave, 1945, Houghton, illustrated by Manning Lee. $15.00

LE MAIR, H. Willebeek, illustrator
Our Old Nursery Rhymes, 1911, Philadelphia, picture book illustrated by Le Mair. $100.00

LENSKI, Lois, b. Ohio, 1893, illustrator-author,
see Series, "Regional Stories."
A-Going Westward, 1937, Lippincott, 368 pages,
b/w illustrations by author. $20.00
Arabella and Her Aunts, 1932, illustrations by
Lenski. $50.00
Bound Girl of Cobble Hill, 1938, Stokes. $35.00
Easter Rabbit's Parade, 1936, Oxford. $45.00
Let's Play House, 1944, Oxford, small oblong,
b/w/blue and red illustrations by author, easy
reader. $25.00
Little Fire Engine, 1946, illustrations by author.
$45.00
Little Engine That Could, 1930, NY, 1st edition,
illustrations by author. $200.00, later editions
$35.00
Now It's Fall, 1948, Oxford, small size, two-color
illustrations by author. $15.00

LENT, Henry
Clear Track Ahead, 1932, Macmillan, photograph frontispiece, b/w illustrations by Earle Winslow. $30.00

LEWIS, C. S.
The Lion, the Witch and the Wardrobe, 1950,
Macmillan, 1st edition, illustrations by Pauline
Baynes. $75.00

LEWIS, Elizabeth, b. Maryland, 1892
Young Fu of the Upper Yangtze, 1932, Winston
(1933 Newbery Medal), 265 pages, color frontispiece, b/w and color plate illustrations by
Kurt Wiese. $15.00

LIENTZ, Thelma
Black Box, 1929, Saalfield, b/w frontispiece. $5.00

LINDERMAN, Frank
How It Came About Stories, ca. 1940s edition, Blue Ribbon. $10.00
Indian Why Stories, 1915, Scribner, illustrations by Charles Russell. $45.00

LINDMAN, Maj, see Series, "Flicka, Ricka and Dicka," "Snipp, Snapp, Snurr."

LINDSAY, Maud
Bobby and the Big Road, Lothrop, small size, color illustrations. $45.00
Choosing Book, 1928, Lothrop, small size, color plate illustrations by Florence Liley Young. $25.00
Little Missy, Lothrop, small size, color illustrations. $45.00
More Mother Stories (1905), 22nd printing, Milton Bradley, b/w illustrations by Sanborn and Railton. $15.00
Silverfoot, Lothrop, small size, color illustrations. $45.00
Story Garden for Little Children, Lothrop, small size, 12 color plate illustrations by Florence Liley Young. $45.00
Story-Teller, The, 1915, Lothrop, small size, color plate illustrations by Florence Liley Young. $25.00

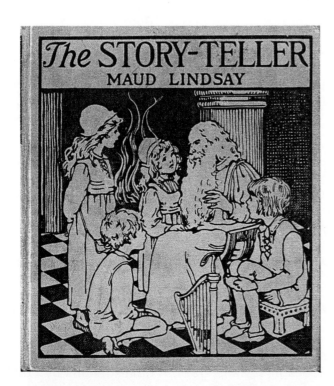

LINDSAY, Norman
The Magic Pudding, 1903, Sydney, illustrated by author. $25.00

LINKLATER, Eric
Pirates in the Deep Green Sea, 1949, London, map endpapers, b/w illustrations by William Reeves. $15.00

LINNELL, Gertrude
Behind the Battlements, 1931, Macmillan, small size, 166 pages, illustrated endpapers, b/w illustrations by Helene Carter. $15.00

LIPPINCOTT, Joseph Wharton
Red Roan Pony, 1934, Lippincott, illustrations by C. W. Anderson. $15.00

LLOYD, Marion
Penny and Peter, 1941, Messner, oversize, 93 pages, illustrations by Agnes Tait. $15.00

LOCKWOOD, Myna
Macaroni, an American Tune, 1939, Oxford, 45 pages, three-color illustrations by author. $15.00
Violin Detectives, 1940, Oxford. $10.00

LOFTING, Hugh, b. England, 1886 – 1947, author-illustrator, see Series, "Doctor Doolittle."

LOMBROSO-CARRARA, Paolo
Adventures of Chicchi, 1927, Putnam, oversize, color paste-on pictorial and gilt trim on cover, 9 color plates by Robert Herbert. $45.00

LONDON GOSPEL TRACT books
My Children's Picture Book, undated, ca. 1880s, b/w illustrations. $25.00

LONDON, Jack
White Fang, 1906, Macmillan, 1st edition. $150.00

LONG, John Luthar
Billy-Boy, 1906, Dodd, oversize, 4 color plates by Jessie Willcox Smith. $150.00

LONG, Lucile
Anna Elizabeth, 1942, Brethren. $5.00

LONGFELLOW, Henry Wadsworth
Story of Evangeline, 1905, Bobbs Merrill, paste-on pictorial cover illustration with gilt lettering, illustrations by Howard Chandler Christy. $50.00
Story of Evangeline, adapted to prose by Clayton Edwards and containing the original poem, 1916 Stokes, oversize, color paste-on pictorial cover, 6 color plate illustrations by M. L. Kirk. $45.00

LOUNSBERRY, Lieut.
Kit Carey's Protege, 1899 edition, Street. $10.00
In Glory's Van (1904 Street), undated, McKay edition. $10.00

LOVELACE, Maud Hart, b. Minnesota, 1892
Betsy in Spite of Herself, 1946, Crowell, illustrated by Lois Lenski. $10.00
Betsy-Tacy, 1940, Crowell, illustrations by Lois Lenski. $15.00.
Golden Wedge, 1942, Crowell, 190 pages, two-color illustrations by Charlotte Chase. $20.00

LOWE, Samuel E.
In the Court of King Arthur, 1918, Whitman, color plate illustrations by Neil O'Keefe. $30.00
New Story of Peter Rabbit, 1926, Whitman, small size, color illustrations by Allan Wright. $35.00

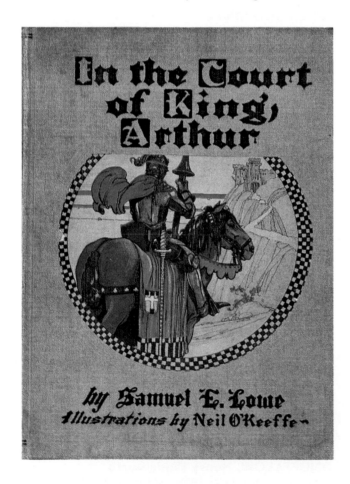

LOWE, V. R.
Boys' Book of Adventures, 1931, Whitman, oversize, 40 pages, color illustrated cover, color illustrations by Joseph Kraemer. $30.00

LUCAS, E. V.
Playtime & Company, 1925, NY, illustrated by Ernest Shepard. $25.00

LUCIA, Rose, see Series, "Peter and Polly."

LYDEN, Clara
Children Come and Sing, 1937, Hale, b/w illustrations by Mary Hellmuth. $15.00

LYONS, Dorothy
Midnight Moon, 1941, Harcourt, b/w illustrations by W. C. Nims. $10.00

───── ═ **M** ═ ─────

MAC DONALD, Betty
Mrs. Piggle-Wiggle, 1947, Lippincott, 1st edition, illustrated by Hilary Knight. $60.00

MAC DONALD, George, 1824 – 1905
At the Back of the North Wind, 1871, Strahan, illustrations by Arthur Hughs. Rare
At the Back of the North Wind, 1910, illustrations by Maria Kirk. $45.00
At the Back of the North Wind, 1919 edition, McKay, color plate illustrations by Jessie Willcox Smith. $85.00
Dealings with Fairies, 1867, Strahan, illustrations by Arthur Hughes. $700.00
Gutta Percha Willy, 1873. Rare
Light Princess, 1926 edition, Macmillan, small, color frontispiece, b/w illustrations by Dorothy Lathrop. $20.00
Light Princess and Other Fairy Stories, 1890. Rare
Light Princess and Other Fairy Stories, 1893 edition, Putnam, impressed cover illustration, b/w illustrations by Maud Humphrey. $40.00
Princess and Curdie, 1883. Rare
Princess and Curdie, 1907 edition, Philadelphia, 12 color plate illustrations by Maria Kirk. $50.00
Princess and Curdie, 1927 edition, Macmillan, illustrations by Dorothy Lathrop. $35.00
Princess and the Goblin, 1872, Strahan, illustrations by Arthur Hughes. Rare
Princess and the Goblin, 1907 edition, Philadelphia, color plate illustrations by Maria Kirk. $50.00
Ranald Bannerman's Boyhood, 1871, Strahan, illustrations by Arthur Hughes. Rare

MAC DONOUGH, Glen and Alice Chapin
Babes in Toyland, 1924, NY, illustrations by Ethel Betts. $200.00

MAC GREGOR, Ellen, 1906 – 1954
Tommy and the Telephone, 1947, Whitman, illustrations by Zabeth. $15.00

MAC HARG, William
Let's Pretend, 1914, Volland, color illustration on cover, color illustrations throughout by Bonnibel Butler. $55.00

MACKALL, Lawton
Scrambled Eggs, 1920, Stewart, illustrations by Oliver Herford. $85.00

MACKENZIE, Compton
Kensington Rhymes, 1912, London, 8 color plate illustrations by J. R. Monsell. $55.00

MAETERLINCK, Maurice
Blue Bird , 1911 edition, Dodd Mead, oversize, 25 color plate illustrations by F. Robinson. $50.00

MALCOLMSON, Anne
Yankee Doodle's Cousin, 1941, Houghton, illustrations by Robert McCloskey. $35.00

MALKUS, Alida Sims
Citadel of a Hundred Stairways, 1941, Winston, color frontispiece, b/w illustrations by Henry Pitz. $15.00

MALOT, Hector
Nobody's Boy, 1916, Cupples, oval paste-on illustration on cover, 3 color plate illustrations by Johnny Gruelle. $45.00

MARAIS, Josef
Koos the Hottentot, 1945, Knopf, 196 pages, b/w illustrations by Henry Stahlhut. $20.00

MARGE (Marjorie Henderson Buell), cartoonist. See Thompson, Ruth.
Little Lulu, 1935, Curtis, collection of previously published b/w cartoons. $50.00
Little Lulu on Parade, 1941, David McKay, b/w/red cartoons. $40.00

MARSH, D. E.
Fighting Seagull, 1937, Harrap, illustrations by Somerfield. $10.00

MARSHALL, Archibald
Audacious Ann, 1926, Dodd, b/w illustrations by Rita Zian. $15.00

MARTIN, George Madden
Emmy Lou (1901), 1903, McClure, red cover with gilt, b/w illustrations by Charles Louis Hinton. $15.00

MASON, Arthur
Wee Men of Ballywooden, 1930, Doran, illustrated by Robert Lawson. $35.00

MASON, Miriam E.
Middle Sister, 1947, Macmillan, b/w illustrations by Grace Paull. $10.00

MATTHEWS, Franklin, editor
Boy Scout Yearbook of Fun and Fiction, 1938, Appleton, a collection of material printed earlier, 274 pages, b/w illustrations by R. M. Brinkerhoff. $15.00

MAUGHAM, W Somerset
Princess September and the Nightingale, 1930, Oxford University, oversize, color illustrations by Richard C. Jones. $55.00

MAURY, Jean West
Old Raven's World, 1931, Little Brown, 284 pages, arts and crafts style two-color frontispiece, 6 b/w full-page illustrations by Ben Kutcher. $20.00

MAVOR, William
English Spelling Book, 1884, Routledge, small size, illustrations by Kate Greenaway. $125.00

MAY, Robert L. (adman for Montgomery Ward)
Rudolph the Red-Nosed Reindeer, 1939, Montgomery Ward Co., a Christmas give-away, oversize, 32 pages, red paper cover, color illustrations by Denver Gillen. $55.00

MAY, SOPHIE (Rebecca Sophia Clarke, 1833 – 1906), see Series, "Little Prudy," "Dotty Dimple Stories," "Quinnebasset," "Flaxie Frizzle Stories."

MAYOL, Lurine
Talking Totem Pole, 1930, Saalfield, color plates and b/w illustrations by Edward Morgan. $30.00

MC CAY, Winsor, 1871 – 1934
Little Nemo, 1906, Doffield, Sunday cartoon strips reprinted in color, 11" x 16", 30 pages, illustrated boards.   Rare
Little Nemo, 1909 edition, Cupples Leon, Sunday cartoon strips reprinted in color, 10" x 14", 30 pages, illustrated boards. Rare

MC CLOSKEY, Robert, b. Ohio 1914, illustrator-author
Blueberries for Sal, 1948, Viking, illustrations by author. $25.00
Homer Price, 1943, Viking, b/w illustrations by author. $20.00
Lentil, 1940, Viking, illustrations by author. $20.00
Make Way for Ducklings, 1941, Viking (1942 Caldecott for art), 1st edition, b/w illustrations by author. $50.00

MC DOUGALL, Walt
Rambillicus Book, 1903, Philadelphia, printed illustration on cover, illustrations by author. $200.00

MC EVOY, J. P.
Bam Bam Clock, 1920, Volland, small size, color illustrations by Johnny Gruelle. $50.00

MC GINLEY, Phyllis, 1905 – 1978
Plain Princess, 1945, Lippincott, illustrations by Helen Stone. $40.00
Horse Who Lived Upstairs, 1944, Lippincott, illustrations by Helen Stone. $40.00

MC GRAW, Eloise Jarvis
Sawdust in His Shoes, 1950, Coward McCann. $15.00

MC LEAN, Sally Pratt
Towhead, 1882, Williams, impressed design with gilt on cover, b/w frontispiece. $10.00

MC NEER, May
Prince Bantam and His Faithful Henchmen, 1929, Macmillan, 229 pages, b/w wood block illustrations by Lynn Ward. $20.00

MC NICHOLS, Charles
Crazy Weather, 1944, Macmillan, 195 pages. $5.00

MC SPADDEN, J. Walker
Robin Hood and His Merry Outlaws (ca. 1923), 1946, World "Rainbow Classics" edition, 288 pages, color illustrations by Louis Slobodkin. $20.00

MEADER, Stephen W.
Away to Sea, 1931, Harcourt, illustrations by Clinton Balmer. $15.00
Bat, 1939, Harcourt, illustrations by Edward Shenton. $10.00
Black Buccaneer, 1920, Harcourt, illustrations by Edward Shenton. $15.00
Blueberry Mountain, 1941, Harcourt, illustrations by Edward Shenton. $10.00

Boy With a Pack, 1939, Harcourt, illustrations by Edward Shenton. $10.00
Red Horse Hill, 1930, Harcourt, illustrations by Lee Townsend. $10.00.

MEEKER, Charles H.
Folk Tales from the Far East, 1927, Winston, color paste-on pictorial on cover, color frontispiece and b/w full-page illustrations by Frederick Richardson. $30.00

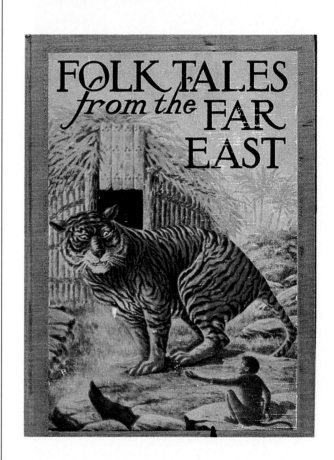

MEIGS, Cornelia, b. Illinois, 1884 – 1973
Call of the Mountain, 1940, Little Brown, illustrations by James Daugherty. $20.00
Clearing Weather, 1928, Little Brown, color illustrations by Frank Dobias. $15.00
Covered Bridge, 1936, Macmillan, illustrations by Marguerite De Angeli. $20.00
Invincible Louisa, 1933, Little Brown (1934 Newbery Medal), 1st edition. $50.00
Mother Makes Christmas, 1940, Grosset, illustrations by Lois Lenski. $25.00
New Moon, 1924, Macmillan, illustrations by Marguerite de Angeli. $25.00
Rain on the Roof, 1925, Macmillan, illustrations by Edith Ballinger Price. $20.00
Scarlet Oak, 1938, Macmillan, color frontispiece, b/w illustrations by Orton Jones. $25.00

Willow Whistle, 1931, Macmillan, color frontispiece, b/w illustrations by E. Boyd Smith. $45.00

MERCHANT, Eilzabeth Lodor
King Arthur and His Knights, 1927, Winston, color paste-on-illustration on cover, 16 color plate illustrations by Frank Godwin. $30.00

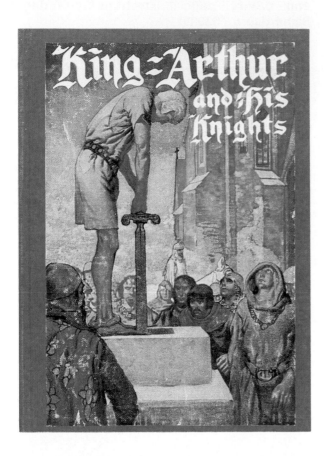

MERRYMAN, Mildred Plew
Daddy Domino, 1929, Volland, small size, color and silhouette illustrations by Janet Laura Scott. $35.00

METCALF, Susanne (L. Frank Baum)
Annabel, 1906, Reilly Britton, 6 plate illustrations, 1st edition. Rare, 1912 edition, 3 plate illustrations. $200.00

METZGER, Bertha
Picture Tales from the Chinese, 1934, Stokes, small size oblong, 110 pages, b/w illustrations by Eleanor Lattimore. $15.00
Picture Tales from India, 1942, Stokes, small oblong, 88 pages, b/w illustrations by Mina Buchanan. $10.00
Tales Told in Hawaii, 1929, Stokes, 116 pages, b/w illustrations by Verna Talman. $15.00

MIKOVARO, E.
Book of Pirates, 1932, Whitman, oversize with color pictorial on cover, color plate illustrations by G. R. Taylor. $30.00

MILLER, Agnes, see Series, "Linger-Nots."

MILLER, Anne Archibald
Huldy's Whistle, 1919, Reilly, b/w illustrations by William Dohahey. $20.00

MILLER, Basil, see Series, "Patty Lou."

MILLER, Elizabeth C.
Young Trajan, 1931, Doubleday, color frontispiece by Maud and Miska Petersham. $30.00

MILLER, Joaquin
True Bear Stories, 1900, Rand, color paste-on pictorial cover, color plate ilustrations initialed W. C. $20.00

MILLER, Olive Beaupre, see Series, "My Book House."
Heroes, Outlaws, & Funny Fellows of American Popular Tales (1939), 1942 edition, Doubleday, oversize, 332 pages, map endpapers, b/w illustrations by Richard Bennett. $15.00
My Travel Ship, editor, 1925 – 26, 3 volumes. $20.00 ea.
Picturesque Tales of Progress, with H. T. Baum, 1935, 8 volumes. $20.00 ea.
Sunny Rhymes for Happy Children, 1917, Volland, illustrations by Carmen L. Browne. $35.00

MILNE, A. A. 1882 – 1956
(Because of the popularity of these books, price range is wide, affected by minor changes in printings, cover embossing, etc. Most of his work was issued first in limited editions of 200 to 500 copies, and these are now rare.)
Christopher Robin Story Book, 1926, London, b/w illustrations by E. H. Shepard. $300.00
Gallery of Children, 1925, McKay 1st trade edition, illustrations by Saida $150.00
House at Pooh Corner, 1928, Metheun, 1928 Dutton, 1st trade editions, b/w illustrations by E. H. Shepard. $150.00
Now We Are Six, 1927, b/w illustrations by E. H. Shepard. $150.00
Once on a Time, 1922, Putnam, illustrations by H. M. Brock. $75.00
Toad of Toad Hall (play based on Grahame's *Wind in the Willows*), 1929, Longmans, 1st trade edition, illustrated. $125.00
When We Were Very Young, 1924, 1st trade edition. $150.00

Winnie-the-Pooh, 1926, Metheun, 1926, Dutton, b/w illustrations by E. H. Shepard. $400.00

MILNE SONG BOOKS, 1929 (Methuen, London, issued song books based on Milne's books, music by H. Fraser-Simson, folio size, illustrations by E. H. Shepard, all are rare.)
Fourteen Songs
King's Breakfast
Teddy Bear and Other Songs
Songs from "Now We Are Six"
More Very Young Songs
Hums of Pooh

MIRZA, Youel B.
Myself When Young (first copyright 1929), 1939 edition, Doubleday, illustrations by Theodore Nadejen. $10.00

MITCHELL, Edith
Betty, Bobby and Bubbles, Volland, color illustrations by author. $55.00
Otherside Book, 1915, Reilly Britton, oversize, color illustrations by author. $45.00

MITCHELL, Lebbeus
Bobby in Search of a Birthday, 1916, Volland, color illustrations by J. P. Nuyttons. $35.00

MOLESWORTH, Mary Louisa, 1839 – 1921 (early pseudonym was Ennis Graham), work included over one hundred children's books.
Adventures of Herr Baby, 1881, illustrations by Walter Crane. $100.00
Bewitched Lamp, 1891, Chambers, small size, printed illustration on red cover. $20.00
Christmas Child, 1880, Macmillan, illustrations by Walter Crane. $75.00
Enchanted Garden, 1892, Unwin, London. Rare
Little Miss Peggy, Only A Nursery Story, 1896, Macmillan, blue cover with gilt, illustrations by Walter Crane. $75.00
Tapestry Room, 1897, London, illustrations by Walter Crane. $75.00
Tell Me a Story, 1875, Macmillan, illustrations by Walter Crane. $100.00
"Us," an Old Fashioned Story, 1885, Macmillan, gold imprinted cover, illustrations by Walter Crane. $125.00

MONTGOMERY, Frances, see Series, "Billy Whiskers."

MONTGOMERY, L. M., see Series, "Anne Shirley."

MONTGOMERY, Rutherford
Trail of the Buffalo, 1939, Macmillan, b/w illustrations by Kurt Wiese. $15.00

MOODY, Ralph
Little Britches, 1950 edition, Norton, illustrated by Edward Shenton. $20.00

MOON, Grace and Carl
Wongo and the Wise Old Crow, 1923, Reilly Lee, b/w illustrations by Carl Moon. $60.00

MOORE, Bertha, see Series, "Triplets."

MOORE, Clement C., 1779 – 1863
Night Before Christmas, poem, first appeared in 1823, has been published in numerous editions and is generally valued for illustrations, see Denslow.
Night Before Christmas, 1928, Donohue, color illustrated cardboard cover, b/w illustrations. $20.00
Night Before Christmas, 1931, Harrap, illustrated by Arthur Rackham. $125.00
Night Before Christmas, ca. 1940s, Saalfield, picture book, oversize, color illustrations by Frances Brundage. $35.00
Night Before Christmas and Jingles, 1908, Hurst, illustrations by Grace Duffie Boylan and Ike Morgan. $35.00
'Twas the Night Before Christmas, 1912, oversize

oblong, 12 color plates by Jessie Willcox Smith. $145.00

Visit from St. Nicholas, 1869, McLoughlin, b/w and color illustrations by Thomas Nast. $250.00

MOORE, Colleen
Enchanted Castle, 1935, Garden City, oversize, 64 pages, blue and white illustrations by Marie Lawson. $20.00

MOORE, Fenworth
Cast Away in the Land of Snow, Jerry Ford Wonder series, 1931, Cupples, b/w illustrations. $10.00

MOORE, Gertrude
Christmas Star, undated, ca. 1900, Tuck, small size, chromolith illustrations, gilt edged pages. $45.00

MORLEY, Christopher
I Know a Secret, 1927, Doubleday, color frontispiece, b/w illustrations by Jeanette Warmuth. $15.00

MOROSO, John
Nobody's Buddy, 1936, Goldsmith. $10.00

MORRIS, Kenneth
Book of Three Dragons, 1930, Longmans 1st edition, 8 b/w plate illustrations by Huszti Howath. $25.00

MORRIS, Rhoda
Bad Penny, 1937, Little Brown, b/w illustrations by Arthur Nelson. $10.00
Susan and the Little Lost Bird, 1941, Little Brown, illustrations by George and Doris Hauman. $10.00

MORRISON, Gertrude, see Series, "Girls of Central High."

MORRISON, Lucile
Lost Queen of Egypt, 1937, Stokes, illustrated by Franz Geritz and Winifred Brunton. $20.00

MORRISON, Mary Whitney (Jenny Wallis)
Stories True and Fancies New, 1898, Dana Estes Boston, illustrations by L. J. Bridgman. $35.00

MUKERJI, Dhan Gopal, b. India, 1890 – 1936
Gay-Neck, 1927, Dutton, (1928 Newbery Medal), limited edition with illustrations by Artzybasheff. $90.00.
Ghond the Hunter, 1928, Dutton, illustrations by Artzybasheff. $50.00
Kari the Elephant, 1922, Dutton, illustrations by J. E. Allen. $20.00
Master Monkey, 1932, Dutton, 261 pages, b/w illustrations by Florence Weber. $15.00

MULLINS, Isla May, see Series, "Blossom Shop."

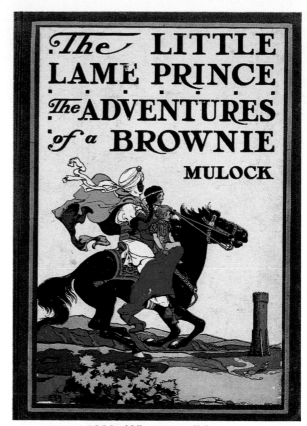

1920s Winston edition

MULOCK, Dinah Maria
The Little Lame Prince and His Travelling Cloak, 1874, London.   Rare
The Little Lame Prince, 1909, Rand McNally, cover with color paste-on illustration, color illustrations throughout by Hope Dunlap. $30.00
The Little Lame Prince and His Travelling Cloak, 1928 edition, Winston, 6 full-page illustrations by Edwin Prittie and John Fitz Jr. $30.00
The Little Lame Prince and The Adventures of a Brownie, ca. 1920s, Winston, color paste-on pictorial cover, b/w illustrations by Edwin Prittle and John Fitz Jr. $30.00
The Little Lame Prince and The Adventures of a Brownie, ca. 1947 edition, Grosset Dunlap, full color wraparound illustration on paper-on-boards cover, color frontispiece, 8 color plates plus b/w illustrations by Lucille Corcos. $20.00

·⇒ N ⇐·

NEALE, Dr.
Good King Wenceslas, introduction by W. Morris, 1895, Cornish Brothers, oversize, illustrations by Arthur Gaskin. Rare

NEILL, John R., illustrator, see Series, "Oz Books."

NELSON, Emile, illustrator
Magic Aeroplane, 1911. $100.00

NESBIT, E. (Edith), 1858 – 1924
Beautiful Stories from Shakespeare, 1907, Hertel Jenkins, 8 color plate illustrations & b/w illustrations by Max Binh. $95.00
Book of Dragons, 1900, London, illustrations by H. R. Millar. $100.00
Five Children and It (copyright 1902) 1948 edition, Random House, b/w illustrations by J. S. Goodall. $10.00
Magic City, 1930 edition, Ernest Benn, b/w illustrations by H. R. Millar. $25.00
New Treasure Seekers, 1904, London, illustrations by Gordon Browne and Lewis Baumer. $60.00
Phoenix and the Carpet, 1904, b/w illustrations by H. R. Millar. $60.00
Railway Children, 1906, London, 1st edition, illustrations by C. E. Brock. $300.00
Royal Children of English History, 1905, NY, printed illustration on cover, illustrations by Frances Brundage. $75.00
Would Be Goods, 1901, NY, illustrations by Reginald Birch. $95.00
Would Be Goods, 1947 edition, Benn, b/w illustrations by Walter Hodges. $15.00

NESBIT, Wilbur
Oh Skin-nay! The Days of Real Sport, 1913, Volland, oversize oblong, 2-color cartoon illustrations by Briggs. $45.00
Tumbledown Town, 1926, Volland, small size, color illustrations by John Gee. $45.00

NEWBERY, Clare Turlay
April's Kittens, 1940, Harper, illustrations by author. $20.00
Babette, 1937, Harper, illustrations by author. $30.00
Barkis, 1938, Harper, illustrations by author. $25.00
Cousin Toby, 1939, Harper, illustrations by author. $25.00
Marshmallow, 1942, Harper, illustrations by author. $20.00
Mittens, 1936, Harper, illustrations by author. $40.00

NEWBERY MEDAL
American award for year's best contribution to children's literature, awarded annually since 1922, named after John Newbery (1713 – 1767) a London bookseller.

NEWELL, Peter, b. Illinois 1862 – 1924, author-illustrator
Hole Book, 1908, Harper, 1st edition, illustrations by author. $200.00
Rocket Book, 1912, NY, 22 color plate illustrations by author. $200.00
Slant Book, 1910, NY, 22 color plate illustrations by author. $200.00
Shadow Show, 1896, NY, 36 color plates. $350.00
Topsys and Turvys, 1893, oversize oblong, 2 volumes, color illustrations by author, 1st edition. $700.00. Later printings. $150.00. 1902 edition. $75.00

NEWTON, Ruth, artist, also well known for doll and toy designs.
Mother Goose, 1934, Whitman, oversize, cloth cover, color illustrations. $30.00

NICHOLS, Ruth Alexander
Betty and Dolly, 1932, Merrill, square book with cardboard covers, photo illustrations. $30.00

NIELSEN, Kay, illustrator
East O' the Sun and West O' the Moon, original stories by Asbjornsen and Moe, 1924 edition, Doran, 25 color plates by Nielsen. $250.00
Hansel and Gretel, ca. 1900, illustrations by Nielsen. $225.00

NOKES, Ethel
Old Lollipop Shop, undated ca. 1930s, London, b/w frontispiece. $10.00

NORTH, Grace May b. Utica, NY, 1876, see Series, "Adele Doring."
Virginia Davis Ranch Stories, 1924. $10.00

NORTH, Sterling
Five Little Bears, 1935, Rand McNally, illustrations by Clarence Biers and Hazel Frazee. $20.00
Greased Lightning, 1940, Winston, illustrations by Kurt Wiese. $15.00
Midnight and Jeremiah, 1943, Winston, illustrations by Kurt Wiese. $15.00

NORTON, Andre (Alice Mary Norton)
(Her work is sought after both by collectors of children's books and collectors of science fiction).
Prince Commands, 1934, Appleton, 1st edition, illustrations by Kate Seredy. $200.00
Ralestone Luck, 1938, Appleton 1st edition, illustrations by James Reid. $150.00
Sword in Sheath, 1949, Harcourt, illustrations by Lorence Bjorklund. $30.00.
Sword is Drawn, 1944, Houghton, 1st edition, illustrations by Duncan Coburn. $50.00

NORTON, Carol, see Series, "Adventure And Mystery For Girls."

NORTON, Mary
Magic Bedknob, 1943, Putnam, color illustrations by Waldo Peirce. $45.00

NURA
Nura's Garden of Betty and Booth, 1935, Morrow. $45.00

NUSBAUM, Aileen
Zuni Indian Tales, 1926, Putnam, illustrated by Margaret Finnan. $20.00

--- ⇒ **O** ⇐ ---

O'BRIEN, Jack
Silver Chief, 1937, Winston, b/w illustrations by Kurt Wiese. $15.00

O'HARA, Mary (Mary Sture-Vasa), 1885 – 1980
My Friend Flicka, 1941, Lippincott. $20.00
Thunderhead, 1943, Lippincott. $20.00
Green Grass of Wyoming, 1946, Lippincott, 319 pages. $20.00.

OLCOTT, Frances
Book of Fairies and Elves, 1918, Houghton, 4 color plate illustrations by Milo Winter. $35.00
Good Stories for Great Holidays, 1914, color plate illustrations by C. M. Burd. $45.00
Good Stories for Great Holidays, 1942 edition, Houghton, color plate illustrations by C. M. Burd. $15.00

OLCOTT, Virginia
Anton and Trini, 1930, Silver Burdett, color illustrations by Constance Whittemore. $20.00
Erik and Britta, 1937. $20.00
Jean and Fanchon, 1931. $20.00

OLMSTEAD, Florence, b. Georgia
Mrs. Eli and Policy Ann, 1912, Reilly Britton, b/w illustrations by Durwin Myers. $25.00

OLMSTED, Millicent, b. Cleveland
Land of Really True, The, 1909, Jacobs, b/w/yellow/orange color plate illustrations by Elenore Abbott and Helen Knipe. $45.00
Land That Never Was, 1908. $45.00

O'NEILL, Rose, illustrator-author
Kewpies, Their Book, 1913, Stokes, author-illustrations. $100.00

ORTON, Helen F., see Series, "Cloverdale Farm."

Gold Laced Coat, 1934, Stokes, b/w illustrations by Robert Ball. $15.00

Mystery at the Old Place, 1943, Lippincott, b/w illustrations by Sandra James. $10.00

Secret in the Rosewood Box, 1937, Stokes, illustrated by Robert Ball. $15.00

Treasure in the Little Trunk, 1932, Stokes, illustrations by Robert Ball $15.00

OTIS, James (James Otis Kaler), 1848 – 1912

Mr. Stubbs's Brother (1882), 1910 edition, Harper, b/w illustrations. $20.00

Teddy (1893), 1900 edition, Donahue, b/w illustrations. $10.00

Toby Tyler, 1881, Harper, 1st edition, illustrated by R. H. Rodgers. $350.00

OUTCAULT, R. F., b. Ohio, 1863 – 1928, author-illustrator-cartoonist, see Series, "Buster Brown."

OWEN, Dora

Book of Fairy Poetry, 1920, Longmans, illustrations by W. Goble. $100.00

OWEN, Ruth Bryan

Picture Tales from Scandanavia, 1939, Stokes, small size oblong, 109 pages, b/w illustrations by Emma Brock. $15.00

OXENHAM, Elsie J.

Abbey Girls, 1920, London. $25.00

Goblin Island, 1907, London, illustrations by Heath Robinson. $45.00

P

PACKER, Eleanor

Day With Our Gang, 1929, Whitman. $20.00

PAINE, Albert Bigelow

Arkansas Bear, 1902 edition, Altemus, b/w/orange full-page illustrations by Frank ver Beck. $45.00

Dumpies, and the Arkansas Bear, 1895, written with Frank ver Beck, illustrations by ver Beck. $65.00

PANSY (Isabell Alden), edited *Pansy,* a children's magazine, published 1874 – 1896, Boston.

Four Girls at Chatauqua, 1876. $20.00

PARRISH, Anne, b. 1888, author-illustrator

Dream Coach, written with brother Dillwyn Parrish, 1924, Macmillan, illustrations by authors. $35.00

Floating Island, 1930, Harper, b/w illustrations by author. $45.00

Knee-High to a Grasshopper, written with brother Dillwyn Parrish, 1923, Macmillan, illustrations by authors. $35.00

Story of Appleby Capple, 1950, Harper, illustrations by author. $20.00

PARRISH, Maxfield, illustrator, see Grahame, Baum, and Series, "Scribner Classics;" for additional information, see Illustrators.

Knave of Hearts, 1925, picture book, color illustrations, 1st edition. Rare

PARTON, Ethel, b. NY 1862, staff member of *Youth's Companion* magazine

House Between, 1943, Viking, illustrations by Platt. $10.00

Runaway Prentice, 1939, Viking, b/w illustrations by Margaret Platt. $15.00

PAULL, Minnie E, see Series, "Ruby And Ruthy."

PAULL, Mrs. George, see Series, "Marjorie."

PAULSEN, Martha

Nice Puppy!, 1943, Saalfield, color illustrations by Mabel Hatt. $30.00

PEABODY, Josephine

Book of the Little Past, 1912, Houghton, oversize, paste-on cover illustration, 6 color plate illustrations by Elizabeth Green. $85.00

PEASE, Howard, 1894 – 1974

Gypsy Caravan, 1930, Doubleday, illustrations by H. Wood. $15.00

Secret Cargo, 1931, Doubleday, illustrations by Paul Forster. $15.00

Foghorns, 1937, Doubleday, illustrations by Anton Otto Fischer. $15.00

Shanghai Passage, 1929, Doubleday, illustrations by Paul Forster. $15.00

Jinx Ship, 1927, Doubleday, illustrations by Mahlon Blaine. $15.00

Tattooed Man, 1926, Doubleday, illustrations by Mahlon Blaine. $15.00

PEAT, Fern Bisel, author-illustrator, colorful picture books

Calico Pets, 1931, Saalfield, oversize, 12 pages, paper cover, full page color illustrations by author. $45.00

Mother Goose, 1929, Saalfield, color illustrations by author. $85.00

Stories Children Like, 1933, Saalfield, color illustrations by author. $35.00

Story of a Happy Doll, 1928, Saalfield, color illustrations by author. $40.00

Storyland, 1930, Saalfield, color illustrations by author. $25.00

PECK, Leigh
Don Coyote, 1942, Houghton, 78 pages, color illustrations by Virginia Burton. $25.00
Pecos Bill and Lightning, 1940, Houghton, illustrations throughout by Kurt Wiese. $25.00

PENROSE, Margaret. See Series, "Dorothy Dale," "Motor Girls, Radio Girls."

PERKINS, Lucy Fitch, author-illustrator, see series, "Twins of the World."
Book of Joys, 1907. $20.00

PERRAULT, Charles 1628 – 1703
  Perrault collected fairy tales. There are numerous editions, and their value is based on illustration, print quality, rarity.
Fairy Tales, 1913 edition, E. P. Dutton, small, paste-on illustration and gilt on cover, 8 color plate illustrations by Charles Robinson. $35.00
Tales of Passed Time, 1922, Selwyn and Blount, oversize, illustrated by John Austin. $150.00

PETERSHAM, Maude and Miska, author-illustrators
American Alphabet, 1941, Macmillan, color illustrations by authors. $45.00
Get-A-Way and Hary Janos, 1933, Viking, oversize, color illustrations throughout by authors. $65.00
Gold, 1935, Winston. $35.00
Rooster Crows, 1945, Macmillan 1st edition (1946 Caldecott art), illustrations by authors. $65.00
Stories from the Old Testament, 1938, Winston, color illustrations. $40.00
Story Book of Clothes, 1933, Winston, square, paste-on pictorial, color illustrations by authors. $25.00
Story Book of Houses, 1933, Winston, illustrations by authors $25.00
Story Book of Ships, 1947, Winston, color illustratons by authors. $20.00
Story Book of Trains, 1935, Winston, illustrations by authors. $25.00

PHELPS, Elizabeth Stuart
Loveliness, 1900, Houghton, small size, b/w paste-on pictorial on cover, b/w illustrations by Sarah Stillwell. $20.00

PHILLPOTTS, Eden
Girl and the Fawn, 1916, London, illustrations by Branquyn. $75.00

PIPER, Watty
(Edited children's picture books)

Children of Other Lands, 1933 edition, Platt Munk, illustrations by Lucille and H. C. Holling. $25.00
Gateway to Storyland, The, 1925, Platt Munk, oversize, color paste-on pictorial cover, color illustrations throughout by Eulalie. $65.00
Road to Storyland, 1932, Platt, oversize, color paste-on pictorial cover, color illustrations by Lucille and Holling C. Holling. $65.00

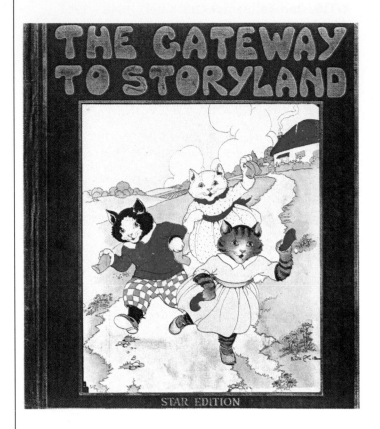

PITZ, Henry, b. Philadelphia, 1895, illustrator, see Series, "Scribner Classics."

PLOWHEAD, Ruth Gipson
Lucretia Ann and the Sagebrush Plains, 1936, Caxton, color plates by Agnes Moore. $30.00
Mile High Cabin, 1945, Caxton, b/w illustrations by Johanna Lund. $10.00

POGANY, Willy, illustrator
My Poetry Book, edited by Huffard, Carlisle, Ferris, 1934, Winston, color and b/w illustrations by Pogany. $50.00
Peterkin, written with Elaine Pogany, 1940, Philadelphia, illustrations by Willy Pogany. $60.00
Wimp and the Woodle, collected stories of other writers, 1935, Sutton, oversize, 180 pages, color plates and b/w illustrations by Willy Pogany. $50.00

PORTER, see Stratton-Porter.

PORTER, Bertha, see Series, "Trudy And Timothy."

PORTER, Eleanor, 1868 – 1920, see Series, "Glad Books."
Pollyanna, 1913, Page, illustrations by Stockton Mulford. $100.00
Pollyanna Grows Up, 1915, illustrations by H. Weston Taylor. $50.00
Turn of the Tide, 1908, Wilde, illustrations by Frank Merrill. $40.00.
Cross Currents, 1907, Wilde, illustrations by William Stecher. $40.00

PORTER, Katherine
Scottish Chiefs, 1900, Dent, illustrations by Thomas Heath Robinson. $50.00

POTTER, Beatrix author-illustrator
(As her picture books remain constantly in print, later editions have average book value unless early date or unique presentation limit the edition.)
Fairy Caravan, 1929 edition, McKay, color plates. $40.00
Ginger and Pickles, 1909, London. $250.00
Pie and the Patty Pan, 1905, London. $$100.00
Roly-Poly Pudding, 1908, Warne. $200.00
Tailor of Gloucester, 1903, Warne. $200.00
Tale of Mrs. Tiggle-Winkle, 1905, Warne, color plate illustrations. $250.00
Tale of Mrs. Tittlemouse, 1910, Warne and NY, color plate illustrations. $200.00
Tale of Flopsy Bunnies, 1909, Warne and NY, color plate illustrations $200.00
Tale of Peter Rabbit, 1901, London. Rare (Limited first printings, sale prices up to $12,000.00)
Tale of Peter Rabbit, 1902, Warne. $500.00
Tale of Peter Rabbit, 1904, Altemus. $45.00
Tale of Squirrel Nutkin, 1903, Warne. $200.00
Tale of Tom Kitten, 1907, Warne. $200.00

POWER, Effie
Stories to Shorten the Road, 1936, Dutton, 1st edition, small size, 126 pages, b/w illustrations by Dorothy Bailey. $15.00

PRATT, Marjorie, editor
Read Another Story, 1939, Sanborn, reader picture book with color illustrations. $15.00

PRICE, Margaret Evans, illustrator
Angora Twinnies, 1917 NY. $35.00
Jack and the Beanstalk, 1927, Rand McNally Book-Elf edition, small size, color illustrations. $35.00

Myths and Enchantments, 1940, Rand, 12 color illustrations. $35.00

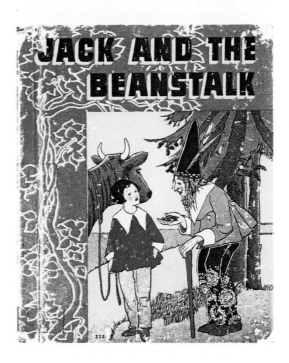

PROUDFIT, Isabel
Treasure Hunter, 1939, Messner. $15.00

PUTNAM, Nina Wilcox
Sunny Bunny, 1918, Volland, small size, color illustrations by Johnny Gruelle. $50.00

PYLE, Howard, b. Delaware, 1853 – 1911, author-illustrator, see Series "Scribner Classics." Pyle wrote and illustrated his own books, and also illustrated the works of other writers. See Illustrators for more information.
Garden Behind the Moon, 1895, Scribner. $150.00
Howard Pyle's Book of Pirates, 1921 trade edition, paste-on pictorial cover. $100.00
Howard Pyle's Book of the American Spirit, 1923 Harper trade edition, color paste-on pictorial. $100.00
Otto of the Silver Hand, 1888, NY. $150.00
Merry Adventures of Robin Hood, 1883, NY, stamped leather cover. $400.00
Merry Adventures of Robin Hood, 1883, London edition. $250.00
Merry Adventures of Robin Hood, 1933 edition, Scribner (pre-series edition). $65.00
Merry Adventures of Robin Hood, ca. 1947 edition, Grosset Dunlap, full color wraparound illustration on paper-on-boards cover, color frontispiece, 8 color plates plus b/w illustrations by Lawrence Beall Smith. $20.00

Pepper and Salt (1885), 1913 edition, Harper, line drawings and illustrations, margin graphics by author. $60.00

Story of King Arthur and His Knights, 1933 edition Scribner (pre-series edition). $65.00

Wonder Clock, 1887, Harper, w/verses by Katherine Pyle, oversize, b/w full page illustrations. $125.00

Wonder Clock, The, 1915 edition, Harper, w/verses by Katherine Pyle, b/w full page illustrations. $25.00

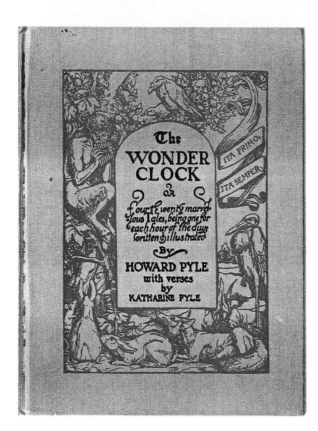

PYLE, Katherine, b. Delaware

Black-Eyed Puppy, 1923, Dutton, small size, paste-on pictorial and gilt lettering on cover, b/w/orange color illustrations by author. $25.00

Christmas Angel, 1900, Little Brown. $50.00

─── ◆══ Q ══◆ ───

QUILLER-COUCH, Sir Arthur

Sleeping Beauty and Other Fairy Tales, undated, Doran, 16 color illustrations by Edmund Dulac. $150.00

Twelve Dancing Princesses, undated, Doran, 16 color plate illustrations by Kay Nielsen. $150.00

─── ◆══ **R** ══◆ ───

RACKHAM, Arthur, illustrator

Aesop's Fables, 1912 signed limited edition, NY & London. to $1000.00

Aesop's Fables, 1912 trade edition, NY & London. $200.00

Allies' Fairy Book, 1916, Heinemann, trade edition. $85.00

Arthur Rackham Fairy Book, 1933, Lippincott, 1st American edition, 8 color plates. $100.00

Arthur Rackham's Book of Pictures, 1913, Heinemann. $175.00

Cinderella, 1919, Philadelphia, trade edition, silhouette illustrations. $90.00

Mother Goose, The Old Nursery Rhymes, 1913, Heinemann London, trade edition. $150.00

Sleeping Beauty, 1920 Philadelphia, trade edition, silhouette illustrations. $130.00

RADFORD, Alice E.

Little Brown Bruno, 1931, Rand, b/w illustrations by Clayton Rawson. $15.00

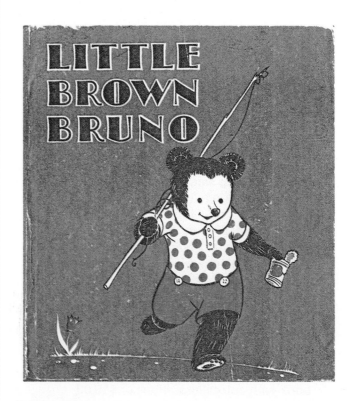

RAE, John

Grasshopper Green, Volland, color illustrations. $35.00

Grasshopper Green and the Meadow Mice, 1922 edition, Algonquin. $25.00

RANKIN, C. W, see Series,"Dandelion Cottage."

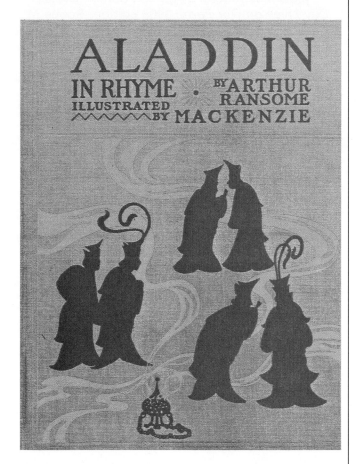

RANSOME, Arthur, 1884 – 1967, author-illustrator

(Although many of his books were illustrated by other artists, after 1932 Ransome began providing simple pen-and-ink drawings for his stories.)

Aladdin and His Wonderful Lamp in Rhyme, undated Brentano's, NY, illustrations dated 1916, oversize, b/w illustrated endpapers, 12 color plates with tissue overlays by Thomas MacKenzie, limited edition. Rare. Trade edition. $100.00

Coot Club, 1935, Lippincott, illustrations by author and Helene Carter. $20.00

Peter Duck, 1933, Lippincott, illustrations by Helene Carter. $20.00

Pigeon Post, 1937, Lippincott, illustrations by Mary Shepard. $20.00

Swallows and Amazons, 1931 edition, Cape, illustrations by Clifford Webb. $65.00

Swallows and Amazons, 1931 edition, Lippincott, illustrations by Helene Carter. $35.00

Swallowdale, 1932, Lippincott, illustrations by Helene Carter. $25.00

We Didn't Mean to Go to Sea, 1938, Lippincott, illustrations by author. $25.00

Winter Holiday, 1934, Lippincott, illustrations by Helene Carter. $25.00

RAWLINGS, **Marjorie**, see Series, "Scribner Classics."

Yearling, The, 1939, Scribner (Pulitzer Prize), 1st trade edition, 14 color plate illustrations by N. C. Wyeth. $65.00

RAYMOND, Evelyn, see Series, "Dorothy."

RAYMOND, Margaret Thomsen

Roberta Goes Adventuring, 1931, Volland, color illustrations by Eleanor Campbell. $45.00

Roberta Goes Adventuring, 1931 edition, Wise-Parslow, color illustrations by Eleanor Campbell. $25.00

Endpaper, Wise-Parslow edition

REID, Sydney

How Sing Found the World is Round, Volland, small size, color illustrations. $35.00

REY, H. A. and Margret

How Do You Get There?, 1941, Houghton, illustrations by H. A. Rey. $40.00

Curious George, 1941, Houghton, color illustrations by H. A. Rey. $55.00

Cecily G. and the Nine Monkeys (1939 London), 1942, Houghton, illustrations by H. A. Rey. $60.00

Elizabite, 1942, Harper, color illustrations by H. A. Rey. $35.00.

Tommy Helps Too, 1943, Houghton, color illustrations by H. A. Rey. $40.00

How the Flying Fishes Came Into Being, 1938, London, illustrations by H. A. Rey. $40.00

RHYS, Ernest

True Annals of Fairyland, undated edition, Dutton, (1917 inscription), small size, red leather cover with gilt trim, gilt page tops, b/w illustrations by Charles Robinson. $35.00

RICE, Alice Hegan

Lovey Mary, 1903, Century, b/w illustrations by Florence Shinn. $20.00

Mrs. Wiggs of the Cabbage Patch (copyright 1901), 1903 edition, Century, color plate illustrations by Florence Shinn. $55.00

RICE, Rebecca

Brown Castle, 1926. $25.00

Carolina's Toy Shop, 1928. $20.00

Giles of the Star, 1928, Lothrop Lee, 6 color plate illustrations by W. M. Berger. $30.00

RICHARDS, Laura E. 1850 – 1943, see Series, "Margaret."

Captain January (1890 Estes), Baby Peggy edition, 1924, L. C. Page, Boston, illustrations are photos from the film. $45.00

Five Mice in a Mouse Trap, 1880, Estes, illustrations by Kate Greenaway. $125.00

Joyous Story of Toto, 1885, Roberts, illustrations by E. H. Garrett. $40.00

Nautilus, 1895, Estes, small size, 120 pages, impressed color illustration on cover. $15.00

RICHARDS, Lela, see Series, "Blue Bonnet."

RICHARDSON, Alfred

King of the Grizzlies, 1925, Rand McNally, color paste-on pictorial, illustrated endpapers, b/w illustrations by Walter Wildering. $15.00

RIGGS, Strafford

Story of Beowulf, 1933, Appleton, illustrated by Henry Pitz. $40.00

RILEY, James Whitcomb, 1849 – 1916

Riley Child Verse, 1906, Bowen Merrill, 8 color plate illustrations by Ethel F. Betts. $75.00

Boy Lives on Our Farm, 1908 edition, Bobbs Merrill, oversize, cloth cover with pictorial insert, color plate and decorative line illustrations by Ethel Betts. $150.00

Runaway Boy, 1906 edition, Bobbs Merrill, cloth cover, pictorial insert, color plate and tinted illustrations by Ethel Betts. $125.00

RINEHART, Mary Roberts, 1876 – 1958

Bab: a Sub-Deb, 1917, Burt. $15.00

RIPPEY, Sarah Cory

Goody-Naughty Book, The, 1913, Rand McNally, color illustrations by Blanche Fisher Wright. $45.00

Sunny-Sulky Book, The, Rand McNally, color illustrations. $35.00

RIX, Herbert

Prince Pimpernel, ca. 1900, color paste-on pictorial cover, illustrations by Frank C. Pape. $145.00

ROBERTS, Elizabeth Madox, 1886 – 1941

Under the Tree, 1922, Viking, 1st edition, illustrated by F. D. Bedford. $60.00

ROBERTSON, Keith

Ticktock and Jim, 1948, Winston, illustrations by Wesley Dennis. $15.00.

Ticktock and Jim, Deputy Sheriffs, 1949, Winston, illustrations by Everett Stahl. $15.00

Dog Next Door, 1950, Viking, illustrations by Morgan Dennis. $15.00.

ROBINSON, Charles, illustrator

ROBINSON, W. Heath illustrator, see Illustrators section.

Adventures of Uncle Lubin, 1902, Grant Richards, illustrations by author. $85.00

Bill the Minder, 1912, London, 16 color plates by author. $200.00

ROBINSON, Mabel, see Series, "Little Lucia."

ROCKWOOD, Roy, see Series, "Bomba," "Dave Dashaway."

ROLLESTON, T. W.

High Deeds of Finn (copyright 1910), 1926 edition Harrup, small size, 214 pages, b/w illustrations by Stephen Reid and dated 1909. $15.00

Tale of Lohengrin, undated, Crowell, oversize art book with color illustrations throughout by Willy Pogany. $200.00

ROLLINS, Philip Ashton

Jinglebob, 1927, Scribner, color illustrations by N. C. Wyeth. $50.00

ROSS, Patricia

Hungry Moon, 1946, Knopf, oversize, 74 pages, color illustrations by Carlos Merida. $20.00

ROSSETTI, Christina

Goblin Market, 1862, small size, illustrated by Dante Rossetti. Rare

Goblin Market, 1893 edition, Macmillan, small size, cover with gilt, illustrations throughout by Laurence Housman. $450.00

Goblin Market, 1893 edition, Macmillan, limited edition (160 copies), oversize, illustrations throughout by Laurence Housman. Rare

Goblin Market and Other Poems, 1919 edition, Blackie & Son, 8 color plates plus b/w illustrations by Florence Harrison. $135.00

Sing-Song, A Nursery Rhyme Book, 1872, Routledge, green cover with gilt, b/w illustrations by Arthur Hughes. $800.00

Sing-Song, A Nursery Rhyme Book, 1872, Roberts, 1st American edition, cover with gilt, illustrations by Arthur Hughes, engraved by The Brothers Dalziel. $385.00

Sing-Song, 1924, Little Library edition Macmillan, illustrated by Marguerite Davis. $45.00

ROUNDS, Glen

Blind Colt, 1941, Holiday House, easy-read book, b/w illustrations by author. $15.00

Lumbercamp, 1937, Holiday House, b/w illustrations by author. $15.00.

Pay Dirt, 1938, Holiday House, b/w illustrations by author. $15.00

Whitey's First Round Up, 1942, Grosset, b/w illustrations by author. $15.00.

Whitey and Jinglebob, 1946, Grosset, b/w illustrations by author. $15.00

Whitey Looks for a Job, 1944, Grosset, b/w illustrations by author. $15.00

Whitey's Sunday Horse, 1942, Grosset, b/w illustrations by author. $15.00

ROWSELL, Mary C.

Honor Bright, 1900, Altemus, color illustration printed on cover with gilt decoration, b/w illustrations by S. Hardy. $25.00

ROY, Lillian, see Series, "Five Little Starrs," "Girl Scouts," "Polly Brewster."

RUSKIN, John

King of the Golden River, 1851, Smith Elder, illustrations by Richard Doyle. $150.00

King of the Golden River, 1932 edition, London, illustrations by Arthur Rackham, signed-by-artist limited edition. to $800.00

King of the Golden River, 1947 edition, World, illustrations by Fritz Kredel. $30.00

◦⇒ **S** ⇐◦

SAGE, Betty

Rhymes of Real Children, 1903, Fox Duffield, color paste-on pictorial, illustrations by Jessie Willcox Smith. $200.00

SAINSBURY, Noel, see Series, "Bill Bolton Aviation," "Champion Sports," "Great Ace," "Malay Jungle."

SAINT EXUPERY, Antoine de

Little Prince, translated by Katherine Woods, 1943, Reynal & Hitchcock, color illustrations by author. $45.00

SALTEN, Felix (Salzmann, Sigmund)

Bambi (1926 Germany, translated by Whittaker Chambers), 1928, NY, 1st American edition. $90.00

Bambi, 1929 edition, Grosset, b/w illustrations by Kurt Wiese. $25.00

Bambi's Children (1939, Bobbs Merrill), undated, Grosset, b/w illustrations by Erna Pinner. $10.00

Jibby the Cat, 1948, Messner, illustrations in b/w by Fritz Kredel. $15.00

SAMUELS, Adelaide, see Series, "Dick Travers."

SANDBURG, Carl, b. Illinois, 1878
Abe Lincoln Grows Up, 1929, Harcourt, illustrations by James Daugherty. $50.00
Early Moon, 1930, Harcourt 1st edition, illustrations by James Daugherty. $80.00
Rootabaga Stories, 1922, Harcourt, 1st edition, illustrations by Maud and Miska Petersham. $125.00
Rootabaga Pigeons, 1923, Harcourt, 1st edition, illustrations by Maud and Miska Petersham. $125.00

SANDERSON, Margaret, see Series, "Camp Fire Girls."

SARG, Tony, 1882 – 1942, author-artist
Tony Sarg's Animal Book, 1925, NY, illustrations by author. $50.00
Tony Sarg's Book for Children, 1924, NY, illustrations by author. $50.00
Tony Sarg's Wonder Zoo, 1927, NY, illustrations by author. $55.00
Where Is Tommy?, 1932, Greenberg. $50.00

SARI
Jeanne Marie Goes to Market, 1938, Grosset, oversize, easy read, color illustrations. $20.00
Ten Little Servants, 1939, Grosset, oversize, easy read, color illustrations. $20.00

SAUER, Julia
Fog Magic, 1943, Viking, illustrations by Lynd Ward. $10.00

SAWYER, Ruth, b. Massachusetts, 1880 – 1970
This Way to Christmas, 1916, Harper, illustrations by Maginal Wright Barney. $55.00

SCHUETTE, Walter
When Stubby Got His Start, undated ca. 1920, Book Concern, small size, 63 pages, color illustrated cardboard cover. $10.00

SCHWATKA, Frederick
Children of the Cold, (1895), 1899 edition, Boston, b/w illustrations. $15.00

SCOTT, J. M.
Cold Lands, 1939, Metheun, small size, paste-on pictorial b/w photo on cover, 12 b/w photograph illustrations. $10.00

SCOTT, Michael
Tom Cringle's Log, 1927, Dodd Mead, illustrated by Mead Schaeffer. $40.00

SCUDDER, Horace E.
Children's Book, 1909, Boston, cover illustrations by Maxfield Parrish. $65.00

SEGUR, Comtesse de
Princess Rosette and Other Fairy Tales, translated by Virginia Olcott, 1930, Macrae, b/w illustrations by Ben Kutcher. $20.00

SEREDY, Kate, b. Hungary, 1899 – 1938, author and illustrator
Listening, 1936, Viking, author illustrated. $20.00
Tree for Peter, 1941, Viking. $15.00
White Stag, 1937, Viking, (1938 Newbery Medal). $35.00
Chestery Oak, 1948, Viking. $20.00

SETON, Ernest Thompson, 1860 – 1946
Trail of the Sandhill Stag, 1899, Scribner, author illustrated. $30.00
Biography of a Grizzly, 1900, Century, author illustrated. $30.00.
Raggylug the Cottontail Rabbit, 1900, London, author illustrated. $30.00
Wild Animals I Have Known, 1899, Scribner, author illustrated. $30.00

SEUSS, Dr. (Theodor Seuss Geisel, b. 1904), author-illustrator
And to Think that I Saw It on Mulberry Street, 1937, Vanguard, oversize, color illustrations by author. $125.00
Bartholomew and the Oobleck, 1949, Random House, oversize, color illustrations by author. $65.00
500 Hats of Bartholomew Cubbins, 1938, Vanguard, oversize, color illustrations by author. $85.00
Horton Hatches the Egg, 1940, Random House, oversize, color illustrations by author. $45.00
King's Stilts, 1939, Random House, oversize, color illustrations by author. $55.00
McElligot's Pool, 1947, Random House, oversize, color illustrations by author. $35.00
Thidwick, 1948, Random House, oversize, color illustrations by author. $35.00

SEWELL, Anna, 1820 – 78
Black Beauty (1877 London), 1912 edition, Jarrold, illustrations by Cecil Aldin. $50.00
Black Beauty, 1946 edition, World, illustrations by Wesley Dennis. $25.00
Black Beauty, ca. 1947 edition, Grosset Dunlap, full color wraparound illustration on paper-on-boards cover, color frontispiece, 8 color plates

plus b/w illustrations by Fritz Eichenberg. $20.00

SEWELL, Helen, 1896 – 1957, author-illustrator, see Series, "Little House."

SEYMOUR, Alta Halverson
Timothy Keeps a Secret, 1939, G & D, illustrations by Gertrude Herrick Howe. $10.00

SHAKESPEARE, William
Under the Greenwood Tree, songs from the plays, edited by Julia Reynolds, 1940 Oxford edition, illustrated by Leonard Weisgard. $40.00
Midsummer Night's Dream A, undated edition, ca. 1908, Doubleday, illustrations dated 1908, oversize, line drawings and color plates with tissue overlays by Arthur Rackham. $100.00

SHANNON, Monica
Tawnymore, 1931, Doubleday, illustrations by Jean Charlot. $15.00

SHAPIRO, Irwin
How Old Stormalong Captured Mocka Dick, 1942, Messner, illustrations by Donald McKay. $10.00
Yankee Thunder, 1944, Messner, 205 pages, endpapers and b/w illustrations throughout by James

Daugherty. $10.00
SHARP, Annabel, see Series, "Peggy Parson."

SHEPARD, Esther
Paul Bunyan, 1941, Harcourt, illustrated by Rockwell Kent. $35.00

SHERMAN, Harold
Beyond the Dog's Nose, 1927, Appleton. $15.00

SHIRLEY, Penn, see Series, "Silver Gate."
Little Miss Weezy, Lothrop, impressed cover, b/w illustrations. $10.00
Little Miss Weezy's Brother, 1888, Lothrop, b/w illustrations. $10.00
Little Miss Weezy's Sister, Lothrop, b/w illustrations. $10.00

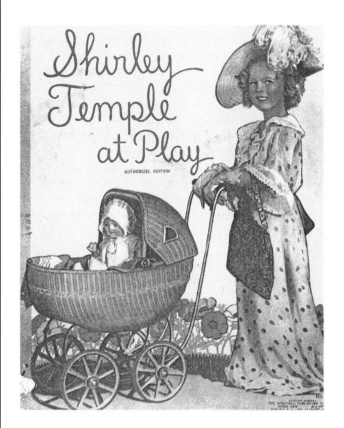

SHIRLEY TEMPLE BOOKS
Heidi, Shirley Temple Edition, Johanna Spyri, 1937 Saalfield, 404 pages, 12 photo illustrations from the Darryl Zanuck production. $45.00
Movie of Me, ca. 1935, Fox Films, small size, 32 pages, b/w photo cover, flip-book. $35.00
Shirley Temple at Play, 1935, Saalfield, OH, oversize, paper cover, full page color drawings from photos, no author or illustrator credits. $65.00
Shirley Temple Story Book, by Dean O'Day, 1935, Saalfield, illustrations by Corinne and Bill Bailey. $45.00
Shirley Temple's Book of Fairy Tales, 1936, Saal-

field, cover illustration of Shirley, Shirley picture endpapers and story illustrations with Shirley. $65.00

Story of My Life, 1935, Fox Film, small booklet, promotional item for "Curly Top" film, photo on cover. $35.00

SIDNEY, Margaret, see Series, "Five Little Peppers."
Five Little Peppers and How They Grew, ca. 1947 edition, Grosset Dunlap, full color wraparound illustration on paper-on-boards cover, color frontispiece, 8 color plates plus b/w illustrations by William Sharp. $20.00

SINDELAIR, Joseph, see Series, "Nixie Bunny."

SINGMASTER, Elsie
Bred in the Bone, 1925, Houghton, b/w illustrations by Elizabeth Shippen Green. $55.00
Rifles for Washington, 1938, Houghton, illustrations by F. E. Schoonover. $40.00
Swords of Steel, 1933, Houghton, illustrations by David Hendrickson. $30.00
You Make Your Own Luck, 1929, Longmans, b/w illustrations signed V. V. $10.00

SKINNER, Cornelia Otis
Little Child's Book of Stories, 1922, NY, 9 color plate illustrations by Jessie Willcox Smith. $125.00

SLOBODKIN, Louis, b. New York, 1903, illustrator, see Thurber and Estes.

SMITH, George Henry, 1873 – 1931, editor of children's page of several newspapers, he wrote syndicated story columns under the pen names of "Uncle Henry" and "Farmer Smith."
Daddy's Goodnight Stories, 1910. $30.00
Dollie Stories, 1912. $35.00
Oh, Look Who's Here, 1911. $30.00

SMITH, Gertrude
Arabella and Araminta, 1895, Thompson. $35.00
The Lovable Tales of Janey & Josey & Joe, 1902, NY, color illustration on cover, illustrations by E. Mars and M. Squires. $100.00. Later editions, $40.00

SMITH, Harriet Lummis, see Series, "Friendly Terrace," "Peggy Raymond," "Pollyanna."

SMITH, Jennie S.
Madge, a Girl in Earnest, ca. 1900 edition, Lee & Shepard. $10.00

SMITH, Jessie Willcox, illustrator
Baby's Red Letter Days, 1901, Just's Food Company, embossed and color illustrations. $95.00
Child's Book of Old Verses, 1910, NY, color paste-on pictorial cover, color illustrations. $180.00
Jessie Willcox Smith's Mother Goose, 1914, New York, oversize oblong with paste-on pictorial, color illustrations. $250.00

SMITH, Laura Rountree, b. Chicago, 1876 – 1924, also used pseudonym Caroline Silver June, see Series "Bunny Cottontail."
Mother Goose Stories, ca. 1915, Whitman, illustrated. $20.00

SMITH, Mabell, see Series, "Ethel Morton."

SMITH, Mary P. W, see Series, "Jolly Good, Summer Vacation," "Young Puritan."
Jolly Good Times at Hackmatack, 1892, Boston, b/w illustrations. $15.00

SMITH, Nora Archibald
Boys and Girls of Bookland, 1923, McKay, oversize, illustrations by Jessie Willcox Smith. $95.00

SNEDDEN, Genevra
Docas, Indian Boy, 1899, Heath, illustration printed on cover, b/w illustrations. $15.00

SNEDEKER, Caroline Dale, 1871 – 1956
Coward of Thermopylae, 1911, Doubleday. $30.00
Forgotten Daughter, 1933, Doubleday, illustrations by Dorothy Lathrop. $40.00
Downright Dencey, 1927, Doubleday, illustrations by Maginal Wright Barney. $40.00.
Theras and His Town, 1924, Doubleday, illustrations by Mary Haring. $20.00

SNELL, Roy, b. Missouri, 1878
Black Schooner, 1923. $15.00
Eskimo Robinson Crusoe, 1917. $15.00
Johnny Longbow, 1928. $15.00
Skimmer and His Thrilling Adventures, 1919. $15.00
Told Beneath the Northern Lights, 1925. $15.00

SNYDER, Fairmont
Rhymes for Kindly Children, 1916, Volland, illustrations by Johnny Gruelle. $65.00

SOGLOW, Otto, cartoonist-author

Little King, The, 1945, John Martin's House, over-size, color boards, 29 pages, color illustrations by author. $40.00

SOUTHWOLD, Stephen
Book of Animal Tales, undated, ca. 1930, Crowell, illustrated. $50.00

SOUTHWORTH, May E.
Great Small Cats and Others, 1914, Paul Elder, San Francisco, photo plates by Pedro Lemos. $25.00

SPEED, Nell (Emma Speed Sampson), 1868 – 1947), see Series, "Miss Minerva," "Molly Brown," "Tucker Twins."

SPERRY, Armstrong, b. Conn, 1892
Call It Courage, 1940, Macmillan (1941 Newbery Medal). $35.00
Little Eagle, a Navajo Boy, 1938. $15.00

SPYRI, Johanna
Heidi (1880 Switzerland), 1885, Boston, translation by Louise Brooks. $200.00
Heidi, 1919 edition, Lippincott, 14 color plate illustrations by Maria Kirk. $65.00
Heidi, 1922 edition, Philadelphia, illustrations by Jessie Willcox Smith. $200.00
Heidi, 1923 edition, Philadelphia, illustrations by Anne Anderson. $85.00
Heidi, 1923 edition, Boston, illustrations by Gustaf Tenggren. $65.00
Heidi, 1924, Saalfield, illustrations by Frances Brundage. $20.00
Heidi, ca. 1947 edition, Grosset Dunlap, full color wraparound illustration on paper-on-boards cover, color frontispiece, 8 color plates plus b/w illustrations by William Sharp. $20.00
Mazli, 1921, Lippincott, white illustration on red cover, color plate illustrations by Maria Kirk. $45.00

STAFFORD, Marie, b. Greenland, 1893, daughter of Josephine and Robert Perry, childhood nickname "the Snowbaby."
Snowbaby's Own Story, 1934. $15.00

STANDISH, Burt (William Patten), see Series, "Big League," "Frank Merriwell."

STEEL, Flora A.
English Fairy Tales (retold by Steel), 1918, MacMillan, color plate illustrations by Arthur Rackham. $150.00
Tales of the Punjab, 1894, Macmillan, illustrations by J. L. Kipling. $60.00

STEINER, Charlotte
Lulu, 1939, Doubleday, oversize oblong picture book, color illustrations by author. $65.00

STEPHENS, Robert Neilson
Enemy to the King, ca. 1907 edition, Grosset Dunlap, cloth cover with gilt trim, illustrations by H. De M. Young. $20.00

STERRETT, Frances, see Series, "Tales Of A Minnesota Girl."

STEVENS, James
Paul Bunyan's Bears, 1947, McCaffrey, Seattle, b/w illustrations by Phyllis Heady. $7.00

STEVENSON, Robert Louis, b. Scotland, 1850 – 1894
Child's Garden of Verses, A, (1885) 1896 edition London, color illustrations by Charles Robinson. $200.00
Child's Garden of Verses, A, 1900 edition, Rand McNally, small size, impressed cover illustration, color plates and color illustrations throughout by E. Mars and M. H. Squire. $35.00
Child's Garden of Verses, A, 1905 edition, NY, color plate illustrations by Jessie Willcox Smith. $150.00
Child's Garden of Verses, A, 1905 edition, NY, illus-

trated by Bessie Pease Gutmann. $50.00

Child's Garden of Verses, A, 1919 edition, Rand McNally, color illustrations by Ruth Mary Hallock. $50.00

Child's Garden of Verses, A, 1934 Book-Elf edition of above, small size, b/w illustrations by Ruth Mary Hallock. $35.00

Child's Garden of Verses, A, 1919 edition, Scribner's, color plate illustrations by Florence Edith Storer. $45.00

Child's Garden of Verses, A, 1931 edition, Whitman, b/w silhouette illustrations by Paula Rees Good. $45.00

Child's Garden of Verses, A, 1929 edition, Saalfield OH, oversize, color plate illustrations by Clara Burd. $65.00.

Child's Garden of Verses, A, 1947 edition, Oxford, illustrations by Tasha Tudor. $60.00

Kidnapped, 1925 edition, Macmillan, illustrations by Warwick Goble. $35.00

Kidnapped, ca. 1947 edition, Grosset Dunlap, full color wraparound illustration on paper-on-boards cover, color frontispiece, 8 color plates plus b/w illustrations by Lynd Ward. $20.00

Kidnapped, see Series, "Scribner Classics."

Treasure Island, 1883, Cassell, cloth-on-boards with gilt, frontispiece map in two colors, with map still in book. Rare

Treasure Island, 1923, Macmillan, illustrations by Warwick Goble. $35.00

Treasure Island, 1927, Doran, illustrations by Edmund Dulac. $150.00

Treasure Island, 1928, NY, illustrations by Paul Bransom. $100.00

Treasure Island, 1928, Macmillan, illustrations by Henry Matthew Brock. $50.00

Treasure Island, ca. 1947 edition, Grosset Dunlap, full color wraparound illustration paper-on-boards cover, color frontispiece, 8 color plates plus b/w illustrations by Norman Price. $20.00

STEWART, Jane, see Series, "Campfire Girls."

STOCKTON, Frank, b. Philadelphia, 1834 – 1902, editor at *St. Nicholas* magazine.

Personally Conducted, 1889, Scribner, b/w illustrations by Joseph Pennell and Alfred Parsons. $25.00

Queen's Museum and Other Fanciful Tales (1887), 1906 edition, Scribner, color paste-on pictorial cover, illustrated endpapers, 9 color plate illustrations by Frederick Richardson. $65.00

Poor Count's Christmas, 1927 edition, Stokes, color frontispiece, b/w illustrations by E. B. Bennett. $20.00

Reformed Pirate (1881), 1936 edition, Scribner,

color frontispiece, b/w illustrations by Reginald Birch. $20.00

STONG, Phil

Honk the Moose, 1935, Dodd, illustrated by Kurt Wiese. $20.00

STORM, John

Faraway Tree, 1948, Lothrop, illustrations by George McVicker. $20.00

STOWE, Harriet Beecher 1811 – 96

Uncle Tom's Cabin, 1852, Boston, 2 volumes, 1st edition. Rare

STRATEMEYER, Edward, see Series, "Stratemeyer."

STRATTON-PORTER, Mrs. Gene, 1863 – 1924

At the Foot of the Rainbow, 1907, Outing. $35.00

Freckles, 1904, 1st edition. $150.00

Freckles, later editions. $15.00

Girl of the Limberlost, 1909, Doubleday, 1st edition. $30.00

Laddie, 1913, Doubleday, 1st edition. $35.00

Music of the Wild, 1910, Abingdon Press. $85.00

STREATFEILD, Noel

Ballet Shoes, 1937, Random House, illustrations by Richard Floethe. $15.00

Circus Shoes, 1939, Random House, illustrations by Richard Floethe. $15.00

Theatre Shoes, 1945, Random, illustrations by Richard Floethe. $15.00

STREETER, James

Biscuit Eater, 1941, Dial, illustrated by Arthur Fuller. $15.00

STRETTON, Hesba (Sarah Smith), 1832 – 1911 (Mentored by Dickens, she wrote novels about street children.)

Fern's Hollow, 1865, London, Religious Tract Society, 1st edition. Rare

Jessica's Last Prayer, 1882, London, 1st edition. Rare

STUART, Ruth McEnery, b. Louisiana, 1849 – 1917

Sonny's Father, 1910, Century, cover with gilt, illustrations by several artists including Jessie Willcox Smith. $85.00

STUDDY, G. E., author-illustrator

Bomzoobo Book, 1929, Partridge, color plates. $50.00

SUTTON, Adah Louise

Little Maid in Toyland, 1908, Saalfield, color frontispiece, b/w illustrations by A. Russell. $25.00

Mr. Bunny, His Book, Saalfield. $25.00

Teddy Bears, Saalfield. $25.00

SUTTON, Margaret, see Series, "Judy Bolton Mysteries."

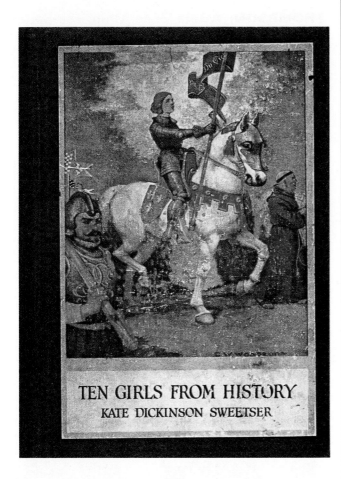

TEN GIRLS FROM HISTORY
KATE DICKINSON SWEETSER

SWEETSER, Kate Dickinson, b. New York

Book of Indian Braves, ca. 1910, Harper, color paste-on pictorial cover, color frontispiece, b/w plates $35.00

Boys and Girls from Eliot, ca. 1910, Harper, color paste-on pictorial cover, color frontispiece, b/w plates $35.00

Boys and Girls from Thackeray, ca. 1910, Harper, color paste-on pictorial cover, color frontispiece, b/w plates. $35.00

Ten American Girls from History, ca. 1910, Harper, color paste-on pictorial cover, color frontispiece, b/w plates. $35.00

Ten Boys from Dickens, ca. 1910, Harper, color paste-on-pictorial cover, color frontispiece, b/w plates $35.00

Ten Boys from History, ca. 1910, Harper, color paste-on pictorial cover, color frontispiece, b/w plates $35.00

Ten Girls from Dickens, ca. 1910, Harper, color paste-on pictorial cover, color frontispiece, b/w plates $35.00

Ten Girls from History, 1912, Harper, paste-on pictorial cover, color frontispiece, b/w illustrations. $35.00

Ten Great Adventures, ca. 1910, Harper, color paste-on pictorial cover, color frontispiece, b/w plates $35.00

SWIFT, Jonathan, 1667 – 1745

(*Gulliver's Travels* was first published in 1726, and was a satire meant for adults. Condensed and adapted versions for children were produced by a number of publishers. Value generally depends on the popularity of the illustrator, quality of product, etc.)

Gulliver's Travels, Arranged for Young Readers, undated ca. 1900, Altemus, small size, impressed cover with gilt trim and pictorial paste-on, b/w illustrations. $20.00

Gulliver's Travels, 1917, illustrations by Willy Pogany. $50.00

Gulliver's Travels, ca. 1947 edition, Grosset Dunlap, full color wraparound illustration on paper-on-boards cover, color frontispiece, 8 color plates plus b/w illustrations by Aldren Watson. $20.00

SWINBURNE, Algernon Charles

Springtide of Life Poems of Childhood, 1918, London signed-by-artist limited edition, color plate illustrations by Arthur Rackham. to $1000.00

Springtide of Life Poems of Childhood, 1918 trade edition, London & NY, Rackham illustrations. $250.00

 **T**

TAGGART, Marion Ames, see Series, "Six Girls."

Captain Sylvia, 1918. $10.00

TARKINGTON, Booth, b. Indiana, 1869 – 1946, author, illustrator, playwright

Penrod, 1914, Doubleday, 1st edition, illustrated by Gordon Grant. $100.00

Penrod, 1914, Grosset edition, Grant illustrations $30.00

Penrod & Sam, 1931, illustrations by Grant. $20.00

TARN, W. W.

Treasure of the Isle of Mist, 1934, Putnam, b/w illustrations by Robert Lawson. $25.00

TATE, Sally Jane

Sally's ABC Sewed in a Sampler, 1929, Harcourt,

illustrated by Dugald Walker. $60.00

TAYLOR, Bryson C.
Nicanor, Teller of Tales, 1906, McClurg, paste-on illustration on cover, 5 color plate illustrations by Troy and Margaret West Kinney. $45.00

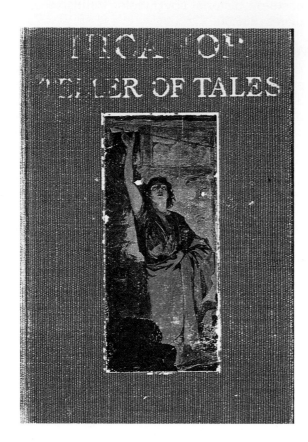

TAYLOR, Jane and Ann
Little Ann and Other Poems, 1883, Routledge, illustrations by Kate Greenaway. $150.00

TEASDALE, Sara, b. Missouri, 1884 – 1933, poet
Stars To-night, 1930, Macmillan, 1st edition, color frontispiece and b/w illustrations by Dorothy Lathrop $25.00

TENGGREN, Gustaf, illustrator, see Woodruff and Spyri.

THACKERAY, William Makepeace, 1811 – 1863
Rose and the Ring, 1855, Smith Elder, illustrations by author.   Rare
Rose and the Ring, 1907 edition, Wessels, oversize, 129 pages, b/w/orange illustrations. $40.00

THAYER, Tiffany Ellsworth, b. Illinois, 1902 – 1959

Rabelais for Boys and Girls, 1939. $20.00

THOMAS, Eleanor
Becky and Tatters, a Brownie Scout Story, 1940, Scribner, b/w illustrations by Gertrude Howe. $15.00

THOMPSON, Adele E., b. Ohio, see Series, "Brave Heart."
American Patty, 1909, Lee & Shepard. $15.00
Beck's Fortune, 1899, Lee & Shepard. $15.00
Betty Seldon, Patriot, 1901. $15.00
Nobody's Rose, 1911, Lee & Shepard. $15.00
Polly of the Pines, 1906, Lee & Shepard. $15.00

THOMPSON, Blanche Jennings
Silver Pennies, 1926, (in Little Library series) Macmillan, illustrations by Winifred Bromhall. $45.00
More Silver Pennies, 1938, Macmillan, b/w illustrations by Pelagie Doane. $35.00

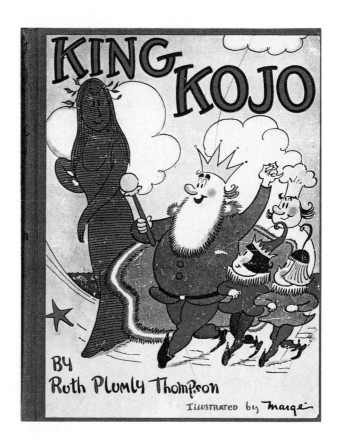

THOMPSON, Ruth Plumly, b. Philadelphia, 1895, see Series, "Oz."
King Kojo, 1938, McKay, Philadelphia, color plate illustrations by Marge. $95.00
Wonder Book, 1929, Reilly Lee, color plate illustrations by William Donahey. $55.00

THORNDYKE, Helen Louise, see Series, "Honey Bunch."

THURBER, James
Many Moons, 1943, Harcourt, illustrations by Louis Slobodkin (1944 Caldecott for art). $65.00
Thirteen Clocks, 1950, Simon Schuster, illustrations by Marc Simont. $85.00

TOLKIEN, J. R. R., b 1892
The Hobbit, 1938, Houghton, 1st American edition, illustrations by author. $500.00
Farmer Giles of Ham, 1949, Allen and Unwin, illustrated by Pauline Baynes. $50.00

TOMLINSON, Everett Titsworth, b. New Jersey, 1859 – 1931
Camping Out on the St. Lawrence, 1899. $25.00
Fort in the Forest, 1904. $20.00
Four Boys in the Yellowstone, 1906. $20.00

TOMPKINS, Jane
Beaver Twins, 1940, Stokes, b/w illustrations by Enos Comstock. $15.00
Penguin Twins, 1939, Lippincott, b/w illustrations by Kurt Wiese. $25.00

TOURTEL, Mary author-illustrator, see Series, "Rupert Little Bear."

TOUSEY, Sanford
Airplane Andy, 1942, Doubleday Junior Books, color illustrations. $10.00

TRAVERS, P. L.
Continually in print, later editions at average book prices:
Mary Poppins, 1934, Reynal, 1st American edition, illustrations by Mary Shepard. $100.00
Mary Poppins Comes Back, 1935, Reynal, illustrations by Mary Shepard. $85.00
Mary Poppins Opens the Door, 1944, illustrations by Mary Shepard. $55.00

TREADGOLD, Mary
We Couldn't Leave Dinah, 1941, London. $15.00

TRENT, Margaret, see Series, "American Adventure."

TRESSELT, Alvin
White Snow, Bright Snow, 1947, Lothrop, illustrations by Roger Duvoisin, (1948 Caldecott art). $50.00

TRITTEN, Charles

Heidi Grows Up, 1938, Grosset, b/w illustrations by Jean Coquillot. $5.00

TROWBRIDGE, J. T., see Series, "Jack Hazard."

TUCKER, Charlotte Marie, 1825 – 93
(Pen name A.L.O.E., which stood for A Lady of England, her books were published by Thomas Nelson, and Gall & Inglis, Scotland. First editions are difficult to identify because later editions are identically marked; 1st editions, rare.)
Fairy Know a-bit, 1866.
Giant-Killer, 1856.
Rambles of a Rat, 1857.
Roby Family, 1857.
Silver Casket, 1864.
Story of a Needle, 1858

TUCKER, Elizabeth S., author-illustrator
Cup of Tea, 1892, Worthington, oversize, illustrations. $65.00
Make-Believe Men and Women, 1897, Stokes, see Humphrey, Maud.

TUDOR, Tasha, b. Boston, 1915, author-illustrator
Alexander the Gander, 1939, NY. $95.00
County Fair, 1940, NY. $65.00
Dorkus Porkus, 1942, London. $40.00
Pumpkin Moonshine, 1938, Oxford. $125.00
Snow Before Christmas, 1941, NY. $100.00

TUNIS, John R.
All-American, 1942, Harcourt, illustrations by Hans Walleen. $15.00
Duke Decides, 1939, Harcourt, illustrations by James MacDonald. $15.00
Iron Duke, 1938, Harcourt, illustrations by Johan Bull. $15.00
Keystone Kids, 1943, Harcourt. $15.00
Kid Comes Back, 1946, Morrow. $15.00
Kid from Tomkinsville, 1940, Harcourt, illustrations by J. H. Barnum. $15.00

TURNER, Nancy Byrd, b. Virginia, 1880, editor at *Youth's Companion.*
Zodiac Town, 1921, Atlantic Monthly, illustrated. $65.00

TURNEY, Ida Virginia
Paul Bunyan Marches On, illustrated by Norma Lyon. $25.00
Paul Bunyan the Work Giant, 1941, Binfords, illustrations by Norma Lyon and Harold Price. $25.00

TWAIN, Mark (Samuel Clemens), 1835 – 1910
Adventures of Huckleberry Finn, 1885, Webster. Rare

Adventures of Huckleberry Finn, 1940 edition, NY, color illustrations by Norman Rockwell. $45.00

Adventures of Huckleberry Finn, ca. 1947 edition, Grosset Dunlap, full color wraparound illustration on paper-on-boards cover, color frontispiece, 8 color plates plus b/w illustrations by Donald McKay. $20.00

Adventures of Tom Sawyer, 1876, Roman.   Rare

Adventures of Tom Sawyer, 1936 edition, NY, 8 color illustrations by Norman Rockwell. $45.00

Adventures of Tom Sawyer, ca. 1947 edition, Grosset Dunlap, full color wraparound illustration on paper-on-boards cover, color frontispiece, 8 color plates plus b/w illustrations by Donald McKay. $20.00

Connecticut Yankee in King Arthur's Court, 1889, Webster. Rare

Prince and the Pauper, 1881. Rare

Prince and the Pauper, 1917 edition, illustrations by Booth. $45.00

Tom Sawyer Abroad: Tom Sawyer, Detective and Other Stories, 1896, Webster, illustrated by Arthur Frost. $100.00

────── ⊷⊜ **U** ⊜⊶ ──────

UNCLE HENRY, see Smith, George Henry.

UNCLE MILTON
Little Susie Sunbonnet, 1907. $150.00

UNTERMEYER, Louis, editor
Rainbow in the Sky, 1935, Harcourt Brace, poetry collection, 498 pages, b/w illustrations by Reginald Birch. $25.00

This Singing World, 1923, Harcourt Brace, poetry collection, b/w illustrations by Florence Wyman Ivins. $35.00

UPHAM, Elizabeth
Little Brown Bear, 1942, Platt Munk, oversize, color illustrations by Marjorie Hartwell. $40.00

UPTON, Bertha, 1849 – 1912
(Illustrations for Bertha Upton's picture books are by her daughter, Florence Upton. These books renewed demand for old-style peg wooden dolls and created an enormous market for stuffed cloth golliwog dolls.)

Adventures of Barbie and Wisp (1905), 1920s editions. $45.00

Adventures of Two Dutch Dolls, 1895, Longmans Green London, oversize size, color illustrations, 1sts, Rare. 1920s editions. $45.00

Golliwogg's Circus, 1903, Longmans, oblong oversize, color illustrations. $150.00

Golliwogg's Desert Island, 1906, Longmans, oblong oversize, color illustrations. $100.00

────── ⊷⊜ **V** ⊜⊶ ──────

VANCE, Eleanor
Tall Book of Fairy Tales, 1947, Harper, 5" x 11", b/w and color illustrations by William Sharp. $40.00

VANDEGRIFF, Peggy
Dy-Dee Doll Days, 1937, Rand, illustrated. $20.00

VANDERCOOK, Margaret, see Series, "Girl Scout," "Ranch Girls," "Red Cross."

VAN DERVEER, Helen
Little Sallie Mandy Story Book, 1935 edition, Platt Munk, color illustrations throughout by Bess Goe Willis. $35.00

VAN DRESSER, Jasmine Stone
Little Pink Pig, The, (copyright 1924 Rand McNally), 1938 edition, Rand McNally, oblong small size, color illustrations by Clarence Biers and Joan Harman. $35.00

VAN DYKE, Henry
First Christmas Tree, 1897, NY, impressed cover, illustrations by Howard Pyle. $50.00

Mansion, 1911 edition, Harper, color paste-on illustration on embossed cover, b/w illustrations by Elizabeth Shippen Green. $40.00

VAN DYNE, Edith (L. Frank Baum), see Series, "Aunt Jane's Nieces."

VAN EPPS, Margaret, see Series, "Nancy Pembroke."

VAN LOON, Hendrik, 1882 – 1944
Story of Mankind, 1921, Liveright (1922 Newbery Medal). $30.00

VER BECK, William Francis, b. Ohio, 1858 – 1933, author, illustrator, see Paine.

VERNE, Jules
Mysterious Island, 1918, Scribner, illustrated by N. C. Wyeth. $90.00

VOLKMANN, Richard von
Rusted Knight and Other Stories, 1933, Humphries, Boston, silhouette illustrations by Marte Landsberger. $45.00

W

WADSWORTH, Leda
Mystery at the Black Cat, 1941, Rinehart, illustrations by George Porter. $10.00

WAGNER, Richard
Siegfried and Twilight of the Gods, translated by Margaret Armour (this translation dated 1911), undated edition, ca. 1930 – 50, Garden City, color illustrations by Arthur Rackham. $30.00

WAHLERT, Jennie
Neighbors Near and Far, 1935, Houghton, school reader, orange/black impressed cover illustration, three-color illustrations throughout by Marguerite Davis and Hildegarde Woodward. $20.00

WALDECK, Theodore J.
Jamba the Elephant, 1942, Viking, illustrated by Kurt Wiese. $15.00
Lions on the Hunt, 1942, Viking, illustrated by Kurt Wiese. $15.00
White Panther, 1941, Viking, illustrated by Kurt Wiese. $15.00

WALKER, Abbie Phillips, 1867 – 1943, see Series, "Sandman."

WALL, Dorothy
Bridget and the Bees, 1935, Artists and Writers Guild, 45 pages, 4 color plates plus b/w illustrations by author. $15.00

WARE, Buzz, and **MATTHEWS, H. B.**, illustrators
Mother Goose Her Chimes, 1915 Saalfield, cover and b/w illustrations by Buzz Ware, color plates mounted on brown paper pages by Matthews. $45.00

WARREN, George, see Series, "Banner Boy Scouts," "Revolutionary."

WATKINS-PITCHFORD, Denys
Little Grey Men, 1949, Scribner, illustrated by author. $20.00

WATSON, Virginia
Princess Pocahontas, 1922, Philadelphia, illustrated by George W. Edwards $100.00
With Cortes the Conqueror, 1917, color paste-on pictorial and gilt lettering, illustrated by Frank Schoonover. $50.00

WAUGH, Ida
Bonny Bairns, 1888, full-page color illustrations. $200.00

WEBER, Sarah Stilwell
Musical Tree, 1925, Penn, oversize, songs and b/w/yellow illustrations by Weber. $50.00

WEBSTER, Frank, see Series, "Webster."

WEBSTER, Jean, b. NY, 1876 – 1916
Daddy Long Legs, 1912, Century, illustrations by author. $20.00
Dear Enemy, 1915, Century, illustrations by author. $20.00
Just Patty, 1911, illustrations by C. M. Relyea. $15.00
When Patty Went to College, 1903, Grosset Dunlap, illustrations by C. D. Williams. $15.00

WEISGARD, Leonard b. Connecticut, 1916, illustrator, see Brown, Margaret.
Pelican Here, Pelican There, 1948, Scribner, illustrations and story by Weisgard. $35.00
Suki, 1937, Nelson, oversize, illustrations by author. $35.00

WELLES, Winifred, b. Connecticut, 1893 – 1939, poet
Skipping Along Alone, 1931, Macmillan, illustrations by Marguerite Davis. $35.00

WELLS, Carolyn, see Series, "Marjorie," "Patty."

WELLS, Helen, see Series, "Cherry Ames," "Vicki Barr."

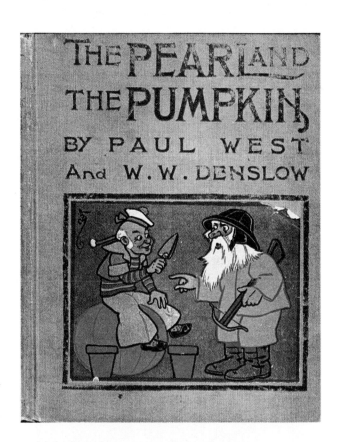

WEST, Paul, b. Boston, 1871 – 1918
Pearl and the Pumpkin, The, 1904, Dillingham, color illustrations by W. W. Denslow. $200.00

WETMORE, Claude
Queen Tiny's Little People, 1914, NY, illustrations by Mildred Bailey. $65.00

WHEELER, Janet D., see Series, "Billie Bradley."

WHEELER, Ruth, see Series, "Janet Hardy."

WHITE, E. B.
Stuart Little, 1945, Harper, b/w illustrations by Garth Williams. $45.00
Stuart Little, 1945, Harper Book Club Edition, b/w illustrations by Garth Williams. $10.00

WHITE, Edward Stewart
Conjuror's House, ca. 1907 edition, Grosset Dunlap, illustrated with scenes from the stage play. $20.00

WHITE, Gwen
Book of Toys, 1946, King Penguin Books, London, small size, color illustrations by author. $35.00

WHITE, Margaret
Boys and Girls at Work and Play, American Book Company, illustrations. $15.00

WHITE, S.
Daniel Boone, Wilderness Scout, 1926, Doubleday, illustrations by James Daugherty. $50.00

WHITE, T. H.
Sword in the Stone, 1938, London. $200.00
Sword in the Stone, 1939 edition, Putnam. $55.00

WHITEHALL, Dorothy, see Series, "Polly Pendleton," "Twins."

WHITEMAN, Edna
Playmates in Print, 1926, Nelson, a poetry collection, 6 color plates by Earl Oliver Hurst. $55.00

WIDDEMER, Margaret, see Series, "Wohelo Camp Fire Girls."

WIECHERS, Jerome
Conquerors of the Sea, 1924, Whitman, color illustrated cardboard cover, 60 pages, b/w illustrations on newsprint paper by Ray Gleason. $10.00

WIESE, Kurt, author-illustrator, see Waldeck.

WIGGIN, Kate Douglas, b. Philadelphia, 1857 (sister Nora Smith), see Series, "Scribner Classics," "Rebecca."
Birds' Christmas Carol, limited 1st edition.   Rare
Birds' Christmas Carol, 1912 edition, NY, illustrations by K. Wireman. $25.00
Mother Carey's Chickens, 1911, Houghton Mifflin, color plate illustrations by Alice Barber Stephens. $45.00
Old Peabody Pew, 1907 edition, Grosset Dunlap, illustrations by Alice Barber Stephens. $25.00
Penelope's Progress, ca. 1907 edition, Grosset Dunlap. $20.00

Rose O' the River, 1905 Houghton, 1st edition, three-color illustrations by George Wright. $20.00
Susanna and Sue, 1909, Riverside, illustrations by N. C. Wyeth and Alice Barber Stephens. $55.00
Tales of Laughter (1908), 1938 edition, Garden City, color paste-on pictorial cover, color frontispiece, 10 full-page b/w illustrations by Elizabeth McKinstry. $15.00

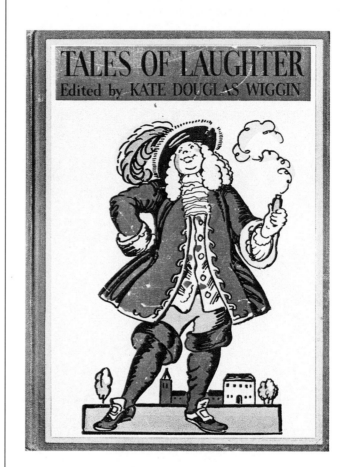

WILDE, Oscar
Birthday of the Infanta, 1929, Macmillan, illustrations by Pamela Bianco. $30.00
Happy Prince, 1913, Putnam, 1st American edition, oversize, 12 color plate illustrations w/tissue guards by Charles Robinson. $150.00
Happy Prince and Other Fairy Tales, 1913, Stokes, illustrations by Spencer Baird Nichols. $200.00
Happy Prince and Other Tales, 1888, D. Nutt, illustrations by Walter Crane and G. P. Hood.   Rare

WILDER, Laura Ingalls, b. Wisconsin, 1867 – 1957, see Series, "Little House."

WILL, Bess Goe
Peter Rabbit Story Book (copyright 1932), 1935 edition, Platt Munk, oversize, color illustrations. $20.00

WILLIAMS, Adene
Girl Warriors, 1901, David Cook, b/w illustrations. $35.00

WILLIAMS, Herschel
Children of the Clouds, 1929, Nelson, color frontispiece, b/w illustrations by Kurt Wiese. $20.00

WILLIAMS, Margery, see Bianco.

WILLIAMSON, Julia
Stars Through Magic Casements, 1931, Appleton, small size, b/w illustrations by Edna Reindel. $20.00

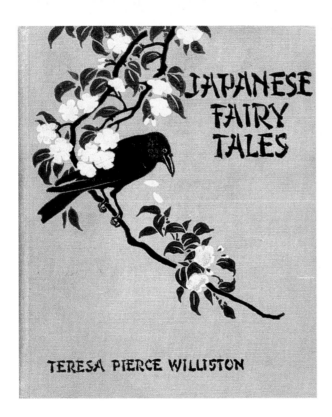

WILLISTON, Teresa
Japanese Fairy Tales, 1904, Rand McNally, illustrations by Sanchi Ogawai. $40.00

WILLSON, Dixie
Honey Bear, 1923, Volland, small size, color illustrations by Maginal Wright Barney. $35.00
Once Upon a Monday, 1931, Volland, color illustrations by Erick Berry. $35.00

WILSON, Edward A.
Pirate's Treasure, 1926, Volland, oversize, color illustrations by author. $40.00

WILSON, Richard
Talk of Many Things, undated, ca. 1930s, Nelson, 224 pages, color illustrations by Phyllis Denton. $15.00

WINLOW, Clara, see Series, "Our Little Cousin."

WINTER, Milo, illustrator, see Series, "Windemere."
Aesop for Children, 1919, Chicago. $75.00
Arabian Nights, The, no author credit, 1914, Rand McNally, 16 color plates. $65.00

WIRRIES, Mary Mabel, see Series, "Mary Rose."

WIRT, Mildred 1905, see Series, "Nancy Drew," "Penny Parker," "Ruth Darrow," "Flying Stories", "Trailer Stories."
(Wirt, a journalist, pilot and amateur archaeologist, used many of her own travel and adventure experiences in her stories. She wrote the first seven Nancy Drew books plus later ones, and is credited with inventing Nancy's independent personality. Pseudonyms include Carolyn Keene, Joan Clark, Frank Bell, Don Palmers, Dorothy West.)
Brownie Scouts at Snow Valley, 1949, Cupples. $10.00
Carolina Castle, 1936. $15.00

Clock Strikes Thirteen, 1942. $15.00
Swamp Island, 1947. $10.00

WISE, Daniel see Series,"Lindendale," "Winwood Cliff."

WISE, John R.
New Forest, 1895 edition, Gibbings, cloth cover with gilt, illustrations by Walter Crane. $95.00

WOOD, Esther
Pepper Moon, 1940, Longmans, illustrations by Laura Bannon. $20.00
Silk and Satin Lane, 1939, Longmans, illustrations by Kurt Wiese. $20.00

WOODRUFF, Elizabeth
Dickey Byrd, 1928 edition, Springfield, illustrations by Gustaf Tenggren. Rare

WOOLLEY, Lazelle, see Series, "Faith Palmer."

WRIGHT, Blanche Fisher, illustrator
Goody-Naughty Book, The, see Rippey.
Peter Patter Book, see Jackson, Leroy F.
Real Mother Goose, 1916, Rand, oversized picture book, color paste-on picture on cover, illustrated endpapers and color illustrations throughout. $65.00

WRIGHT, Harold Bell
Uncrowned King, 1910, Book Supply Co, small size, gilt decoration on red cover, color illustrations by John R Neill. $45.00

WRIGHT, Isa
Remarkable Tale of a Whale, Volland, small, color illustrations. $40.00

WURTH, A.
Rag Doll Susie, 1939, Saalfield picture book, color illustrations by Fern Bisel Peat. $45.00

WYETH, N. C. 1882 – 1945, illustrator, see Series "Scribner Classics."
Robin Hood, 1917 edition, McKay, illustrations by N. C. Wyeth. $90.00

WYMAN, Levi, see Series, "Hunniwell Boys," "Lakewood Boys."

WYNNE, Annette
Treasure Things, Volland, illustrated. $45.00

WYSS, Johann Rudolf
Swiss Family Robinson, 1853 edition, Willis Hazard, illustrated. $125.00
Swiss Family Robinson, 1909 edition, Harper, illustrations by Louis Rhead. $35.00
Swiss Family Robinson, 1913, Doran, illustrations by Thomas Heath Robinson. $50.00
Swiss Family Robinson, ca. 1947 edition, Grosset Dunlap, full color wraparound illustration on paper-on-boards cover, color frontispiece, 8 color plates plus b/w illustrations by Lynd Ward. $20.00

 **Y**

YONGE, Charlotte, 1823 – 1901
Heir of Redclyffe (copyright 1879 Macmillan), 1902 edition, Macmillan, illustrations by Kate Greenaway. $150.00
Little Duke (1854 London), 1927 edition, Macmillan, color frontispiece and b/w illustrations by Marguerite de Angeli. $10.00

YOUNG, Clarence, see Series, "Jack Ranger", "Motor Boys."

YOUNG, Ella
Tangle-coated Horse and Other Tales, 1929, Longmans, oversize, b/w woodblock style illustrations by Vera Bock. $50.00
Unicorn with Silver Shoes, 1932, Longmans, illustrations by Robert Lawson. $65.00

 **Z**

ZEITLIN, Ida
Skazki: Tales and Legends of Old Russia, 1926, Doubleday, color plus gold and black illustrations by Theodore Nadejen. $25.00

ZOLLINGER, Gulielma
Boy's Ride, 1909, McClurg, color paste-on pictorial cover, b/w illustrations by Fanny Chambers. $15.00

BOOK LIST BY SERIES

Prices for series books are for each book without dust jacket. Each book should be clean and in good condition (no tears, missing pages, mold spots or other damage.) A clean dust jacket usually doubles the price of a series book written for younger children, and adds 50 percent to the price of books written for older children.

Most series books were originally written to be part of a series. However, as the popularity of series books increased, publishers put together unrelated titles, sometimes by the same author, sometimes by a variety of authors (see Windemere, Scribner, and Rainbow), to make up a series. Therefore, the same title may appear in more than one series, but its edition in each series will have an exterior appearance that matches the other books in the series.

A

ADELE DORING SERIES, by Grace North, 1919 – 23, 5 books. $10.00

ADVENTURE GIRLS, Clair Bank, 1920, Burt, 3 books. $7.00
Adventure Girls at K-Bar-O
Adventure Girls in the Air
Adventure Girls at Happiness House

ADVENTURE AND MYSTERY SERIES FOR GIRLS, 1930, Burt. $10.00
Phantom Yacht, Carol Norton
Bobs, a Girl Detective, Carol Norton
Seven Sleuths Club, Carol Norton
Phantom Treasure, Harriet Grove
Mystery of the Sandalwood Boxes, Harriet Grove

Black Box, Thelma Lientz
Kay and the Secret Code, Thelma Lientz

ADVENTUROUS ALLENS, Harriet Grove, 1932, Burt, 3 books. $7.00

AEROPLANE SERIES, John Langworthy, ca. 1910, Donohue. $20.00
Aeroplane Boys
Aeroplane Boys on the Wing
Aeroplane Boys Among the Clouds
Aeroplane Boys' Flights
Aeroplane Boys on a Cattle Ranch

ALL ABOUT SERIES, Johnny Gruelle illustrations and re-tellings, ca. 1916, Cupples & Leon, small size, pictorial paste-on covers. $50.00.   1920s reprints, Cupples. $40.00

All About Cinderella, 1916, Cupples, color illustrations

All About Little Red Riding Hood, 1916, Cupples, color illustrations

All About Mother Goose, 1916, Cupples, color illustrations

All About the Little Small Red Hen, 1917, Cupples, color illustrations

All About Little Black Sambo, (retelling of Bannerman story), 1917, Cupples, color illustrations

ALTEMUS' MOTHER STORY SERIES, ca. 1908, Henry Altemus Co., Philadelphia, standard size, color and b/w illustrations, about 100 pages, collections of poetry and short stories. $35.00

Mother Stories

Mother Nursery Rhymes and Tales

Mother Nature Stories

Mother Stories from the Old Testament

Mother Bedtime Stories

Mother Animal Stories

Mother Bird Stories

Mother Santa Claus Stories

AMELIARANNE, Constance Heward and illustrator Susan Beatrice Pearce originated the series for children, continued by other authors, London and McKay. $30.00.

Ameliaranne and the Green Umbrella, 1920

Ameliaranne Keeps Shop, 1928

Ameliaranne, Cinema Star, 1929

Ameliaranne at the Circus, by Margaret Gilmour, 1931 McKay, black print illustration on red cover, small size, 64 pages, color illustrations by Susan Beatrice Pearse.

Ameliaranne at the Farm, 1937

Ameliaranne Gives a Christmas Party, 1938

Ameliaranne Camps Out, 1939

Ameliaranne Keeps School, 1940

AMERICAN ADVENTURE SERIES, Margaret Trent, 1932, Burt, 3 books. $10.00

AMERICAN GIRLS SERIES, Mary Darling, ca. 1900, Lee & Shepard, 35 books. $15.00

Battles at Home, first published in 1871

Captain Molly

Daisy Travers

Deerings of Medbury

ANNE SHIRLEY, L. M. Montgomery, novels for girls, written as individual novels with a continuing character by the same author, published by different publishers, later published in series formats.

Anne of Green Gables, 1908, L. C. Page, 1st edition. $250.00

Anne of Avonlea, 1909, Boston. $65.00

Chronicles of Avonlea, 1912, Page, color paste-on pictorial and color frontispiece by George Gibbs. $45.00

Anne of the Island (1915 Page), 1921 edition, Burt. $15.00

Anne's House of Dreams, 1917 edition, Stokes. $20.00

Further Chronicles of Avonlea, 1920, Boston. $20.00

Anne of Windy Poplars, 1936, NY. $20.00

Anne of Ingleside, 1939, Boston. $20.00

ANN STERLING, Harriet Grove, 1926, Burt, 7 books. $7.00

APPLE MARKET STREET SERIES, Mabel Hill, 1934 – 43, Stokes, 5 books. $10.00

ARDEN BLAKE MYSTERY SERIES, Cleo Garis, 1934, Burt. $15.00

ARMY BOY SERIES, by Charles Kilbourne, 1913 – 16, 4 books. $15.00

AUGUSTUS SERIES, Le Grand (Henderson), 1940s, Bobbs Merrill, oversize, about 130 pages, illustrations by author. $25.00

Augustus and the River

Augustus Goes South

Augustus and the Mountains, 1941

Augustus Helps the Navy, 1942

Augustus Helps the Army

Augustus Helps the Marines, 1943

Augustus Drives a Jeep, 1944

Augustus Rides the Border, 1947

AUNT JANE'S NIECES, Edith Van Dyne (L. Frank Baum), novels for girls, created as a series for Reilly Britton, small size, cloth covers, impressed and color paste-on cover illustration, illustrations E. A. Nelson, advertising page lists titles. (1st editions will be last title in list.) Reilly Britton. 1st editions, $55.00; later editions, $35.00

Aunt Jane's Nieces, 1906.

Aunt Jane's Nieces Abroad, 1906

Aunt Jane's Nieces at Millville, 1908

Aunt Jane's Nieces at Work, 1909

Aunt Jane's Nieces in Society, 1910

Aunt Jane's Nieces and Uncle John, 1911

Aunt Jane's Nieces on Vacation, 1912

Aunt Jane's Nieces on the Ranch, 1913

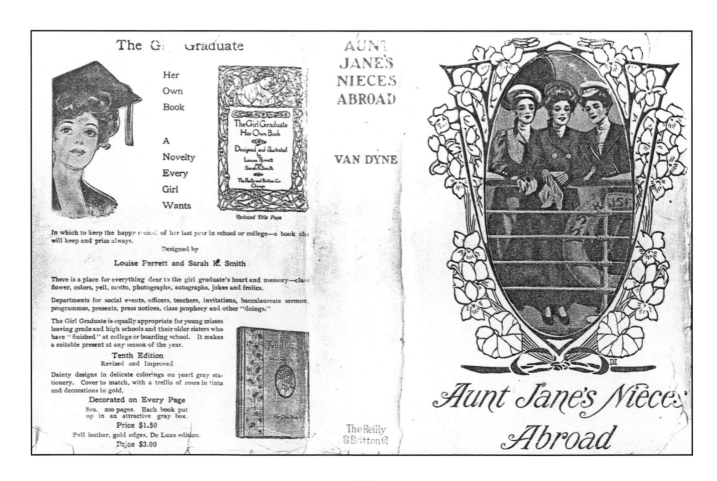

Aunt Jane's Nieces Out West, 1914
Aunt Jane's Nieces in the Red Cross, 1915

AUSTIN BOYS SERIES, Ken Anderson, 1944,
Zondervan.
Marooned $5.00

AUTOMOBILE GIRLS SERIES, Laura Crane,
1910, Altemus, 6 books. $10.00
Automobile Girls at Newport
Automobile Girls in the Berkshires
Automobile Girls Along the Hudson
Automobile Girls at Chicago
Automobile Girls at Palm Beach
Automobile Girls at Washington

B

BABAR SERIES, Jean de Brunhoff, 1899 – 1937,
author-illustrator
(The Babar books were originally written in
French. Some of the English translations were
published posthumously. These are oversize
picture books, color illustrations throughout.)
The Story of Babar (1931 France), trans. by Merle
Haas, 1934, London, 1933, Random House, 1st
edition. $150.00
Babar's Travels, 1934, Random House. $65.00
Babar the King, 1935, Random House. $65.00
Babar's Friend Zephyr, 1937, Random House.
$55.00
Babar's ABC, 1936, Random House. $65.00
Babar and His Children, 1938, Random House. $55.00
Babar and Father Christmas, 1940, Random House.
$125.00

BABAR SERIES, continued by Laurent de Brunhoff, b. 1925 (son of Jean de Brunhoff).
Babar and that Rascal Arthur (1947 France), trans.
by Olive Jones ,1948, London. $50.00

BABY ANIMALS BOOKS SERIES, Charles Kilbourne, 1913 – 17, 10 books. $15.00

BABS SERIES, Alice Colver, 1917, Penn Pub. 4
books. $10.00

BANNER BOY SCOUTS SERIES, George War-
ren, ca. 1920, Cupples & Leon. $10.00
Banner Boy Scouts
Banner Boy Scouts on Tour
Banner Boy Scouts Afloat
Banner Boy Scouts Snowbound

BANNER CAMPFIRE GIRLS SERIES, Julianne
DeVries, 1933, World, 6 books. $15.00

BARBARA HALE SERIES, Lilian Garis, ca. 1930s,
Grosset Dunlap. $15.00
Barbara Hale
Barbara Hale's Mystery Friend

BARNEY GOOGLE SERIES, cartoon books, ca.
1920s, Cupples & Leon, 10 " x 10 ", color illustrated cardboard covers, b/w cartoon strip stories. $75.00

BARTON BOOKS, by May Hollis Barton, ca. 1920,
Cupples, small size, cloth cover stamped in
color. $10.00
Girl from the Country
Three Girl Chums at Laurel Hall
Nell Grayson's Ranching Days
Four Little Women of Roxby
Plain Jane and Pretty Betty

BASEBALL JOE SERIES, Lester Chadwick, ca.
1920s, Cupples & Leon. $15.00
Baseball Joe of the Silver Stars
Baseball Joe on the School Nine
Baseball Joe at Yale
Baseball Joe in the Central League
Baseball Joe in the Big League
Baseball Joe on the Giants
Baseball Joe in the World Series
Baseball Joe around the World
Baseball Joe: Home Run King
Baseball Joe: Saving the League
Baseball Joe: Captain of the Team

BAUM, L. Frank, See under series:
AUNT JANE'S NIECES, pseudonym Edith Van
Dyne
BOY FORTUNE HUNTERS, pseudonym Floyd
Akers
MARY LOUISE, pseudonym Edith Van Dyne
OZ, L. Frank Baum
SAM STEELE'S ADVENTURES, pseudonym Capt.
Hugh Fitzgerald
TWINKLE TALES, pseudonym Laura Bancroft

BED TIME ANIMAL STORIES, Howard R. Garis
(see Series, Garis Family), lst copyrights are to
R. F. Fenno Co. These stories were published as
individual stories in newspapers and used on
radio, then collected into books ca. 1920, 31 sto-
ries per book (one for each night in month), 8
color plate illustrations by Lang Campbell, A. L.
Burt editions. $35.00
Sammy and Susie Littletail
Johnnie and Billie Bushytail
Lulu, Alice and Jimmie Wibblewobble
Jackie and Petie Bow Wow
Buddy and Brighteyes Pigg

Joie, Tommie and Kittie Kat
Charlie and Arabella Chick
Neddie and Beckie Stubtail
Bully and Bawly No-Tail
Nannie and Billie Wagtail
Jollie and Jillie Longtail
Jacko and Jumpo Kinkytail
Curly and Floppy Twistytail
Toodle and Noodle Flat-Tail
Dottie and Willie Flufftail
Dickie and Nellie Fliptail, 1921
Woodie and Waddie Chuck

BEDTIME STORY-BOOKS SERIES, Thornton Burgess, 20 vol., 1913 – 20, Little Brown, small size, stamped illustrations on cloth covers, illustrated by Harrison Cady. $40.00
Adventures of Reddy Fox
Adventures of Johnny Chuck
Adventures of Peter Cottontail
Adventures of Unc' Billy Possum
Adventures of Mr. Mocker
Adventures of Jerry Muskrat
Adventures of Danny Meadow Mouse
Adventures of Grandfather Frog
Adventures of Chatterer the Red Squirrel
Adventures of Sammy Jay
Adventures of Buster Bear
Adventures of Old Mr. Toad
Adventures of Prickly Porky
Adventures of Old Man Coyote
Adventures of Paddy the Beaver
Adventures of Poor Mrs. Quack
Adventures of Bobby Coon
Adventures of Jimmy Skunk
Adventures of Bob White
Adventures of Ol' Mistah Buzzard

BEST NURSERY SERIES, Donohue, oversize, cloth cover with full color illustration, picture books, b/w illustrations. $35.00
No. 650 Night Before Christmas, 1928

BETH ANNE SERIES, 1915, 4 volumes, Mrs. Pemberton Ginther. $15.00

BETTER LITTLE BOOKS, Whitman Publishing, extension of Whitman's successful Big Little Books line, advertised as "Better Little Books feature your favorite characters."
Apple Mary and Dennie's Lucky Apples, 1939, by Martha Orr. $25.00
Little Lulu, Alvin and Tubby, 1947, by Marge. $35.00
Popeye and Queen Olive Oyl, 1949, by Bud Sagendorf. $35.00
Uncle Wiggily's Adventures, 1946, by Howard Garis. $30.00

BETTY BOOKS SERIES, Alice Hale Burnett, New York Book Company, small size, 84 pages, color paste-on pictorial covers, 3 color plates by Charles Lester, advertised as "40 cents postpaid" apiece. $20.00
Betty and Her Chums
Betty's Attic Theatre
Betty's Carnival
Betty's Orphans

BETTY GORDAN SERIES, Alice B. Emerson, ca. 1920s, Cupples & Leon, small size, cloth covers, illustrated, 15 books. $10.00
Betty Gordan at Bramble Farm
Betty Gordan in Washington
Betty Gordan in the Land of Oil
Betty Gordan at Boarding School

Betty Gordan at Mountain Camp
Betty Gordan at Ocean Park
Betty Gordan and Her School Chums

BEVERLY GRAY COLLEGE MYSTERY SERIES,
Clair Blank, ca. 1930 – 1950, Grosset, 21 books. $10.00
Beverly Gray, Freshman
Beverly Gray, Sophomore
Beverly Gray, Junior
Beverly Gray, Senior
Beverly Gray's Career
Beverly Gray on a World Cruise
Beverly Gray in the Orient
Beverly Gray on a Treasure Hunt
Beverly Gray's Return
Beverly Gray, Reporter
Beverly Gray's Romance
Beverly Gray's Quest

BIGGLES, Captain W. E. Johns, eighty-plus adventure novels. $15.00
Biggles of the Camel Squadron, 1934, London
Biggles Flies Again, 1934
Biggles Flies East, 1935
Biggles and Co., 1936

BIG LEAGUE SERIES, Burt Standish, 1913 – 28, 14 books. $15.00

BIG LITTLE BOOKS, Whitman, series introduced in 1933, approximately 4½" high x 3½" wide x 1½" thick, color illustrated covers, b/w illustrations facing each page of text, stories generally based on newspaper comic strips, low-end price is about $25.00, with prices ranging up to $200.00 for rare editions. Generally, greatest demand is for Dick Tracy, science fiction characters such as Flash Gordon and John Carter of Mars, and for specific collector favorites, such as Mickey Mouse and Tarzan. Prices quoted are rounded out to give the collector an idea of value. Condition affects value dramatically, and so does changing popularity.
Billy the Kid, 1935, Cocomalt premium. $35.00
Blondie and Dagwood titles, 1940s. $20.00
Buck Rogers City Below the Sea, 1934. $55.00
Buck Rogers and the Doom Planet, 1935. $50.00
Bugs Bunny titles, 1940s. $35.00
Dick Tracy, Boris Arson Gang, 1935. $50.00
Dick Tracy Out West, 1933. $50.00
Flash Gordon titles, 1940s. $35.00
Gene Autry titles, 1940s. $25.00
G-Man Alien, 1939. $25.00
Invisible Scarlet O'Neil titles, 1940s. $25.00
Jack Armstrong and the Ivory Tower Treasure, 1937. $25.00
Little Orphan Annie, 1933. $100.00
Other Litttle Orphan Annie titles, 1930s. $50.00
Mickey Mouse Runs His Own Newspaper. $65.00
Popeye See the Sea, 1936. $55.00

Smilin' Jack titles, 1930s. $30.00
Tarzan titles, 1940s. $50.00
Tom Mix titles, 1940s. $25.00

BILL BOLTON AVIATION SERIES, Noel Sainsbury, 6 books. $15.00

BILLIE BRADLEY SERIES, Janet D. Wheeler, ca. 1920s, Cupples & Leon, small size, cloth covers, illustrations, 9 books. $10.00
Billie Bradley and Her Inheritance
Billie Bradley at Three-Towers Hall
Billie Bradley on Lighthouse Island
Billie Bradley and Her Classmates
Billie Bradley at Twin Lakes

BILLY BUNNY BOOKS SERIES, David Cory, ca. 1920s, Cupples Leon, small size, b/w/orange illustrations by H. Hasting. $25.00
Billy Bunny and the Friendly Elephant
Billy Bunny and Daddy Fox
Billy Bunny and Uncle Bull Frog
Billy Bunny and Uncle Lucky Lefthindfoot
Billy Bunny and Robbie Redbreast
Billy Bunny and Timmie Chipmunk

BILLY TO-MORROW SERIES, Sarah Pratt Carr, 1909 – 19, 4 books. $20.00

BILLY TOPSAIL SERIES, Norman Duncan, 1906 Revell, small, illustration imprinted on cloth cover, 12 b/w illustrations. $15.00
Adventure of Billy Topsail
Billy Topsail and Company
Billy Topsail, M. D.

BILLY WHISKERS SERIES, Frances Montgomery, Saalfield, brown cloth cover with imprint, color plate illustrations .
Billy Whiskers Vacation, 1908 $40.00
Billy Whiskers in an Aeroplane, 1912, illustrations by Constance White. $40.00
Billy Whiskers at the Fair, 1909. $35.00
Billy Whiskers Twins, 1911. $35.00
Billy Whiskers, Tourist, 1929. $25.00
Billy Whiskers in the Movies, illustrations by Paul Hawthorne.   40.00

BLACK STALLION SERIES, Walter Farley, Random House. $15.00
Black Stallion, 1941, illustrations by Keith Ward

90

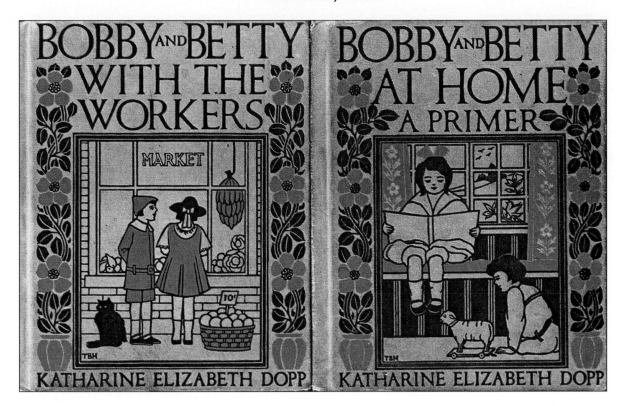

Black Stallion Returns, 1945, illustrations by Harold Eldridge
Son of Black Stallion
Black Stallion and Satan
Black Stallion's Filly
Black Stallion Revolts

BLOSSOM SHOP SERIES, Isla May Mullins, 1913-22, Page, 6 books. $10.00

BLUE BONNET SERIES, Lela Richards, 1910 – 29, Page, 7 books. $10.00

BLYTHE GIRLS, Laura Lee Hope, 1925 – 32, Grosset, illustrations by Thelma Gooch, advertised as "The Blythe girls were left alone in New York City...", 12 books. $7.00
Blythe Girls, Helen, Margy and Rose
Blythe Girls, Margy's Queer Inheritance
Blythe Girls, Rose's Great Problem
Blythe Girls, Helen's Strange Boarder
Blythe Girls, Three on a Vacation

BOBBSEY TWINS, Laura Lee Hope, 1904 – 1950, first editions, Grosset after 1913, 43 books. Pre – 1920 $25.00, post-1920. $15.00
Bobbsey Twins, 1904, Mershon, ca. 1907, Grosset Dunlap, b/w illustrations
Bobbsey Twins in the Country, Chatterton-Peck, ca. 1907, Grosset Dunlap, b/w illustrations by Nuttall

Bobbsey Twins at School
Bobbsey Twins at Snow Lodge
Bobbsey Twins on a Houseboat
Bobbsey Twins at Meadow Brook
Bobbsey Twins at Home
Bobbsey Twins in a Great City
Bobbsey Twins on Blueberry Island
Bobbsey Twins on the Deep Blue Sea
Bobbsey Twins in the Great West

BOBBY AND BETTY SERIES, Kathrine Dopp, 1917 – 27, Rand McNally, school readers, b/w/orange illustrations by Mary Spoor Brand, 4 books
Bobby and Betty at Home. $20.00
Bobby and Betty with the Workers. $20.00

BOB DEXTER SERIES, Willard F. Baker, ca. 1920, Cupples. $10.00
Bob Dexter and the Club-House Mystery
Bob Dexter and the Beacon Beach Mystery
Bob Dexter and the Storm Mountain Mystery

BOB HANSON SERIES, Russell Carter, ca. 1920s, 4 books. $10.00

BOMBA SERIES, Roy Rockwood, ca. 1920s, Grosset, 1st edition, cloth covers. $20.00; later edition illustrated paper-over-boards covers, $10.00
Bomba the Jungle Boy
Bomba at the Moving Mountain

Bomba at the Giant Cataract
Bomba on Jaguar Island
Bomba in the Abandoned City
Bomba on the Terror Trail
Bomba in the Swamps of Death
Bomba Among the Slaves
Bomba on the Underground River
Bomba and the Lost Explorers

BOOKSHELF FOR BOYS AND GIRLS, 1948, University Society, NY, color paste-on pictorial on cloth cover, this series combines material from *Boys and Girls Bookshelf, Young Folks Treasury, Modern Boy's Activity.* $10.00 per volume.

BOONE AND KENTON SERIES, Edward Ellis, ca.1890s, Winston. $15.00
Shod With Silence
In the Days of the Pioneers
Phantom of the River

BOY DONALD SERIES, Sarah Clarke, 1900, 3 books. $15.00

BOY FORTUNE HUNTERS, Floyd Akers (Baum). $75.00
Boy Fortune Hunters in Panama
Boy Fortune Hunters in Alaska
Boy Fortune Hunters in Egypt
Boy Fortune Hunters in China
Boy Fortune Hunters in the South Seas

BOY HUNTER SERIES, Capt. Ralph Bonehill. $15.00
Four Boy Hunters
Guns and Snowshoes
Young Hunters of the Lake
Out With Guns and Camera

BOY INVENTORS SERIES, ca. 1910, Donohue. $15.00
Boy Inventors' Wireless Triumph
Boy Inventors and the Vanishing Sun
Boy Inventors' Diving Torpedo Set
Boy Inventors' Flying Ship
Boy Inventors' Electric Ship
Boy Inventors' Radio Telephone

BOY PIONEER SERIES, Edward Ellis, ca. 1890s Winston. $15.00
Ned in the Block-House
Ned on the River
Ned in the Woods

BOY RANCHERS SERIES, Willard F. Baker, ca.

1920s, Cupples & Leon, small size, cloth cover, b/w illustrations. $10.00
Boy Ranchers
Boy Ranchers in Camp
Boy Ranchers on the Trail
Boy Ranchers among the Indians
Boy Ranchers at Spur Creek
Boy Ranchers in the Desert

BOY SCOUTS SERIES, Lieut. Howard Payson, ca. 1910, Hurst, color printed cover illustration, b/w illustrations by R. M. Brinkerhoff. $20.00
Boy Scouts' Mountain Camp
Boy Scouts of Eagle Patrol
Boy Scouts on the Range
Boy Scouts and the Army Airship

BRAVE HEART SERIES, Adele E. Thompson, ca. 1900, Lee & Shepard, illustrations Lillian Crawford True. $10.00
Betty Seldon, Patriot
Brave Heart Elizabeth
Lassie of the Isles

BRINGING UP FATHER SERIES, George McManus, cartoon books, ca. 1920s, 10" x 10" cardboard cover with b/w cartoon strip stories. $60.00

BROTHER AND SISTER SERIES, Josephine Lawrence, ca. 1920, Cupples & Leon, small size, illustrations by Julia Greene. $20.00
Brother and Sister
Brother and Sister's Schooldays
Brother and Sister's Holidays
Brother and Sister's Vacation

BUDDY BEAR SERIES, Linda Almond, ca. 1920s. $25.00

BUDDY BOOKS SERIES, Howard Garis, ca. 1930s, Cupples & Leon, b/w illustrations. $15.00
Buddy on the Farm
Buddy at School
Buddy's Winter Fun
Buddy at Rainbow Lake
Buddy and His Chums
Buddy at Pine Beach

BUNNY BROWN SERIES, Laura Lee Hope, 1916 – 31, Grosset, 20 books, advertised as "eagerly welcomed by the little folks." $15.00
Bunny Brown and His Sister Sue
Bunny Brown and His Sister Sue on Grandpa's Farm
Bunny Brown and His Sister Sue Playing Circus
Bunny Brown and His Sister Sue at Camp Rest-A-While

BUNNY COTTONTAIL SERIES, Laura Rountree

Smith, ca. 1915, Whitman, reprints of earlier Smith books, small size square, illustrated by Dorothy Aniol. $25.00
Tail of Bunny Cottontail
Bunny Bright Eyes
Three Little Cottontails
Bunny Bear and Grizzly Bear
Little Bear
Bunny Cottontail Jr.
Circus Cottontails
Snubby Nose and Tippy Toes

BUSTER BROWN SERIES, R. F. Outcault, oversize, color and b/w illustrations by author, ca. 1900, London and Stokes, NY.
Buster Brown, His Dog Tige and Their Troubles, 1900, London, color illustrations. $85.00
Buster Brown Abroad, 1904, Stokes, $40.00

BUSTER BROWN NUGGETS SERIES, by R. F. Outcault, ca. 1905 Cupples & Leon, small size, color illustrated paper-covered boards, 36 pages, full-color, full-page illustrations. $75.00
Buster Brown Goes Fishing
Buster Brown Goes Swimming
Buster Brown Plays Indian
Buster Brown Goes Shooting
Buster Brown Plays Cowboy
Buster Brown on Uncle Jack's Farm
Buster Brown, Tige and the Bull

Buster Brown and Uncle Buster
Buddy Tucker Meets Alice in Wonderland
Buddy Tucker Visits the House that Jack Built

BYE-LO SERIES, ca. 1910 Rand McNally, small size, color illustration on cover, approximately 60 pages with b/w/orange illustrations. $35.00
Handy Pandy
Jack and Jill
Tommy Snooks
Hot Cross Buns
Jumping Joan
Betty Blue
Little Jenny Wren
Cinderella, 1914, illustrations by Blanche Fisher Wright

CAMP FIRE GIRLS SERIES, Margaret Sanderson, 1913 – 21, Reilly, 8 books. $10.00

CAMPFIRE GIRLS SERIES, Irene Benson, 1918 Donohue, 10 books. $10.00

CAMP FIRE GIRLS SERIES, Hildegarde Frey, 1916 – 20, Burt, 10 books. $10.00

CAMPFIRE GIRLS SERIES, Jane Stewart, 1914 Saalfield, 6 books. $10.00
Campfire Girl's First Council Fire

Campfire Girl's Chum
Campfire Girl in Summer Camp
Campfire Girl's Adventure
Campfire Girl's Test of Friendship
Campfire Girl's Happiness

CAMPFIRE GIRLS SERIES, Margaret Penrose, Goldsmith, 4 books. $10.00

CARTER GIRLS SERIES, Nell Speed. $10.00

CHAMPION SPORTS SERIES, Noel Sainsbury, 5 books. $10.00

CHERRY AMES, NURSE SERIES, Helen Wells, 1943 – 48, Grosset, 9 books. $10.00

CHICKEN LITTLE JANE SERIES, Lily Ritchie, 1918 – 26, Britton, 5 books. $20.00

CHILDREN'S OWN BOOKS SERIES, ca. 1918 Reilly & Britton, Chicago, small size, 2 stories in each book, color covers, illustrations and endpapers, many by John R. Neill, lists the same 12 books as *Children's Red Books* Series plus volumes 13 and 14. $45.00 ea.
Volume 13: Aladdin and the Wonderful Lamp, Robin Hood
Volume 14: Christmas Carol, Jessica's First Prayer.

CHILDREN'S RED BOOKS SERIES, ca. 1915, Reilly & Britton, Chicago, small size, 2 stories in each book, color covers, illustrations and endpapers, many by John R. Neill, 12 books in series. $45.00 ea.

Peter Rabbit, Dick Whittington
Little Black Sambo, Uncle Tom's Cabin
Night Before Christmas, Mother Goose Rhymes
Black Beauty, Little Lame Prince
Rab and His Friends, J. Cole
Adventures of a Brownie, Swiss Family Robinson
Little Red Riding Hood, Sleeping Beauty
Cinderella, Three Bears
Jack and the Beanstalk, Robinson Crusoe
Alice's Adventures in Wonderland, Through the Looking Glass
Ugly Duckling, Rip Van Winkle
Hansel and Gretel, Snow White and Rose Red

CIRCUS BOYS SERIES, Frank Patchin. $15.00

CLEO SERIES, Lilian Garis, ca. 1930s, Grosset Dunlap. $15.00
Cleo's Misty Rainbow
Cleo's Conquest

CLOVERDALE FARM SERIES, Helen Orton, 1922 – 26, Stokes, 4 books. $10.00

COLLEGE LIFE SERIES, Burt Standish, 1913 – 28, 6 books. $10.00

COLLEGE SPORTS SERIES, Lester Chadwick, ca. 1925, Cupples & Leon. $10.00
Rival Pitchers
Quarterback's Pluck
Batting to Win
Winning Touchdown
For the Honor of Randall
Eight-Oared Victors

CONKEY CO., Chicago, paper or clothlike cover, picture books, oversize size, 12 pages with color illustrations throughout. $30.00
Gulliver's Travels, 1899
Robinson Crusoe, 1899

CONNIE LORING SERIES, Lilian Garis, ca. 1930 Grosset Dunlap. $15.00
Connie Loring
Connie Loring's Gypsy Friend

CONNIE MORGAN SERIES, 7 volumes 1916 – 29, James Hendryx.

CURLYTOPS SERIES, Howard R. Garis, ca. 1920s, Cupples & Leon, small size, illustrations, 14 books. $30.00
Curlytops at Cherry Farm
Curlytops on Star Island
Curlytops Snowed In
Curlytops at Uncle Frank's Ranch
Curlytops at Silver Lake
Curlytops and Their Pets
Curlytops and Their Playmates
Curlytops in the Woods
Curlytops at Sunset Beach

✐ D ✐

DADDY SERIES, Howard Garis, 1920s edition Donohue, small size, paste-on pictorial cover, illustrations by Louis Wisa, Edyth Powers, Eva Dean. $35.00
Daddy Takes Us Camping
Daddy Takes Us Fishing
Daddy Takes Us to the Circus
Daddy Takes Us Skating
Daddy Takes Us Coasting
Daddy Takes Us to the Farm
Daddy Takes Us to the Garden
Daddy Takes Us Hunting Birds
Daddy Takes Us Hunting Flowers
Daddy Takes Us to the Woods

DANA GIRLS MYSTERY STORIES SERIES, Carolyn Keene, ca. 1930s, Grosset. $15.00
By the Light of the Study Lamp
Secret at Lone Tree Cottage
In the Shadow of the Tower
Three-Cornered Mystery
Secret at the Hermitage
Circle of Footprints
Mystery of the Locked Room
Clue in the Cobweb
Secret at the Gatehouse

DANDELION COTTAGE SERIES, C. W. Rankin,

1904 – 21, Holt, 5 books. $20.00

DAVE DASHAWAY SERIES, Roy Rockwood, ca. 1920s, Cupples. $15.00
Dave Dashaway: the Young Aviator
Dave Dashaway and His Hydroplane
Dave Dashaway and His Giant Airship
Dave Dashaway Around the World
Dave Dashaway Air Champion

DAVE DAWSON SERIES, Sidney Bower, ca. 1940s, Saalfield. $10.00

DEARBORN SERIES, Blanche Dearborn, 1936, Macmillan, small size, two-color illustrations. $15.00
Kitten Kat
Winter Time
Country Days
City Friends

DEAR LITTLE GIRL SERIES, Amy Blanchard, 1897 – 1912, Jacobs, 4 books. $20.00

DEERFOOT SERIES, Edward Ellis, ca. 1890s, Winston. $15.00
Hunters of the Ozark
Last War Trail
Camp in the Mountains.

DICK AND JANE SERIES, school readers, teachers' guides by William and Lillian Gray, 1946 – 47 edition.
Guidebook to Our New Friends. $125.00
Guidebook to Fun With Dick and Jane. $125.00

DICK AND JANET CHERRY SERIES, Howard Garis, 1930, McLoughlin, small size, 264 pages, wraparound color illustration on cover boards, b/w endpaper and frontispiece illustrations. $30.00
Dick and Janet Cherry Shipwrecked on Christmas Island
Dick and Janet Cherry in the Gypsy Camp
Dick and Janet Cherry Saving the Old Mill
Dick and Janet Cherry on a Bear Hunt

DICK TRAVERS SERIES, Adelaide Samuels, 1870s, Lee & Shepard, small size, cloth with gilt covers, line drawings. $25.00

DOCTOR DOOLITTLE, Hugh Lofting, Stokes, illustrations by author
Story of Dr. Doolittle, 1920. $175.00
Story of Dr. Doolittle, 1948 edition, Lippincott. $15.00
Dr. Doolittle in the Moon, 1928. $75.00

Dr. Doolittle at the Zoo, 1925. $45.00

DOLLY AND MOLLY SERIES, Elizabeth Gordon,
1914 Rand, 4 books. $30.00

DONOUE & CO. Bright Eyes SERIES 210
undated, ca. 1930s, standard size, hardcover
with full-color illustration on front cover, b/w
illustrations on newsprint pages. $25.00
Childhood's Golden Dreams

**DONOHUE & CO. Linennwear SERIES
802 and 803**
undated, ca. 1930, Chicago & NY, oversize,
color illustrated cloth cover, picture books,
color illustrations. $35.00
Animal Pets
Favorite Picture Book
Wee Folks Picture Book

DONOHUE & CO. Best Nursery SERIES 650
standard size, color illustrated cardboard covers, b/w illustrations on newsprint quality
paper. $20.00
Little Red Riding Hood, 1929
Mother Goose Favorites, 1928
Night Before Christmas, 1928

DON STURDY SERIES, Victor Appleton, by 1907
Grosset Dunlap listed 5 titles, advertised with
"Individual colored wrappers and text illustra-
tions by Walter S. Rogers." $10.00
Don Sturdy on the Desert of Mystery
Don Sturdy with the Big Snake Hunters
Don Sturdy in the Tombs of Gold
Don Sturdy Across the North Pole
Don Sturdy in the Land of Volcanoes

DORIS FORCE SERIES, Julia K. Duncan, ca.
1930, Goldsmith, cover illustration by Thelma
Gooch. $10.00
Doris Force at Locked Gates
Doris Force at Cloudy Cove
Doris Force at Raven Rock
Doris Force at Barry Manor

DOROTHY SERIES, Evelyn Raymond, 1907 – 13,
Chatterton, 11 books. $10.00

DOROTHY DAINTY SERIES, 1902 – 23, Lothrop-
Lee, 22 books. $10.00

DOROTHY DALE SERIES, Margaret Penrose, ca.
1920s, Cupples & Leon, small size, illustrated,
13 books, advertised as "Dorothy Dale is the
daughter of an old Civil War veteran who is
running a weekly newspaper in a small Eastern
town...her trials and triumphs make clean,
interesting and fascinating reading." $10.00
Dorothy Dale: A Girl of To-Day
At Glenwood School
Great Secret

And Her Chums
Queer Holidays
Camping Days
School Rivals
In the City
Dorothy Dale's Promise
In the West
Strange Discovery
Engagement
To the Rescue

DOROTHY DIX AIR MYSTERIES SERIES, Dorothy Wayne (Noel Sainsbury), 6 books. $15.00

DOTTY DIMPLE STORIES, Sophie May, 1867 – 69, 6 books. $25.00

DULCIE SERIES, Jack Bechdolt and Decie Merwin, Dutton, small size, 2-color illustrations. $20.00
Dulcie and Half a Yard of Linsey Woolsey,   1943
Dulcie and Her Donkey, 1944
Dulcie Sews a Sampler, 1945
Dulcie and the Gypsies, 1948

———  ———

ELIZABETH ANN SERIES, Josephine Lawrence, 1923 – 29, Barse, then Grosset, 8 books. $15.00

ELSIE DINSMORE SERIES, Martha Finley, 1867 – 1905, Dodd, 28 books. $10.00

ETHEL MORTON SERIES, Mabell Smith, 1915, NY Books, 6 books. $10.00
At Rose House
Sweet Briar Lodge
Holidays
Enterprise

———  ———

FAIRMONT GIRLS SERIES, Etta Baker, 1904 – 14, Little, 4 books. $10.00

FAITH PALMER SERIES, Lazelle Woolley, ca. 1912, 4 volumes. $10.00

FAMOUS FIVE, Enid Blyton, illustrations Eileen Soper (collectible in Great Britain, not well known in U. S.). $15.00
Five Go to Devil's Rocks
Five on Treasure Island, 1942, London

FATHER TAKES SERIES, Grace Humphrey, 1927, Penn, 4 books. $15.00
Father Takes Us to New York
Father Takes Us to Boston
Father Takes Us to Philadelphia
Father Takes Us to Washington

FELICIA SERIES, Elizabeth Gould, 1908-11, Penn, impressed illustration on cover, b/w illustrations by Mary Price. $15.00
Felicia
Felicia's Friends

Felicia Visits
Felicia's Folks

FIGHTERS FOR FREEDOM SERIES, Whitman, b/w illustrations. $15.00
Barry Blake and the Flying Fortress
Norma Kent of the WACS
Sally Scott of the WAVES
Sparky Ames and Mary Mason of the Ferry Command

FIRESIDE HENTY SERIES, G. A. Henty, ca. 1850s, Donohue, heavily impressed cloth covers, b/w illustrations, this series contains the following sub-series, and each of these contain many titles, including crossovers from individual books and other series by Henty, usually valued more for the covers than the content, so condition of cover should be very good. $35.00
Boy Hunters
Rifle Rangers
Wood Rangers

FIVE LITTLE PEPPERS SERIES, Margaret Sidney (Harriet Lothrop), 1880 – 1916, Lothrop, (high collector demand for specific hard-to-find editions or titles priced to $200.00), 12 books, later printings. $20.00

FIVE LITTLE STARRS, Lillian Roy, 1913 – 19, Platt, 8 books. $10.00

FLAXIE FRIZZLE STORIES, Sophie May, 1876 – 74, Lee & Shepard, b/w illustrations by Elizabeth Tucker, 6 books. $35.00
1910 edition, Lothrop Lee, small size. $20.00

FLICKA, RICKA AND DICKA SERIES, written and illustrated by Maj. Lindman, Whitman, oversize books with color illustrations throughout, 1st editions, $50.00, later printings and library covers. $35.00
Flicka, Ricka and Dicka and the New Dotted Dresses, 1939
Flicka, Ricka and Dicka and the Girl Next Door, 1940
Flicka, Ricka and Dicka and the Three Kittens, 1941
Flicka, Ricka and Dicka and their New Friend, 1942
Flicka, Ricka and Dicka and the Strawberries, 1944

FLORENCE STORIES, Jacob Abbott, ca. 1860s, Sheldon Co., 1sts, $50.00, later editions, $20.00
Florence and John
Florence's Return
Florence's Visit to the Isle of Wight

FLYAWAY STORIES, Alice Dale Hardy, ca. 1907, Grosset Dunlap, advertised three books of its new series with "Individual colored jackets and colored illustrations." $20.00
Flyaways and Cinderella
Flyaways and Red Riding Hood
Flyaways and Goldilocks

FOREST AND PRAIRIE SERIES, Edward S. Ellis
Great Cattle Trail, 1894, Winston, Philadelphia, illustrations by White. $20.00

FOUR CORNERS SERIES, Amy Blanchard, 1906 – 13, Jacobs, 8 books. $15.00

FOUR LITTLE BLOSSOMS, Mabel Hawley, 1920 – 30, Cupples, 7 books, small, cloth cover with color imprint. $10.00
Four Little Blossoms at Brookside Farm
Four Little Blossoms at Oak Hill School
Four Little Blossoms and Their Winter Fun
Four Little Blossoms on Apple Tree Island
Four Little Blossoms Through the Holidays

FRANK MERRIWELL SERIES, Burt Standish, (William Patten 1866 – 1945), 1900 – 1933, 208 books in series. $15.00

FRED FENTON SERIES, Allen Chapman, ca. 1920s, Cupples & Leon. $15.00
Fred Fenton the Pitcher
Fred Fenton in the Line
Fred Fenton on the Crew
Fred Fenton on the Track
Fred Fenton: Marathon Runner

FRIENDLY TERRACE SERIES, Harriet Smith, 1912-22, Page, 5 books. $10.00

FRONTIER GIRLS SERIES, Alice Curtis, 1929 – 37, Penn, 5 books. $10.00

FURRY FOLK STORIES, Jane Fielding, ca. 1920s, Donohoe, cloth cover, illustrations. $20.00
Bear Brownie
Jackie Hightree
Kitty Purrpuss
Master Reynard
Scamp
Wee Willie Mousie

G

GARIS FAMILY: SERIES by Howard Garis, Lilian Garis, and son Roger Garis and daughter Cleo

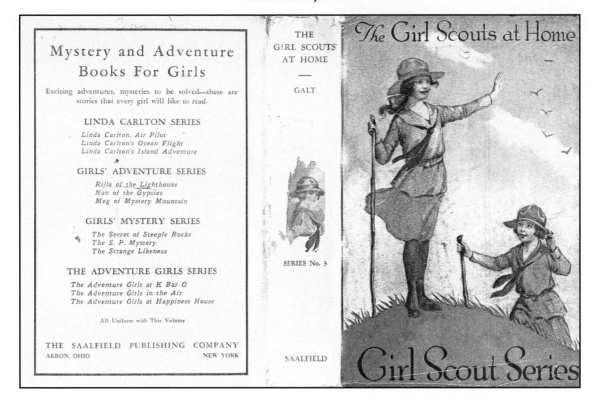

Garis. The four wrote over a thousand books, according to Roger Garis, so many that Roger Garis was not sure of all the titles and series and pseudonyms. Many of their series were written for Stratemeyer. The Garises wrote complete series, or several books in a series, and they wrote under their own names and also under pseudonyms. The following are some of the series to which each Garis contributed:

Howard: (in addition to his famous Uncle Wiggily stories) Daddy Stories, Buddy, Happy Home

Lilian: Girl Scout, Bobbsey Twins, Nancy Brandon, Motor Girls, Melody Lane Mysteries, Barbara Hale, A Girl Called Ted, Two Girls, the Gloria books, Connie Loring, Judy Jordan, the Joan books

Roger: Outboard Boys, Buffalo Hunter series (updated rewrites of an 1890s series owned by Stratemeyer), X Bar X Boys

Cleo: girl mystery books including Missing at Marshlands, Mystery of Jockey Hollow, Orchard Secret, Arden Blake series

GARY GRAYSON SERIES, Elmer Dawson, ca. 1910, Grosset, advertised as "Good clean football at its best and in addition, up-to-the-minute stories of school rivalries and boy life." $10.00
Gary Grayson's Hill Street Eleven
Gary Grayson at Lenox High
Gary Grayson's Football Rivals
Gary Grayson Showing His Speed
Gary Grayson at Stanley Prep

GEORGEY'S MENAGERIE SERIES, Mrs. Madeline Leslie, ca. 1864, Thomas Crowell, 144 pages, illustrations. $35.00
Bear
Deer
Lion
Wolf

GIRL AVIATOR SERIES, Margaret Burnham, 1920s editions, Donahue. $15.00
Girl Aviators and the Phantom Airship
Girl Aviators on Golden Wings
Girl Aviators' Sky Cruise
Girl Aviators' Motor Butterfly

GIRL SCOUT SERIES, Katherine Galt, 1921, Saalfield, 3 books. $10.00
Girl Scouts at Home
Girl Scouts Rally
Girl Scout's Triumph

GIRL SCOUT SERIES, Lilian Garis, ca. 1920s, Cupples & Leon, small size, cloth cover, illustrated, advertised as "The highest ideals of girlhood as advocated by the foremost organizations of America form the background for these stories and while unobtrusive, there is a message in every volume." $15.00
Girl Scout Pioneers
Girl Scouts at Bellaire
Girl Scouts at Sea Crest

Girl Scouts at Camp Comalong
Girl Scouts at Rocky Ledge

GIRL SCOUT SERIES, Edith Lavell, 1922 – 25, Burt, 10 books. $10.00
Girl Scouts' Good Turn
Girl Scouts' Canoe Trip
Girl Scouts' Rivals
Girl Scouts' on the Ranch

GIRL SCOUT SERIES, Margaret Vandercook, 1914 – 20, Winston, 5 books. $10.00

GIRL SCOUT MYSTERY SERIES, Virginia Fairfax, 1933 – 36, Burt, 6 books. $10.00

GIRL SCOUTS SERIES, Lillian Elizabeth Roy, ca. 1915, Grosset, advertised as "The heroines of these pleasant stories are Girl Scouts and woven through the adventures and fun you will find the principles of Scouting carried out." $15.00
Girl Scouts at Dandelion Camp
Girl Scouts in the Adirondacks
Girl Scouts in the Rockies
Girl Scouts in Arizona and New Mexico
Girl Scouts in the Redwoods
Girl Scouts in the Magic City
Woodcraft Girls at Camp
Woodcraft Girls in the City

Woodcraft Girls Camping in Maine
Little Woodcrafter's Book
Little Woodcrafter's Fun on the Farm

GIRLS' ADVENTURE SERIES, ca. 1930, Saalfield. $10.00
Rilla of the Lighthouse
Nan of the Gypsies
Meg of Mystery Mountain

GIRLS' DETECTIVE SERIES, ca. 1930, Saalfield. $15.00
Seven Sleuths' Club
Sisters
Mystery of Arnold Hall

GIRLS MYSTERY SERIES, by Harriet Pyne Grove, ca. 1928, Saalfield. $10.00
Secret of Steeple Rocks
S. P. Mystery
Strange Likeness

GIRLS OF CENTRAL HIGH SERIES, Gertrude Morrison, 1914 – 21, Grosset, 7 books. $7.00

GLAD BOOKS SERIES (POLLYANNA), Eleanor Porter (see author Porter for listing on first edition) and Smith and Chalmers, 1913 – 44, Page Pub., 11 books. $15.00

GLENLOCK GIRLS SERIES, Grace Remick, ca. 1909, 4 books. $10.00

GLORIA SERIES, Lilian Garis, ca. 1930s, Grosset
Dunlap. $15.00
Gloria: A Girl and Her Dad
Gloria at Boarding School

GOLDEN BOOKS, see "Little Golden Books."

GOLDEN BOYS SERIES, Levi Wyman, ca. 1920s,
9 books. $7.00

GRACE HARLOWE COLLEGE GIRLS SERIES,
Jessie Graham Flower, ca. 1915 – 25, Altemus,
cloth cover with imprint, illustrated. $10.00
Grace Harlowe's First Year at Overton College
Grace Harlowe's Second Year at Overton College
Grace Harlowe's Third Year at Overton College
Grace Harlowe's Fourth Year at Overton College
Grace Harlowe's Return to Overton College
Grace Harlowe's Problem
Grace Harlowe's Golden Summer

**GRACE HARLOWE HIGH SCHOOL GIRLS
SERIES**, Jessie Flower, ca. 1915, Altemus, cloth
cover, illustrated. $15.00
Grace Harlowe's Plebe Year at High School
Grace Harlowe's Sophomore Year at High School
Grace Harlowe's Junior Year at High School
Grace Harlowe's Senior Year at High School

GRACE HARLOWE OVERLAND RIDERS SERIES,
Jessie Flower, ca.1920, Altemus, 10 books.
$15.00
On the Old Apache Trail

On the Great American Desert
Among the Kentucky Mountaineers
In the Great North Woods
In the High Sierras
In the Yellowstone National Park
In the Black Hills
At Circle O Ranch
Among the Border Guerrillas
On the Lost River Trail

GRACE HARLOWE OVERSEAS SERIES, Jessie
Flower, ca. 1920s, Altemus, 6 books. $10.00
Grace Harlowe Overseas
Grace Harlowe with the Red Cross in France
Grace Harlowe with the Marines at Chateau Thierry
*Grace Harlowe with the U. S.
Troops in the Argonne*
*Grace Harlowe with the Yankee Shock Boys
at St. Quentin*
Grace Harlowe with the American Army on the Rhine

GRANDPA'S LITTLE GIRL SERIES, Alice Curtis,
1907 – 10, 4 books. $20.00

GREAT ACE SERIES, by Noel Sainsbury, 7 books. $10.00

GREAT MARVEL SERIES, Roy Rockwood, ca.
1925, Cupples & Leon. $15.00
Through the Air to the North Pole
Under the Ocean to the South Pole
Five Thousand Miles Underground
Through Space to Mars
Lost on the Moon
On a Torn-Away World
City Beyond the Clouds

GREEN FOREST SERIES, Thornton Burgess, ca. 1915, Little Brown, color paste-on pictorial covers, 8 color plates by Harrison Cady. $40.00
Lightfoot the Deer
Blacky the Crow
Whitefoot the Mouse

GREEN MEADOW SERIES, Thornton Burgess, ca. 1915, Little Brown. $40.00
Happy Jack
Mrs. Peter Rabbit
Bowser the Hound
Old Granny Fox

GREYCLIFF GIRLS SERIES, Harriet Grove, 1923 – 25 Burt, 8 books. $10.00

GUNBOAT SERIES, Harry Castlemon. 1864 – 68. $25.00

───── ⊷⇒ **H** ⇐⊶ ─────

HAPPY HOME SERIES, Howard Garis, 1926, Grosset, 6 books. $25.00

HARDY BOYS SERIES, F. W. Dixon, ca. 1920s, Grosset & Dunlap. $15.00
Tower Treasure
House on the Cliff
Secret of the Old Mill
Missing Chums
Hunting for Hidden Gold
Shore Road Mystery
Secret of the Caves
Mystery of Cabin Island
Great Airport Mystery
What Happened at Midnight
While the Clock Ticked
Footprints Under the Window
Mark on the Door
Hidden Harbor Mystery
Sinister Sign Post
A Figure in Hiding
Secret Warning
Twisted Claw
Disappearing Floor
Mystery of the Flying Express
Clue of the Broken Blade
Flickering Torch Mystery
Melted Coins
Short-Wave Mystery

HEADLINE BOOKS FOR GIRLS, ca. 1930s Grosset
Divine Corners Stories, Faith Baldwin $15.00
Babs

Judy
Myra
Mary Lou
Mystery Books, $10.00
Blue Junk, Priscilla Holton
At Midnight, Louise Platt Hauck
Nobody's Joan, Helen Berger
Stolen Blueprints, Ruth Grosby
Historical Books, Lucy Foster Madison $10.00
Maid of Salem Towne
Daughter of the Union
Career Books, Helen Diehl Olds $10.00
Barbara Benton, Editor
Joan of the Journal
Western Books, Ann Spence Warner $10.00
Sidesaddle Ranch
Gold is Where You Find It
Days of Gold
Western Book, Marie de Nervaud $10.00
Scarum

HELEN GRANT SERIES, Amanda Douglas, 1903 – 11, Lothrop, 9 books. $10.00

HILDA OF GREYCOT SERIES, Mrs. Pemberton Ginther, 1922 – 25, 4 books. $15.00

HILLTOP SERIES for Boys, ca. 1915, Goldsmith. $10.00
Hill Top Boys
In Camp
Lost Island
On the River

HISTORICAL SERIES, James Johonnot, 1887, Appleton, small size, black print illustration on brown board cover, b/w illustrations. $15.00
Grandfather Stories
Stories of Heroic Deeds
Stories of Our Country
Stories of Other Lands
Stories of Olden Times
Ten Great Events in History
How Nations Grow and Decay

HOME STORIES SERIES, August Larned, 1873, 6 books. $40.00

HONEY BUNCH SERIES, Helen Louise Thorndyke, ca. 1920-on Grosset Dunlap, 30+ books, illustrations by Walter S. Rogers, advertised as "pleasing series of stories for little girls from four to eight years old." $20.00
Honey Bunch: Just a Little Girl
Honey Bunch: Her First Big Adventure
Honey Bunch: Her First Visit to the City

Honey Bunch: Her First Days on the Farm
Honey Bunch: Her First Visit to the Seashore
Honey Bunch: Her First Little Garden
Honey Bunch: Her First Days in Camp

HORATIO ALGER'S SERIES, Horatio Alger Jr., late 1800s, uplifting tales for boys, printed as individual titles and collected and reprinted as series, usually had b/w illustrations and now sell for value of their ornately impressed or illustrated covers. A cover in excellent condition will increase the price. The 1896 advertisement for the Winston series quoted Alger, saying, "A writer for boys should have an abundant sympathy with them. He should be able to enter into their plans, hopes and aspirations. Boys object to being written down to. A boy's heart opens to the man or writer who understands him."

Bound to Win Series, 1930s edition, Grosset, illustrated by Ernest Townsend. $10.00
Phil Hardy's Struggle
Phil Hardy's Triumph

Brave and Bold Series, 1890s, Winston, small size, illustrated. $15.00
Brave and Bold
Jack's Ward
Shifting for Himself
Wait and Hope

Campaign Series, 1890s, Winston, small size, illustrated. $15.00
Frank's Campaign
Charlie Codman's Cruise
Paul Prescott's Charge

Frank and Fearless Series, 1890s, Winston, small size, illustrated. $15.00
Frank Hunter's Peril
Frank and Fearless
Young Salesman

Good Fortune Library Series, 1890s, Winston, small size, illustrated. $15.00
Walter Sherwood's Probation
Boy's Fortune
Young Bank Messenger

Luck and Pluck Series, 1890s, Winston, small size, illustrated. $15.00
Luck and Pluck
Sink or Swim
Strong and Steady
Strive and Succeed
Try and Trust
Bound to Rise
Risen from the Ranks
Herbert Carter's Legacy

New World Series, 1890s, Winston, small size, illustrated. $15.00
Digging Gold
Facing the World

In a New World

Ragged Dick Series, 1890s, Winston, small size, illustrated. $10.00
Ragged Dick
Fame and Fortune
Mark the Match Boy
Rough and Ready
Ben the Luggage Boy
Rufus and Rose

Tattered Tom Series, 1890s, Winston, small size, illustrated. $10.00
Tattered Tom
Paul the Peddler
Phil the Fiddler
Slow and Sure
Julius
Young Outlaw
Sam's Chance
Telegraph Boy

Victory Series, 1890s, Winston, small size, illustrated. $15.00
Only an Irish Boy
Adrift in the City
Victor Vane, or the Young Secretary

"HOW-TO-DO-IT" BOOKS SERIES, ca. 1920s edition, Donahue, advertised as "printed from new plates and bound in cloth, profusely illustrated." $15.00
Carpentry for Boys
Electricity for Boys
Practical Mechanics for Boys

HUNNIWELL BOYS SERIES, Levi Wyman, ca. 1929, 7 books. $10.00

ISLAND STALLION SERIES, Walter Farley, ca. 1940s, Random House. $20.00
Island Stallion, 1948, Random House, b/w illustrations by Keith Ward
Island Stallion's Fury

❧ **J** ❧

JACK HARKAWAY SERIES, Bracebridge Hemyng, undated, ca. 1910, Federal, paste-on pictorial cover with impressed color decorations. $15.00

JACK HAZARD SERIES, J. T. Trowbridge, ca. 1890s, Winston. $15.00
Jack Hazard and His Fortunes
The Young Surveyor
Fast Friends

Doing His Best
A Chance for Himself
Lawrence's Adventures

JACK RANGER SERIES, Clarence Young, ca. 1920s, Cupple & Leon. $15.00
Jack Ranger's School Days
Jack Ranger's Western Trip
Jack Ranger's School Victories
Jack Ranger's Ocean Cruise
Jack Ranger's Gun Club
Jack Ranger's Treasure Box

JANE ALLEN COLLEGE SERIES, Edith Bancroft, ca. 1920, Cupples & Leon, advertised as "a series recognized as an authoritative account of the life of a college girl." $10.00
Jane Allen of the Sub Team
Jane Allen: Right Guard
Jane Allen: Center
Jane Allen: Junior

JANE STUART SERIES, Grace Remick, ca. 1913, 4 books. $10.00

JANET HARDY SERIES, by Ruth Wheeler, ca. 1930s, Goldsmith, Goldsmith advertised its girls and boys books as "modern as radar." $10.00
Janet Hardy in Hollywood
Janet Hardy in Radio City

JERRY FORD WONDER STORIES SERIES, Fenworth Moore, ca. 1920s, Cupples Leon. $10.00
Wrecked on Cannibal Island
Lost in the Caves of Gold
Castaway in the Land of Snow
Prisoners on the Pirate Ship

JERRY TODD SERIES, Leo Edwards, ca. 1910 Grosset, advertised as "Detective stories for boys! Jerry Todd and his trusty pals solve many a baffling mystery in their home town." $15.00
Jerry Todd and the Whispering Mummy
Jerry Todd and the Rose-Colored Cat
Jerry Todd and the Oak Island Treasure
Jerry Todd and the Waltzing Hen
Jerry Todd and the Talking Frog
Jerry Todd and the Purring Egg
Jerry Todd in the Whispering Cave

JOAN SERIES, Lilian Garis, ca. 1930, Grosset Dunlap. $15.00

Joan: Just Girl
Joan's Garden of Adventure

JOE STRONG SERIES, Vance Barnum, 1917 Sully, 7 books. $35.00, 1940s edition Whitman. $10.00
Boy Wizard
On Trapeze
Boy Fish
On the High Wire
Wings of Steel

JOLLY GOOD SERIES, Mary Smith, ca. 1870s – 90s, 8 books. $25.00

JOLLY JUMP-UPS SERIES, McLoughlin, pop-up books with color illustrations by Geraldine Clyne.
Jolly Jump-Ups and Their New House, 1939. $55.00
Jolly Jump-Ups on Vacation, 1942. $60.00
Jolly Jump-Ups Child's Garden of Verse, 1946. $60.00
Jolly Jump-Ups Number Book, 1950. $45.00

JOURNEYS THROUGH BOOKLAND SERIES, Charles Sylvester, ca. 1910 Bellows-Reeve, b/w illustrations, 10 books, each book. $15.00

JUDY BOLTON MYSTERIES SERIES, Margaret Sutton, ca. 1930s, Grosset Dunlap, cover and endpaper illustrations by Pelagie Doane. $10.00
Vanishing Shadow
Haunted Attic
Invisible Chimes
Seven Strange Clues
Ghost Parade
Yellow Phantom
Mystic Ball
Voice in the Suitcase
Mysterious Half Cat
Riddle of the Double Ring
Unfinished House
Midnight Visitor
Name on the Bracelet
Clue in the Patchwork Quilt
Mark on the Mirror

JUST SO STORIES SERIES, stories by Rudyard Kipling, reissued in book form, 1940s, Garden City, color illustrated paper-covered boards, about 28 pages, b/w and color illustrations. $15.00
How the Camel Got His Hump
How the Rhinoceros Got His Skin

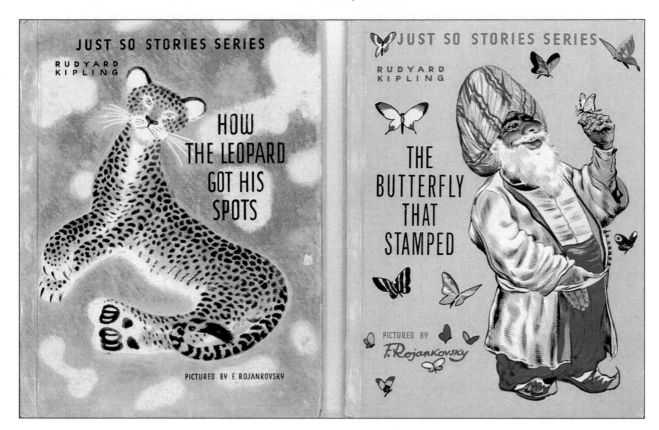

How the Leopard Got His Spots
Cat That Walked by Himself
Elephant's Child
Butterfly That Stamped

K

KATRINKA SERIES, Helen Haskell, 1915 – 39, Dutton, 5 books. $10.00

KATY DID SERIES, Susan Coolidge (Sarah Woolsey), ca. 1860s, 5 books, 1sts, Rare. Later editions. $15.00
 What Katy Did, 1872, Boston
 What Katy Did at School, 1873,
What Katy Did Next, 1886

KAY TRACEY MYSTERY SERIES, Frances Judd, 1934 – 42, Cupples, 18 books. $10.00

KHAKI BOYS SERIES, Capt. Gordon Bates, ca. 1920, Cupples & Leon, small size, cloth cover, illustrations. $10.00
Khaki Boys at Camp Sterling
Khaki Boys on the Way
Khaki Boys at the Front
Khaki Boys Over the Top
Khaki Boys Fighting to Win
Khaki Boys Along the Rhine

KHAKI GIRLS SERIES, Edna Brooks, Cupples & Leon, small size, cloth cover, illustrations $15.00
Khaki Girls Behind the Lines, 1918
Khaki Girls of the Motor Corps, 1918
Khaki Girls at Windsor Barracks, 1919
Khaki Girls in Victory, 1920

KNEETIME ANIMAL STORIES, Richard Barnum, ca. 1916, Barse, small size, print illustrated cloth cover, b/w illustrations by Walter Rogers. $10.00
Squinty, the Comical Pig
Slicko, the Jumping Squirrel
Mappo, the Merry Monkey
Tum Tum, the Jolly Elephant
Don, the Runaway Dog
Dido, the Danger Bear
Blackie, the Lost Cat
Flop Ear, the Funny Rabbit
Tinkle, the Trick Pony
Lightfoot, the Leaping Goat

L

LAKEWOOD BOYS SERIES, Levi Wyman, ca. 1924, 5 books. $10.00

LANG FAIRY BOOKS, 12 in series, Andrew Lang, ca. 1890s editions, gilt design on cloth-covered boards in color corresponding to title, b/w illustrations by H. J. Ford. $150.00;

ca. 1929 Longmans, Green Crown Edition, gilt lettering and design on cloth cover, 4 to 8 color plate illustrations plus b/w illustrations by H. J Ford and Lancelot Speed. $45.00;

ca. 1930s editions, McKay, color paste-on pictorial on cloth cover, 4 color plate illustrations by Jennie Harbor. $35.00.

Blue Fairy Book, 1889
Red Fairy Book, 1890
Green Fairy Book, 1892
Yellow Fairy Book, 1894
Pink Fairy Book, 1897
Grey Fairy Book, 1900
Violet Fairy Book, 1901
Crimson Fairy Book, 1903
Brown Fairy Book, 1904
Orange Fairy Book, 1906
Olive Fairy Book, 1907
Lilac Fairy Book, 1910

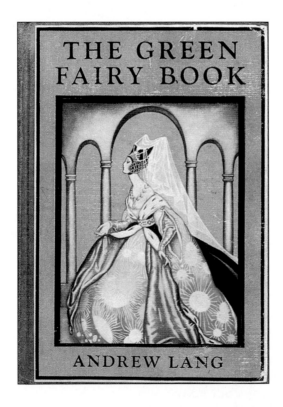

LAVELL SERIES, ca. 1920s, Saalfield. $10.00
Mystery of the Secret Band
Mystery of the Fires
Mystery at Dark Cedar

LET'S MAKE BELIEVE STORIES SERIES, Lilian Garis, ca. 1920s, Donohue, advertised as "large clear type on superior quality paper, fron-

tispiece and jacket printed in full colors." $20.00
Let's Make Believe We're Keeping House
Let's Play Circus
Let's Make Believe We're Soldiers

LETTY SERIES, Helen Griffith, 1910 – 18, Penn, 7 books. $10.00

LIMITED EDITION CLUB SERIES, NY
Alice's Adventures in Wonderland, 1932, limited edition of 500 signed by Alice Hargreaves. $700.00
Complete Anderson, 1949, 6 volume set, illustrated.   Set $130.00
Wind in the Willows, 1940, limited edition of 2020, illustrated by Arthur Rackham, signed by Kenneth Grahame. $550.00

LINDA CARLTON SERIES, Edith Lavell, ca. 1930s, Saalfield. $10.00
Linda Carlton, Air Pilot
Linda Carlton's Ocean Flight
Linda Carlton's Island Adventure

LINDENDALE SERIES, Daniel Wise, ca. late 1800s. $15.00

LINGER-NOTS SERIES, Agnes Miller, Cupples & Leon, small size, impressed cover illustration, b/w frontispiece. $15.00
Linger-Nots and the Mystery House, 1923
Linger-Nots and the Valley Feud
Linger Nots and Their Golden Quest
Linger-Nots and the Whispering Charm, 1925

LITTLE BEAR, see **SERIES**, "Rupert Little Bear."

LITTLE COLONEL, Annie Fellow Johnston, 1894 – 1914, Page, (first editions in excellent condition have higher collector value, generally in the $50.00 range), illustrated cloth covers, 17 books. $25.00
Little Colonel, 1895 Boston
Little Colonel's House Party
Little Colonel's Holidays
Little Colonel's Hero
Little Colonel at Boarding School
Little Colonel in Arizona
Little Colonel's Christmas Vacation, 1905
Little Colonel: Maid of Honor
Little Colonel's Knight Comes Riding, 1907
Little Colonel Good Time Book

LITTLE GIRL SERIES, Amanda Douglas, 1896 –

1909, Dodd, 14 books. $15.00

LITTLE GOLDEN BOOKS, Whitman Publishing, began series in 1942, small size books, with color illustrated paper boards, 42 pages, color illustrations throughout, each book is numbered. The following are the first twelve and were printed in 1942. *Three Little Kittens* and *Poky Little Puppy*, in excellent condition, sell at double the price. The rest of the 1942 books are usually priced at about $20.00.

Three Little Kittens
Bedtime Stories
Alphabet A-Z
Mother Goose
Prayers for Children
Little Red Hen
Nursery Song
Poky Little Puppy
Golden Book of Fairy Tales
Baby's Book
Animals of Farmer Jones
Little Piggy Counting Rhymes

LITTLE HOUSE, Laura Ingalls Wilder, Harper Bros., color frontispiece and b/w illustrations by Helen Sewell. $65.00
Little House in the Big Woods, 1932
Farmer Boy, 1933

Little House on the Prairie, 1935
On the Banks of Plum Creek, 1937
On the Shores of Silver Lake, 1939
Long Winter, 1940
Little Town on the Prairie, 1941
These Happy Golden Years, 1943

LITTLE JOURNEYS TO HAPPYLAND SERIES, David Cory, 1922 – 27, Grosset, small size, color paste-on pictorial covers, color endpapers, b/w illustrations by H. Barbour. $20.00
Cruise of Noah's Ark
Magic Soap Bubble
Iceberg Express
Wind Wagon
Magic Umbrella

LITTLE LUCIA SERIES, Mabel Robinson, ca. 1922, 4 books. $20.00

LITTLE MAID SERIES, Alice Curtis, 1913 – 37, Penn, 24 books. $10.00

LITTLE MISS WEEZY SERIES, Sarah Clarke, 1886 – 89, 3 books. $35.00

LITTLE ORPHAN ANNIE Cartoon Book Series, Harold Gray, ca. 1930s, Cupples & Leon, hardback numbered volumes, about 84 pages of Chicago Tribune comics. $35.00

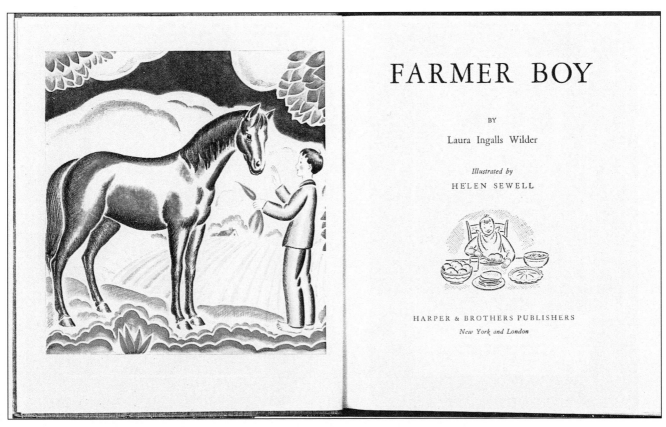

Book 9 *Little Orphan Annie and Uncle Dan*, 1933

LITTLE PEOPLE EVERYWHERE SERIES, McDonald and Dalrymple, 1909 – 16, Little Brown, 14 books. $15.00

LITTLE PILGRIM SERIES, Sophie Titterington, ca. 1897. $15.00

LITTLE PRINCESS SERIES, Aileen Higgins, 1909, Penn Pub., 5 books. $15.00

LITTLE PRUDY SERIES, Sophie May, 1863 – 65, Lee & Shepard. $25.00
Later edition ca. 1920s, Cupples & Leon, small size, illustrations. $15.00
Little Prudy
Little Prudy's Sister Susy
Little Prudy's Captain Horace
Little Prudy's Cousin Grace
Little Prudy's Story Book
Little Prudy's Dotty Dimple

LITTLE PRUDY'S FLYAWAY SERIES, Sophie May, 1870 – 73, Lee & Shepard, 6 books. $25.00

LITTLE RED HOUSE SERIES, Amanda Douglas, 1912 – 16, Lothrop, 5 books. $20.00

LITTLE RUNAWAYS SERIES, Alice Curtis, 1906 – 14, Penn Pub., 4 books. $15.00

LITTLE WOMEN SERIES, Orchard House Edition, Little Brown, Louisa May Alcott, advertised as "The complete story of the Little Women is told in *Little Women, Little Men,* and *Jo's Boys....*The Orchard House edition has been published to answer the need for an attractive, popular-priced, uniform edition of all three books." Endpapers are a two-page spread photograph in sepia tones of the Alcott home, Orchard House, at Concord, Massachusetts. (Later, most of Alcott's books were offered in the Orchard House Edition format.)
Little Women, 1936, 3 illustrations by Jessie Willcox Smith from the 1925 edition. $25.00
Little Men, 1937, 8 color plate illustrations by Reginald Birch. $25.00

LIVE DOLLS SERIES, Josephine Scribner Gates, 1901 – 1912, Bobbs-Merrill, 11 books
Live Dolls, 1901, Bobbs-Merrill $75.00
Live Dolls House Party, 1906, illustrations by Virginia Keeping. $45.00, later editions $20.00
More About Live Dolls, 1903, illustrations by Virginia Keeping. $50.00
Secret of Live Dolls, 1924 edition, Bobbs-Merrill, illustrations by A. L. Archibald. $30.00

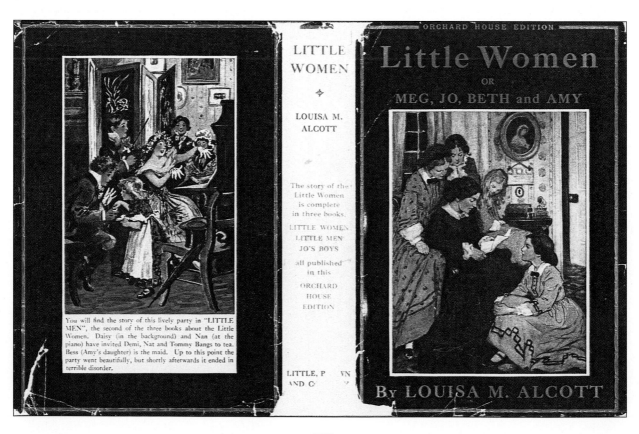

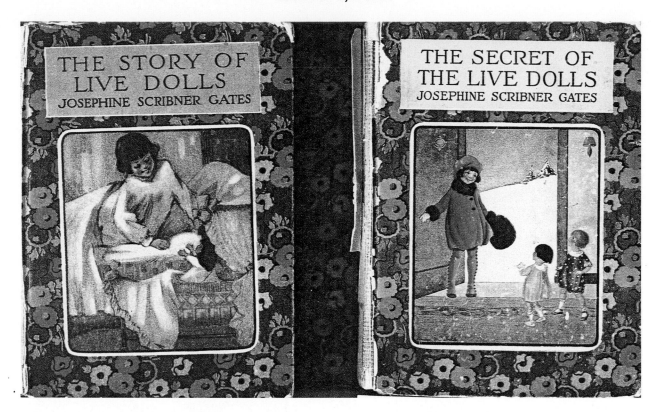

Story of Live Dolls, 1901, Bobbs-Merrill, illustrations by Mabel Rogers. $55.00

Story of Live Dolls, 1920 edition, Bobbs-Merrill, standard size, illustrations by Mabel Rogers. $25.00

LOG CABIN SERIES, Edward Ellis, ca. 1890s, Winston. $15.00
Lost Trail
Footprints in the Forest
Camp-Fire and Wigwam

LOUIE MAUDE SERIES, Helen Griffith, 1924, Penn, 4 books. $10.00

LUCY GORDON SERIES, Aline Havard, Penn. $15.00
Captain Lucy and Lieutenant Bob, 1918
Captain Lucy in France, 1919
Captain Lucy's Flying Ace, 1920
Captain Lucy in the Home Sector,   1921

————— ✎ **M** ✎ —————

MADGE MORTON SERIES, ca. 1930s, Altemus. $10.00
Madge Morton – Captain of the Merry Maid
Madge Morton's Secret
Madge Morton's Trust
Madge Morton's Victory

MAIDA SERIES, Inez Irwin, 1909 – 49, Grosset, 10

books. $10.00

MAKE BELIEVE STORIES SERIES, Laura Lee Hope, 1920 – 23, Grosset, small size, printed illustration on cover, color illustrations by Harry L. Smith, advertised as "In this fascinating line of books Miss Hope has the various toys come to life when nobody is looking." $20.00
Story of a Sawdust Doll
Story of a White Rocking Horse
Story of a Lamb on Wheels
Story of a Bold Tin Soldier
Story of a Candy Rabbit
Story of a Monkey on a Stick
Story of a Calico Clown
Story of a Nodding Donkey
Story of a China Cat
Story of a Plush Bear

MALAY JUNGLE SERIES, Harvey Richards (Noel Sainsbury). $10.00

MARGARET SERIES, Laura Richards, 1897 – 1901, Estes, 5 books. $20.00

MARJORIE SERIES, Alice Curtis, 1905 – 1913, Penn. $15.00

MARJORIE SERIES, Carolyn Wells, 1905 – 12, Grosset, 6 books, advertised as "happiest books that have ever been written especially for

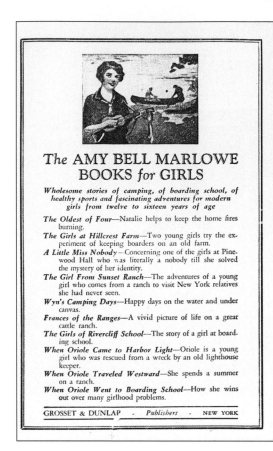

her majesty, the American girl." $20.00
Marjorie's Vacation
Marjorie's Busy Days
Marjorie's New Friend
Marjorie in Command
Marjorie 's MayTime
Marjorie at Seacote

MARJORIE SERIES, Mrs. George Paull, 1900 – 04, Jacobs, 3 books. $15.00

MARLOWE BOOKS FOR GIRLS, Amy Bell Marlowe, ca. 1914, Grosset, advertised as "thoroughly up-to-date and wholly American in scene and action." $15.00
Oldest of Four
Girls at Hillcrest Farm
Little Miss Nobody
Girl from Sunset Ranch
Wyn's Camping Days, 1914, illustrated by W. Rogers
Frances of the Ranges
Girls of Rivercliff School
When Oriole Came to Harbor Light
When Oriole Traveled Westward
When Oriole Went to Boarding School

MARY AND JERRY MYSTERY SERIES, Francis

Hunt, 1935, Grosset, 5 books. $10.00

MARY JANE SERIES, Clara Judson, 1918 – 39, Barse, 19 books. $10.00

MARY LOUISE SERIES, Edith Van Dyne (Baum), 1916 – 22, Reilly, 8 books. $25.00
Mary Louise
Mary Louise and the Liberty Girls
Mary Louise Stands the Test
Mary Louise at Dorfield
Mary Louise Adopts a Soldier
Mary Louise in the Country
Mary Louise Solves a Mystery

MARY ROSE SERIES, Mary Mabel Wirries, 7 books, ca. 1920s. $15.00

MAXIE SERIES, Elsie Gardner, 1932 – 39, Cupples, 7 books. $10.00

MAYFLOWER SERIES FOR GIRLS, ca. 1900, Lee & Shepard, 25 books, illustrations. $35.00
Action Speaks Louder Than Words
Angel Children
Birds of a Feather

MC LOUGHLIN PICTURE BOOKS, oversize,

papercovers, color illustrations
Circus and Menagerie ABC, 1897. $50.00
Three Bears, 1888, illustrated by R. Andre. $50.00

MC LOUGHLIN SUN BEAM SERIES, hard cardboard covers with color illustration, b/w illustration on newsprint quality paper inside. $15.00
To Pass Time, 1908

MC LOUGHLIN WONDER STORY SERIES, standard size, paper covers, color illustrations
Rip Van Winkle, 1889. $50.00

MEADOWBROOK GIRLS SERIES, Janet
Aldridge, 1913, Altemus, 6 books. $10.00
Meadowbrook Girls Under Canvas
Meadowbrook Girls Across Country
Meadowbrook Girls Afloat
Meadowbrook Girls in the Hills
Meadowbrook Girls by the Sea
Meadowbrook Girls on the Tennis Courts

MELODY LANE MYSTERY SERIES, Lilian Garis,
ca. 1930s, Grosset Dunlap. $15.00
Ghost of Melody Lane
Forbidden Trail
Tower Secret
Wild Warning
Terror at Moaning Cliff
Dragon of the Hills

Mystery of Stingyman's Alley
Secret of the Kashmir Shawl

MERRIWEATHER GIRLS SERIES, Lizette Edholm,
1932, Goldsmith, 4 books. $10.00

MERRY MAID SERIES, ca. 1915, Rand McNal-
ly, small size, color illustrated covers, nurs-
ery rhymes in large print, b/w/color
illustrations by Marguerite and Willard
Wheeler. $25.00
Death and Burial of Poor Cock Robin
House That Jack Built
Mother Cary, Mary Hulett Lamont
Frog He Would A-Wooing Go

MERRYVALE GIRLS SERIES, Alice Burnett, 1916,
NY Books, 6 books. $10.00

MILDRED SERIES, Martha Finley, ca. 1870 – 90, 7
books. $15.00

MISS MINERVA SERIES, Nell Speed, 1918 – 39,
Reilly, 11 books. $15.00

MISS PAT SERIES, P. Ginther, 1915 – 17, Winston,
11 books. $10.00

MOLLY BROWN SERIES, Nell Speed, 1912 – 21,
Hurst, 8 books. $10.00

MOTHER WEST WIND SERIES, Thornton Burgess, ca. 1910 – 20, Little Brown, color illustrations by Harrison Cady. $45.00
Old Mother West Wind
Mother West Wind's Children
Mother West Wind's Animal Friends
Mother West Wind's Neighbors
Mother West Wind "Why" Stories
Mother West Wind "How" Stories
Mother West Wind "When" Stories
Mother West Wind "Where" Stories

MOTION PICTURE CHUMS SERIES, Victor Appleton, 1913, Grosset, small size, illustrations. $15.00
First Adventure
Outdoor Exhibition
At Seaside Park

MOTOR BOYS SERIES, Clarence Young, ca. 1920s, Cupples & Leon, illustrations. $15.00
Motor Boys
Motor Boys Overland
Motor Boys in Mexico
Motor Boys Across the Plains
Motor Boys Afloat
Motor Boys on the Atlantic
Motor Boys in Strange Waters
Motor Boys on the Pacific
Motor Boys in the Clouds
Motor Boys Over the Rockies
Motor Boys Over the Ocean
Motor Boys on the Wing
Motor Boys After a Fortune
Motor Boys on the Border
Motor Boys Under the Sea
Motor Boys on Road and River
Motor Boys at Boxwood Hall
Motor Boys on a Ranch
Motor Boys in the Army
Motor Boys on the Firing Line
Motor Boys Bound for Home
Motor Boys on Thunder Mountain

MOTOR BOYS, Second Series, by Clarence Young, ca. 1920, Cupples & Leon. $10.00
Ned, Bob and Jerry at Boxwood Hall
Ned, Bob and Jerry on the Ranch
Ned, Bob and Jerry in the Army
Ned, Bob and Jerry on the Firing Line
Ned, Bob and Jerry Bound for Home

MOTOR GIRLS SERIES, Margaret Penrose, ca. 1920s, Cupples & Leon, small size, cloth covers, illustrations, advertised as "No one is better equipped to furnish these tales than Mrs. Penrose who, besides being an able writer, is an expert automobilist." $15.00
Motor Girls
Motor Girls on a Tour
Motor Girls at Lookout Reach
Motor Girls through New England
Motor Girls on Cedar Lake
Motor Girls on the Coast
Motor Girls on Crystal Bay
Motor Girls on Waters Blue
Motor Girls at Camp Surprise
Motor Girls in the Mountains

MOVING PICTURE BOYS SERIES, Victor Appleton, 1913, Grosset. $15.00
In the West
On the Coast
In the Jungle
In Earthquake Land

MOVING PICTURE GIRLS SERIES, Laura Lee Hope, 1914, Grosset, 7 books. $15.00
Girls at Sea
Girls Snowbound
Oak Farm
Under the Palms
In War Plays
Moving Picture Girls
Rocky Ranch

MRS. MEIGS SERIES, Elizabeth Corbett, 1931 – 43, Appleton, 5 books. $15.00

MUTT AND JEFF SERIES, cartoon books, Bud Fisher, ca. 1920s, Cupples & Leon, 10" x 10", three-color cardboard cover, b/w cartoon strip stories. $50.00

MY BOOK HOUSE SERIES, edited by Olive Beaupre Miller, ca. 1920, Book House for Children, Chicago, and reprinted periodically with color paste-on pictorials on covers, color illustrations throughout, numbered volumes, $25.00 ea., matched set of first six, $200.00; matched set of twelve volumes, $400.00. Later editions, $10.00 ea., set of six $75.00; set of 12, $195.00
Volume 1, In the Nursery
Volume 2, Up One Pair of Stairs
Volume 3, Through Fairy Halls
Volume 4, Treasure Chest
Volume 5, From the Tower Window
Volume 6, Latch Key
Volume 7, Magic Garden
Volume 8, Flying Sails
Volume 9, Treasure Chest

Volume 10, *From the Tower Window*
Volume 11, *Shining Armor*
Volume 12, *Hall of Fame*

——— ⇒ **N** ⇐ ———

NANCY AND NICK SERIES, Olive Barton, 1918, Doran, 6 books. $10.00

NANCY BRANDON SERIES, Lilian Garis, ca. 1930s Grosset. $15.00

NANCY DREW SERIES, Carolyn Keene, pseudonym, idea created by Edward Stratemeyer for his syndicated books, and after 1930, plot outlines were created by his daughter, Harriet S. Adams. *Nancy Drew Scrapbook*, by Karen Plunkett Powell, states that the first seven books, and several later books, were written by Mildred Wirt Benson, others were written by Walter Karig, Harriet Adams, Margaret Sherf Beebe, Iris Vinton, and possibly Lilian Garis, and other writers. 1930 – 1950 b/w illustrations and color dust jackets were drawn by Russell Tandy. Plain cloth covers with small silhouette illustration. First editions in excellent condition draw higher prices, and a good condition dust jacket can double the price. $20.00
Secret of the Old Clock, 1930
Hidden Staircase, 1930

Bungalow Mystery, 1930
Mystery of Lilac Inn, 1930
Secret of Shadow Ranch, 1931
Secret of Red Gate Farm, 1931
Clue in the Diary, 1932
Nancy's Mysterious Letter, 1932
Sign of the Twisted Candles, 1933
Password to Larkspur Lane, 1933
Clue of the Broken Locket, 1934
Message in the Hollow Oak, 1935
Mystery of the Ivory Charm, 1936
Whispering Statue, 1937
Haunted Bridge, 1937
Clue of the Tapping Heels, 1939
Mystery of the Brass Bound Trunk, 1940
Mystery at the Moss Covered Mansion, 1941
Quest of the Missing Map, 1942
Clue in the Jewel Box, 1943
Secret in the Old Attic, 1944
Clue in the Crumbling Wall, 1945
Mystery of the Tolling Bell, 1946
Clue in the Old Album, 1947
Ghost of Blackwood Hall, 1948
Clue of the Leaning Chimney, 1949

NANCY PEMBROKE SERIES, Margaret Van Epps, 1930, Burt, 7 books. $10.00

NEW DEERFOOT SERIES, Edward Ellis, ca. 1890s, Winston. $15.00

Deerfoot in the Forest
Deerfoot on the Prairie
Deerfoot in the Mountains

NIXIE BUNNY SERIES, Joseph Sindelair, ca. 1915, Beckley-Cardy, b/w/green or red three-color illustrations throughout by Helen Geraldine Hodge. $20.00
Nixie Bunny in Manners-Land
Nixie Bunny in Workaday-Land
Nixie Bunny in Holiday-Land
Nixie Bunny in Faraway-Lands

NORTHWEST SERIES, Edward Ellis, ca. 1890s, Winston. $15.00
Two Boys in Wyoming
Cowmen and Rustlers
Strange Craft and its Wonderful Voyage

——— ·⇒ O ⇐· ———

OUR LITTLE COUSIN SERIES, Clara Winlow, 1911 – 25. $15.00

OUR LITTLE FRIENDS SERIES, Frances Carpenter, 1931 – 37, 5 books. $15.00

OUTDOOR GIRLS SERIES, Laura Lee Hope, 1913 – 33, Whitman, 23 books. $10.00
Outdoor Girls at Deepdale
Outdoor Girls at Rainbow Lake
Outdoor Girls in a Motor Car
Outdoor Girls in a Winter Camp

Outdoor Girls in Florida
Outdoor Girls at Ocean View
Outdoor Girls on Pine Island
Outdoor Girls in Army Service
Outdoor Girls at Hostess House
Outdoor Girls at Bluff Point
Outdoor Girls at Wild Rose Lodge
Outdoor Girls in the Saddle
Outdoor Girls Around the Campfire
Outdoor Girls on Cape Cod
Outdoor Girls at Foaming Falls
Outdoor Girls Along the Coast
Outdoor Girls at Spring Hill Farm
Outdoor Girls on a Hike
Outdoor Girls on a Canoe Trip
Outdoor Girls at Cedar Ridge
Outdoor Girls in the Air

OZ BOOKS SERIES, L. Frank Baum
(This extremely popular series was extended to include other authors and illustrators and reprinted numerous times. The following information has been put under sub-headings to try to simplify it.)
A **first edition** Baum book in the original series is slightly larger than standard size, and will have a cloth cover with a printed illustration or a color paste-on pictorial, and tipped-in full-page color illustrations facing text (except in *Ozma, Road to Oz, Patchwork Girl),* plus illustrated endpapers.
Wonderful Wizard, the first Oz book, was illustrated by W. W. Denslow, who also illustrated

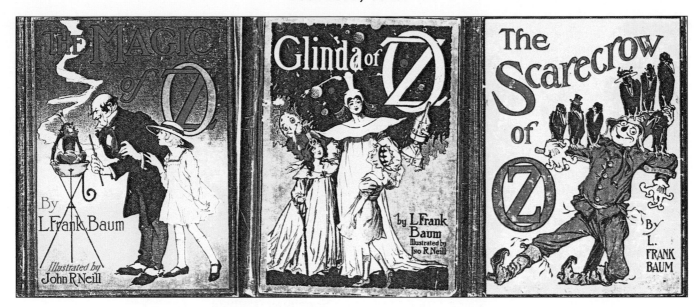

some of L. Frank Baum's non-Oz books. *Marvelous Land of Oz* and all remaining Baum Oz books through *Glinda Of Oz* were illustrated by John R. Neill.

The **first publisher** was Hill; the second book and following books were published by Reilly & Britton and in 1919, the publisher's name changed to Reilly & Lee.

Wonderful Wizard of Oz, 1900, Hill; 24 color plate illustrations by Denslow. Rare

New Wizard of Oz, 1903 edition, (same book, new title), Bobbs-Merrill, used Hill plates except new title and cover, 16 color plate illustrations by Denslow. $150.00

New Wizard of Oz, 1913 edition, Donohue, same plates as Bobbs-Merrill 2nd edition. $100.00

Wizard of Oz, 1944 edition, Bobbs Merrill, color illustrations by E. Copeland. $25.00

Marvelous Land of Oz, 1904, Reilly & Britton, 16 color plate illustrations by John R. Neill. $200.00

Land of Oz, (same book, shortened title) 1904, Reilly & Britton. $200.00

Land of Oz, 1917 variant reduced to 12 color plate illustrations. $100.00

Ozma of Oz, 1907, Reilly & Britton, color throughout text, illustrations including full-page color illustrations but no inserted color plates, illustrations by Neill. $200.00

Dorothy and the Wizard in Oz, 1908, Reilly & Britton, 16 color plate illustrations by Neill. $150.00

Road to Oz, text printed on tinted stock in solid colors (easily faded), line drawings throughout but no color plates, illustrations by Neill. $100.00

Emerald City of Oz, 1910, Reilly & Britton, 16 color plate Neill illustrations embellished with metallic green ink. $300.00

Emerald City of Oz, later printings omitting metallic ink. $100.00

Patchwork Girl of Oz, 1913, Reilly & Britton, colored text illustrations throughout book by Neill, no color plate inserts. $200.00

Tik-Tok of Oz, 1914, Reilly & Britton, colored endpapers are maps of Oz, 12 color plates illustrations by Neill. $150.00

Tik-Tok of Oz, 1920 edition, maps omitted. $60.00

Scarecrow of Oz, 1915, Reilly & Britton, 12 color plate illustrations by Neill. $150.00

Rinkitink in Oz, 1916, Reilly & Britton, 12 color plate illustrations by Neill. $150.00

Lost Princess of Oz, 1917, Reilly & Britton, 12 color plate illustrations by Neill. $150.00

Tin Woodman of Oz, 1918, Reilly & Britton, 12 color plates by Neill. $100.00

Magic of Oz, 1919, Reilly & Lee, 12 color plates by Neill. $100.00

Glinda of Oz, 1920, Reilly & Lee, 12 color plates by Neill. $100.00

Oz Books Series, **Related Stories**, L. Frank Baum. These books came out in different format but with characters that appear in the Oz series.

Woggle-Bug Book, 1905, Reilly Britton, 15" x 11+", 48 pages, board cover, illustrated by Ike Morgan and produced to coincide with the opening in Chicago of Baum's play "The Woggle-Bug," described as a musical extravaganza, stapled gatherings, full-color illustrations, text printed in dark blue. Rare

Little Wizard Series, L. Frank Baum, 1913, Reilly, 6 volumes, small size, 29 pages, full-color illustrations by Neill. $45.00

Cowardly Lion and the Hungry Tiger

Little Dorothy and Toto

Tiktok and the Nome King

Ozma and the Little Wizard
Jack Pumpkinhead and the Sawhorse
Scarecrow and the Tin Woodman
Compiled Little Wizard Series
Little Wizard Stories of Oz, 1914, Reilly, 196 pages, contains all six stories in the series, color illustrations from the series. $150.00
Little Wizard Series, L. Frank Baum, 1939 edition, Rand McNally, 3 volumes, each containing two of the original Little Wizard Stories in abridged form, small size, about 62 pages. $25.00
Little Wizard Jell-O Series, 1932, Reilly, 4 volumes, small size, 29 pages, revised editions of original series with Jell-O advertisments and recipes added. $50.00
Tiktok and the Nome King
Ozma and the Little Wizard
Jack Pumpkinhead and the Sawhorse
Scarecrow and the Tin Woodman

OZ BOOKS SERIES, Ruth Plumly Thompson. After Baum's death, Thompson was hired to continue the series. For sales purposes, Baum's name alone was used on the cover of the first Thompson book, *Royal Book of Oz*. Thereafter, Thompson is credited. Size and format of the original Oz series continued through *Wishing Horse of Oz*, 1935.
For the following books, 1st edition publisher was Reilly & Lee, illustrator was John R. Neill. Cloth covers with color paste-on pictorial, 12 full- color tipped-in illustrations, b/w pictorial endpapers, except *Wishing Horse*. Reminder: prices in this list are for good condition first editions without dust jackets. Prices are sometimes higher than for some of the earlier Baum books. Reason: Baum books went through sev-

eral editions and printings. Many of the post-Baum books were not re-issued in their original format and are therefore harder to find. Generally in good condition they are priced around $125.00. Reprints, 1935 through 1950s, b/w illustrations only $50.00
Royal Book of Oz, 1921
Kabumpo in Oz, 1922
Cowardly Lion of Oz, 1923
Grampa in Oz, 1924
Lost King of Oz, 1925
Hungry Tiger of Oz, 1926
Gnome King of Oz, 1927
Giant Horse of Oz, 1928
Jack Pumpkinhead of Oz, 1929
Yellow Knight of Oz, 1930
Pirates in Oz, 1931
Purple Prince of Oz, 1932
Ojo in Oz, 1933
Speedy in Oz, 1934
Wishing Horse of Oz, 1935, blank endpapers
    The following Thompson books, 1st editions, Reilly & Lee, illustrator Neill, cloth covers with color paste-on pictorial, were issued with b/w illustrations only, b/w pictorial endpapers. $100.00
Captain Salt in Oz, 1936
Handy Mandy in Oz, 1937
Silver Princess in Oz, 1938
Ozoplaning with the Wizard of Oz, 1939

OZ BOOKS, John R. Neill, illustrator, authored and illustrated three books. Same size and format, cloth covers with color paste-on pictorial, b/w illustrations, pictorial b/w endpapers. $55.00
Wonder City of Oz, 1940
Scalawagons of Oz, 1941
Lucky Bucky in Oz, 1942

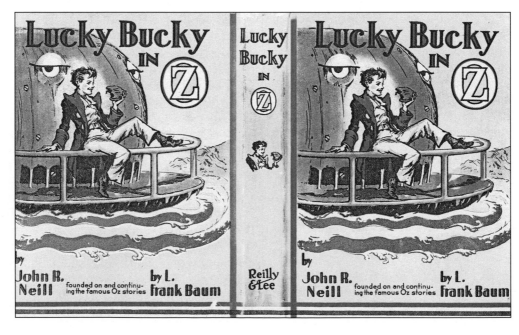

OZ BOOKS, Jack Snow. Same size and format, cloth covers with color paste-on pictorial, b/w illustrations by Frank Kramer. $65.00

Magical Mimics in Oz, 1946, pictorial green print on yellow endpapers.

Shaggy Man of Oz, 1949, b/w endpapers

OZ BOOKS, Frank Joslyn Baum (L. Frank Baum's son)

Laughing Dragon of Oz, 1935, Whitman Big Little Book, illustrations by Milt Youngren, hard-to-find. $200.00

OZ BOOKS, JUNIOR EDITIONS, 1939, Rand McNally, small, 62 pages, color illustrations based on original illustrations, shortened adaptations of Baum books. $55.00

Land of Oz

Road to Oz

Emerald City of Oz

Patchwork Girl of Oz

Rinkitink of Oz

Lost Princess of Oz

— **P** —

PATRIOT LAD SERIES, Russell Carter, 1923 – 36, 12 books. $10.00

PATSY CARROLL SERIES, Grace Gordon, ca. 1920, Cupples, small size, illustrated cloth cover, illustrations, advertised as "a series per-meated with the vibrant atmosphere of the great outdoors." $10.00

Patsy Carroll at Wilderness Lodge

Patsy Carroll under Southern Skies

Patsy Carroll in the Golden West

Patsy Carroll in Old New England

PATTY SERIES, Carolyn Wells, 1901 – 1919, Dodd, 17 books. $10.00

PATTY LOU SERIES, Basil Miller, 1942 – 50, Zondervaan, 9 books. $10.00

PEE-WEE HARRIS SERIES, Percy Fitzhugh, ca. 1910, Grosset. $10.00

Pee-Wee Harris

Pee-Wee Harris on the Trail

Pee-Wee Harris in Camp

Pee-Wee Harris in Luck

PEGGY PARSON'S SERIES, Annabel Sharp, ca. 1920s, Donohoe. $10.00

Peggy Parson Hampton Freshman

Peggy Parson at Prep School

PEGGY RAYMOND SERIES, Harriet Smith, ca. 1915, 3 books. $10.00

PENNY HILL STORIES SERIES, Linda Almond. $15.00

PENNY PARKER MYSTERIES SERIES, Mildred

Wirt, 1941 – 1947 Cupples, 10 books. $15.00

PETER AND POLLY SERIES, Rose Lucia, 1912 – 18, American, 4 books. $10.00

PETER LOOMIS SERIES, Margaret Chalmers, 1914 – 25 Page, 6 books. $10.00

PHANTOM SERIES, ca. 1920s, Saalfield $10.00
Phantom Town Mystery
Phantom Treasure
Black Box

PLATT & MUNK CO. SERIES, ca. 1930s, paper cover picture books, standard size, 12 pages, color illustrations. $35.00
No. 3000C *Jack and the Beanstalk*, illustrations by Eulalie
No. 3000G *Three Bears*, illustrations by Eulalie

PLEASEWELL SERIES, *Dame Trot and Her Comical Cat*, ca. 1890, McLoughlin Bros. $35.00

POLLY SERIES, Emma Dowd, 1912 – 21, Houghton, 5 books. $10.00

POLLYANNA SERIES, see "Glad."

POLLY BREWSTER SERIES, Lillan Roy, 1922 – 32, Grossett, 16 books. $15.00 Ca. 1930s edition Whitman. $10.00
Polly of Pebbly Pit
Polly and Eleanor
Polly in New York
Polly and Her Friends Abroad
Polly's Business Venture
Polly's Southern Cruise
Polly in South America
Polly in the Southwest
Polly in Alaska
Polly in the Orient

POLLY PENDLETON SERIES, Dorothy Whitehall, 1916 – 32, Barse, 13 books. $10.00

POLLY PRENTISS SERIES, Elizabeth Gould, 1913, Penn, 4 books. $10.00

POPPY OTT SERIES, Leo Edwards, ca. 1910, Grosset, advertised as "packed full of the side-splitting adventures which a group of 100% American boys share." $15.00
Poppy Ott and the Stuttering Parrot
Poppy Ott 's Seven League Stilts
Poppy Ott and the Galloping Snail

Poppy Ott 's Pedigreed Pickles

PRINCESS POLLY SERIES, Amy Brooks, ca. 1910. $15.00

PRUE SERIES, Amy Brooks, 1908 – 13, Lothrop, 6 books. $15.00

———— ⊶ **Q** ⊷ ————

QUINNEBASSET SERIES, Sophie May, 1871 – 91, ca. 1891, boxed set, Lee & Shepard, color illustrations, set of 6 in original box. $95.00 or $10.00 ea.
Our Helen
In Old Quinnebasset
Janet, A Poor Heiress
Asbury Twins
Doctor's Daughter
Joy Bells

———— ⊶ **R** ⊷ ————

RADIO BOYS SERIES, Allen Chapman, ca.1907 – 15, Grosset Dunlap, advertised as "Fascinating radio adventures founded on fact and containing full details of radio work. Each volume has a foreword by Jack Binns, the well known

No. 3000C
© PLATT & MUNK CO. INC MADE IN USA.

radio expert." $10.00
Radio Boys' First Wireless
Radio Boys at Ocean Point
Radio Boys at the Sending Station
RAdio Boys at Mountain Pass
Radio Boys Trailing a Voice
Radio Boys with the Forest Rangers
Radio Boys with the Iceberg Patrol
Radio Boys with the Flood Fighters
Radio Boys on Signal Island
Radio Boys in Gold Valley

RADIO BOYS SERIES, ca. 1920, Donohue. $10.00
Radio Boys in the Secret Service, Frank Honeywell
Radio Boys on the Thousand Islands, Frank Honeywell
Radio Boys in the Flying Service, J. W. Duffield
Radio Boys Under the Sea, J. W. Duffield
Radio Boys' Loyalty, Wayne Whipple

RADIO GIRLS SERIES, Margaret Penrose, 1920s, Cupples & Leon. $15.00
Radio Girls of Roselawn
Radio Girls on the Program
Radio Girls on Station Island
Radio Girls at Forest Lodge

RAGGEDY ANN SERIES, Johnny Gruelle, Volland, Donohue, color illustrations throughout by author. Boxed Volland books $200.00; without box $50.00. Later Donohue editions, $25.00.
Raggedy Ann Stories, 1918
Raggedy Andy Stories, 1920
Raggedy Ann's Friendly Fairies, 1919
Raggedy Ann and Andy and the Camel with the Wrinkled Knees, 1924
Raggedy Andy's Number Book, 1924, a linen book for pre-schoolers
Raggedy Ann's Wishing Pebble, 1925
Raggedy Ann and the Paper Dragon, 1926
Raggedy Ann's Magical Wishes, 1928
Raggedy Ann Fairy Stories, 192
Marcella: A Raggedy Ann Story, 1929
Raggedy Ann in the Deep, Deep Woods, 1930
Raggedy Ann in Cookie Land, 1931
Raggedy Ann's Lucky Pennies, 1932

RAGGEDY ANN, books published by Whitman:
Raggedy Ann and the Left-Handed Safety Pin, 1935, Whitman, illustrations by Johnny Gruelle. $45.00
Raggedy Ann in the Golden Meadow, 1935, Whitman, illustrations by Johnny Gruelle $45.00

RAGGEDY ANN, books published by the Johnny Gruelle Company and illustrated by his brother Justin or his son Worth:
Raggedy Ann in the Magic Book, 1939, illustrations by Worth Gruelle. $40.00
Raggedy Ann and the Golden Butterfly, 1940, illus-

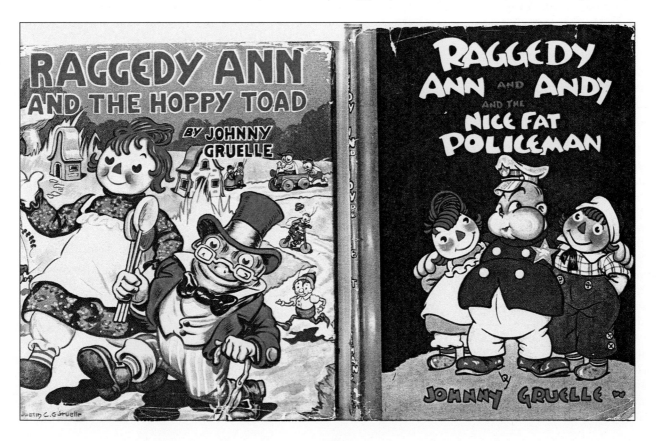

trations by Justin Gruelle. $40.00

Raggedy Ann and Andy and the Nice Fat Policeman, 1942, illustrations by Worth Gruelle. $40.00

Raggedy Ann and Betsy Bonnet String, 1943, illustrations by Justin Gruelle $40.00

Raggedy Ann in the Snow White Castle, 1946, illustrations by Justin Gruelle $45.00

RAGGEDY ANN books published by McLoughlin in its "Westfield Classics" collection: approximately 42 pages, hardboard covers with color illustrations, large "reader" print, b/w endpaper illustrations, b/w and color illustrations. $40.00

Raggedy Ann Helps Grandpa Hoppergrass
Raggedy Ann and the Hoppy Toad, illustrated by Justin Gruelle, 1943
Raggedy Ann in the Garden
Raggedy Ann and the Laughing Brook
Raggedy Andy Goes Sailing
Camel with the Wrinkled Knees

RAILROAD STORIES, Allan Chapman, ca. 1910, Grosset, advertised as "Railroad stories are dear to the heart of every American boy. Ralph is determined to be a railroad man. He starts at the foot of the ladder but through manly pluck wins out." $10.00

Ralph in the Round House
Ralph in the Switch Tower
Ralph on the Engine
Ralph on the Overland Express
Ralph the Train Dispatcher
Ralph on the Army Train
Ralph on the Midnight Flyer
Ralph and the Missing Mail Pouch
Ralph on the Mountain Division

RAINBOW CLASSICS SERIES, ca. 1940s, World Publishing, 250 to 300 pages, hardcover with illustrated endpapers, color and b/w illustrations, advertised as "a series of the world's best-loved children's books in editions distinguished by authoritative texts, beautiful format, and many illustrations." $10.00

Adventures of Huckleberry Finn, Mark Twain, illustrations by Baldwin Hawes

Adventures of Tom Sawyer, Mark Twain, illustrations by Louis Slobodkin

Alice's Adventures in Wonderland, Lewis Carroll, illustrations by John Tenniel

Andersen's Fairy Tales, H. C. Andersen, illustrations by Jean O'Neill

Black Beauty, Anna Sewell, illustrations by Wesley Dennis

Book of Bible Stories, May Lamberton Becker, illustrations by Hilda van Stockum

Book of Sherlock Holmes, Sir Arthur Conan Doyle, illustrations by Charlotte Ross

Child's Garden of Verses, A, Robert Louis Stevenson, illustrations by Alexander Dobkin

Christmas Stories, Charles Dickens, illustrations by Howard Simon

Eight Cousins, Louisa May Alcott, illustrations by C. B. Falls

Five Little Peppers, Margaret Sidney, illustrations by Nettie Weber

Grimm's Fairy Tales, illustrations by Jean O'Neill

Hans Brinker, Mary Mapes Dodge, illustrations by Hilda van Stockum

Heidi, Johanna Spyri, illustrations by Leonard Weisgard

Jack and Jill, Louisa May Alcott, illustrations by Nettie Weber

Jane Eyre, Charlotte Bronte, illustrations by Nell Booker

Jo's Boys, Louisa May Alcott, illustrations by Grace Paull

Kidnapped, Robert Louis Stevenson, illustrations by C. B. Falls

King Arthur and His Knights, Mary MacLeod, illustrations by Alexander Dobkin

King of the Golden River, John Ruskin, illustrations by Fritz Kredel

Last of the Mohicans, James Fenimore Cooper, illustrations by James Daugherty

Little Lame Prince, Dinah Maria Muluck, illustrations by Jon Nielson

Little Men, Louisa May Alcott, illustrations by Hilda van Stockum

Little Women, Louisa May Alcott, illustrations by Hilda van Stockum

Mysterious Island, Jules Verne, illustrations by Henry Pitz

Old-Fashioned Girl, Louisa May Alcott, illustrations by Nettie Weber

Pinocchio, Carlo Collodi, illustrations by Richard Floethe

Pride and Prejudice, Jane Austen, illustrations by Edgard Cirlin

Prince and the Pauper, Mark Twain, illustrations by Howard Simon

Rainbow Mother Goose, illustrations by Lili Cassel

Robin Hood, J. Walker McSpadden, illustrations by Louis Slobodkin

Robinson Crusoe, Daniel DeFoe, illustrations by Roger Duvoisin

Swiss Family Robinson, Johann Wyss, illustrations by Jeanne Edwards

Three Musketeers, Alexandre Dumas, illustrations by C. Walter Hodges

Toby Tyler, James Otis, illustrations by Louis Slobodkin

Treasure Island, Robert Louis Stevenson, illustrations by C. B. Falls

Twenty Thousand Leagues Under the Sea, Jules Verne, illustrations by Kurt Wiese

Two Years Before the Mast, Richard Henry Dana, illustrations by Alexander Dobkin

Wuthering Heights, Emily Bronte, illustrations by Nell Booker

RAINY DAY BOOKS SERIES, ca. 1920s, small size, color board covers, b/w illustrations. $20.00
Rainy Day Book
Rhymes and Riddles
Playtime Book

RANCH GIRLS SERIES, Margaret Vandercook, 1911 – 24, Winston, 9 books. $10.00
Ranch Girls at Rainbow Lodge
Ranch Girls' Pot of Gold
Ranch Girls at Boarding School

RAND MC NALLY SERIES, ca. 1940s, small cardboard cover picture books, often made up of illustrations from large picture books of the 1910 – 30 period. $15.00
Humpty Dumpty and other Mother Goose Rhymes, 1944

RANDOLPH SERIES, ca. 1920s, Saalfield. $10.00
Secret of Casa Grande
Mystery of Carlitos
Crossed Trails in Mexico

RANDY BOOKS SERIES, Amy Brooks, ca. 1900, Lee & Shepard, embossed cloth cover, illustrated by author. $25.00
Randy's Summer
Randy's Winter
Randy and Her Friends
Randy and Prue

RAPHAEL TUCK & SONS SERIES, London, Juvenile Gift and Toy Books, soft covers, color illustrations throughout, numbered, illustrations sometimes signed, authors seldom indicated.
No. 7438 *Father Tuck's Cats and Dogs, ca.1880s.* $35.00
No. 1448 *From Across the Sea,* 1895, diecut outline. $55.00
No. 413 *Peep at the World's Fair,* 1884, illustrations A. Marie, Hodgson, Brundage. $50.00
Beauty and the Beast, 1900, diecut outline. $45.00

Well-Known Creatures, 1900, 8 pages. $50.00
Father Christmas, 1903. $35.00

REBECCA SERIES, Kate Douglas Wiggins
Rebecca of Sunnybrook Farm, 1903, Riverside, cloth cover, color plate illustrations. $75.00
Rebecca of Sunnybrook Farm, 1931 edition, Riverside, color paste-on pictorial on cloth cover, color plates and b/w illustrations by Helen Mason Grose. $20.00
More About Rebecca, 1907 edition, Grosset Dunlap. $25.00
New Chronicles of Rebecca, 1907 Houghton, b/w paste-on pictorial on cover, b/w illustrations by F. C. Yohn. $35.00

RED CROSS SERIES, Margaret Vandercook, 1916-20, Winston, 10 books. $15.00

RED RANDALL SERIES, Sidney Bowen, ca. 1940s, Grosset. $10.00

REGIONAL STORIES SERIES, written and illustrated by Lois Lenski. $20.00
Bayou Suzette, 1943, Stokes
Strawberry Girl, 1945, Lippincott
Blue Ridge Billy, 1946, Lippincott

Judy's Journey, 1947, Lippincott
Boom Town Boy, 1948, Lippincott
Cotton in My Sack, 1949, Lippincott
Texas Tomboy, 1950, Lippincott

REVOLUTIONARY SERIES, George Warren, ca.
  1920, Cupples & Leon. $10.00
Musket Boys of Old Boston
Musket Boys under Washington
Musket Boys on the Delaware

RICK AND RUDDY SERIES, Howard Garis,
  1930s, McLoughlin, 256 pages, wraparound
  color illustration on cover boards, b/w fron-
  tispiece. $30.00
Mystery of the Brass Bound Box
Swept from the Storm
Face in the Dismal Cavern
Secret of Lost River
On the Showman's Trail

RIDDLE CLUB SERIES, Alice Hardy, ca. 1920s,
  Grosset, 6 books, advertised as "full of
  adventures and doings of six youngsters, but
  as added attraction, each book is filled with a
  lot of the best riddles you ever heard."
  $15.00
Riddle Club at Home
Riddle Club in Camp
Riddle Club Through the Holidays
Riddle Club at Sunrise Beach
Riddle Club at Shadybrook

RIVERBOAT SERIES, Rose Knox, 1930 – 37, Doubleday, 6 books. $10.00

ROCKY MOUNTAIN SERIES, Harry Castlemon,
  1868 – 71. $10.00

ROD AND GUN SERIES, Harry Castlemon, 1883
  – 84. $10.00

ROLLO SERIES, Jacob Abbott, 28 titles, Reynolds
  first editions with cloth cover, gilt cover letter-
  ing, engraving illustrations. $50.00. Later
  printings $20.00
Nursery tales (possibly based on author's son),
  include:
Rollo on the Atlantic, 1853
Rollo in Paris, 1854
Rollo on the Rhine, 1855
Rollo and Lucy Books of Poetry, ca. 1864

ROSALIE DARE SERIES, Amy Brooks, ca. 1924
  $15.00

ROVER BOYS SERIES, Arthur Winfield.
  $20.00
Rover Boys in the Air, 1912

ROY BLAKELY SERIES, Percy Fitzhugh, ca.
  1910, Grosset. $10.00
Roy Blakely
Roy Blakely 's Adventures in Camp
Roy Blakely's Camp on Wheels
Roy Blakely, Pathfinder

RUBY AND RUTHY SERIES, Minnie E. Paull, ca.
  1920s, Cupples & Leon. $15.00
Ruby and Ruthy
Ruby's Ups and Downs
Ruby at School
Ruby's Vacation

RUPERT LITTLE BEAR SERIES, Mary Tourtel
  author-illustrator, series based on a daily pictorial series in the *London Daily Express*. After
  1936, the strip and annuals were continued by
  A. E. Bestall.
Rupert Little Bear books with color illustrations,
  ca. 1930 – 36, London. $45.00

RUTH DARROW FLYING STORIES SERIES,
  Mildred Wirt, 1930 – 31, Barse. $15.00
In the Air Derby
In the Fire Patrol
In the Yucatan
And the Coast Guard

RUTH FIELDING SERIES, Alice B. Emerson,
  ca. 1920s, Cupples & Leon, small, illustrat-
  ed cover, advertised as "Ruth Fielding was
  an orphan and came to live with her miser-
  ly uncle. Her adventures and travels make
  stories that will hold the interest of every
  reader." $15.00
Ruth Fielding at the Red Mill
Ruth Fielding at Briarwood Hall
Ruth Fielding at Snow Camp
Ruth Fielding at Lighthouse Point
Ruth Fielding at Silver Ranch
Ruth Fielding on Cliff Island
Ruth Fielding at Sunrise Farm
Ruth Fielding and the Gypsies
Ruth Fielding in Moving Pictures
Ruth Fielding Down in Dixie
Ruth Fielding at College
Ruth Fielding in the Saddle
Ruth Fielding in the Red Cross
Ruth Fielding at the War Front
Ruth Fielding Homeward Bound

Ruth Fielding Down East
Ruth Fielding in the Great Northwest
Ruth Fielding on the St. Lawrence
Ruth Fielding Treasure Hunting
Ruth Fielding in the Far North

RUTH FIELDING IN THE GREAT NORTHWEST

ALICE B· EMERSON

⊶ **S** ⊷

SAALFIELD PICTURE BOOKS, no author credit, paper and clothlike covers, color illustrations
Bad Little Billy Goat, 1915, Linen series. $25.00
Pets of the Farm, 1916, Linen series. $25.00
Pets, 1917, oversize size $30.00
Rhymes for Baby, 1918, Linen series. $25.00
Goldilocks and the Three Bears, 1919. $35.00
ABC of Animals, 1921, Linentex series. $25.00
Friendly Animals, 1928, oversize size, illustrations by C.M.Burd. $55.00
Kitty Cat Stories, 1930, cover illustrations Frances Brundage. $35.00

SADDLE BOYS SERIES, Captain James Carson, ca. 1920s, Cupples & Leon. $10.00
Saddle Boys of the Rockies
Saddle Boys in the Grand Canyon
Saddle Boys on the Plains
Saddle Boys at Circle Ranch
Saddle Boys on Mexican Trails

SALLY SERIES, Lilian Garis, ca. 1930s, Grosset, illustrations by Thelma Gooch. $15.00
Sally for Short
Sally Found Out

SANDMAN SERIES, Abbie Phillips Walker, 12 volume set, ca. 1920s. $15.00 ea. Complete set, $250.00

SCALLY ALDEN SERIES, Ada Claire Darby, ca. 1930, Stokes, impressed color illustration on cover, color map endpapers, unusual three-color illustrations printed on tipped-in pink pages, illustrations by Gaye Woodring. $30.00

SCRANTON HIGH SERIES for Boys, ca. 1915, Goldsmith. $10.00
Chums
Pennant
Cinder Path
Ice Hockey

SCRIBNER CLASSICS SERIES, listed on dust jackets as "Scribner's Junior Classics" and "Scribners Illustrated Classics" with crossovers in titles to both series, Charles Scribner's Sons, NY, color paste-on pictorials on cloth covers, color endpapers, color plate illustrations. First editions in this series are new editions of previously published books, some using illustrations from an earlier edition, some using new illustrations. The Scribner Illustrated Classics series was advertised as "books of rare beauty and tested literary quality, presented in handsome format and strikingly illustrated in color by such famous artists as N. C. Wyeth, Maxfield Parrish, Jessie Willcox Smith and others. ... They are to be found in two groups — the Popular Group, issued at a remarkably low price, and the Quality Group, published at a higher but still very reasonable price." The higher priced books were printed on better quality paper and often contained 12 color plates. The lower priced books usually contained 8 or less color plates.
Arabian Nights, edited by Wiggins & Smith, 1909, illustrator Maxfield Parrish. $100.00
Black Arrow, R. L. Stevenson, 1916, illustrator N. C. Wyeth, $100.00
Boy's King Arthur, Sidney Lanier, 1947 edition, 9 color plates by N. C. Wyeth. $50.00
Drums, Boyd, illustrator Wyeth. $75.00
Hans Brinker, Mary Mapes Dodge, 1936, illustrator George Wharton Edwards. $40.00

Sampo, James Baldwin, illustrator Wyeth. $75.00

Poems of Childhood, Eugene Field, ca. 1932, title page dated 1904 but on the reverse side, copyright dates for individual poems in the collection are dated up to 1922. This is oversize, 200 pages, printed on a lesser quality paper, and contains 8 color plates from the original 1904 Maxfield Parrish illustrated edition $55.00

Treasure Island, R. L. Stevenson, 1911, illustrator Wyeth. $100.00

Westward Ho!, Charles Kingsley, 1940s edition, illustrations by N. C. Wyeth. $50.00

Wind in the Willows, Kenneth Grahame, 1928, 12 color plate illustrations by Nancy Barnhart. $40.00

Yearling, The, Marjorie Rawlings, 1939, illustrator Wyeth. $65.00

SHERBURNE SERIES, Amanda Douglas, 1892 – 1907, Dodd, 12 books. $10.00

SILVER GATE SERIES, Penn Shirley, 1897, Lothrop Lee, b/w illustrations. $10.00
Young Master Kirke
Merry Five
Happy Six

SIX GIRLS SERIES, Marion Taggart, 1906 – 12, Wilde, 7 books. $10.00

SIX LITTLE BUNKERS SERIES, Laura Lee Hope, ca. 1905, Grosset Dunlap, illustrated. $15.00
Six Little Bunkers at Grandma Bell's
Six Little Bunkers at Aunt Jo's
Six Little Bunkers at Grandpa Ford's

SKY BUDDIES, E. J. Craine, 1931, World, color frontispiece. $5.00
Air Mystery of Isle La Motte
Cap Rock Flyers
Sky Buddies Secrets of Cuzko
Flying to Any-Ran Fastness

SLEEPY-TIME TALES SERIES, Arthur Scott Bailey, ca. 1916, Grosset, small size, illustrated cover and color illustrations by Harry L. Smith, advertised as "series of animal stories for children from three to eight years, tell of the adventures of the four-footed creatures of our American woods and fields in an amusing way, which delights small two-footed human beings." Books in this series can also be found with b/w/orange illustrations by Diane Peterson. $20.00
Tale of Cuffy Bear
Tale of Frisky Squirrel

Tale of Tommy Fox
Tale of Fatty Coon
Tale of Billy Woodchuck
Tale of Jimmy Rabbit
Tale of Peter Mink
Tale of Sandy Chipmunk
Tale of Brownie Beaver
Tale of Paddy Muskrat
Tale of Ferdinand Frog
Tale of Dickie Deer Mouse
Tale of Timothy Turtle
Tale of Benny Badger
Tale of Major Monkey
Tale of Grumpy Weasel
Tale of Grandfather Mole
Tale of Master Meadow Mouse

SLIM TYLER AIR STORIES SERIES, Richard Stone, ca. 1920s, Cupples & Leon. $15.00
Sky Riders of the Atlantic
Lost Over Greenland
Air Cargo of Gold
Adrift Over Hudson Bay
Airplane Mystery
Secret Sky Express

SMILING POOL SERIES, Thornton Burgess, 1920s, G & D, small size, paste-on pictorial covers, color plate illustrations by Harrison Cady. $40.00
Jerry Muskrat at Home, 1926
Little Joe Otter

SNIPP, SNAPP, SNURR SERIES, written and illustrated by Maj. Lindman, Whitman, oversize books with bright colored cover illustrations, color illustrations throughout. $45.00
Snipp, Snapp, Snurr and the Red Shoes, 1932
Snipp, Snapp, Snurr and the Buttered Bread, 1934
Snipp, Snapp, Snurr and the Magic Horse, 1935

SPEEDWELL BOYS SERIES, Captain James Carson, ca. 1920s, Cupples & Leon. $10.00
Speedwell Boys on Motor Cycles
Speedwell Boys and Their Racing Auto
Speedwell Boys and Their Power Launch
Speedwell Boys in a Submarine
Speedwell Boys and Their Ice Racer

STAMPKRAFT SERIES, Barse & Hopkins, NY, ca. 1920, oversize oblong, b/w illustrations with sheets of colored illustrations on stamps to paste on story pages, no author or illustrator identification. $45.00
Alice in Wonderland.
Anderson's Fairy Tales

Cinderella
Favorite Rhymes from Mother Goose
Kiddie Kapers
King Parrot and His Court
Mother Goose and Other Rhymes
Puss in Boots
Stories from the Bible
Robinson Crusoe
Three Bears
Tiny Tot Rhymes

ST. NICHOLAS, An Illustrated Magazine Series, ca. 1873 – 1880 Scribner, 1880 – 1930, Century Co., NY, hardbound oversize volumes, each 900 pgs., with paste-on color illustration on cover and b/w illustrations throughout. $40.00 ea.

STORIES ABOUT CAMP FIRE GIRLS SERIES, Margaret Vandercook, 1913 – 21, Winston, 14 books. $15.00

STRATEMEYER, Edward, 1862 – 1930, NJ. Wrote Rover Boys series under pseudonym Arthur M. Winfield, and founded the Stratemeyer syndicate, creating series ideas and plot outlines, then hiring writers at a flat fee per book. His series included Rover Boys, Motor Boys, Tom Swift, Bobbsey Twins, Rocket Riders, Melody Lane, Tom Cardiff's Circus, X Bar X Boys, Outboard Boys, and the runaway bestselling series, Nancy Drew.

STRATEMEYER SYNDICATE created series ideas and plots and pseudonyms, with writers writing under several names, several writers often using the same pseudonyms. Syndicate pseudonyms include Alice Emerson, Laura Lee Hope, Margaret Penrose, Carolyn Keene, Victor Appleton, Mabel Hawley, Frances Judd.

SUE BARTON, Helen Boylston. $15.00
Sue Barton, Student Nurse, 1936, Boston
Sue Barton, Senior Nurse, 1937
Sue Barton, Visiting Nurse, 1938
Continuing titles through 1952.

SUMMER VACATION SERIES, Mary Smith. $10.00

— T —

TALES OF A MINNESOTA GIRL SERIES, Frances Sterrett, 1928 – 31, Penn, 4 books. $15.00

TARZAN, Edgar Rice Burroughs, 24 books.

Tarzan and the Jewels of Opar, 1919, McClurg. $150.00

TOM FAIRFIELD, Allen Chapman, ca. 1925, Cupples & Leon. $10.00
Tom Fairfield's School Days
Tom Fairfield at Sea
Tom Fairfield in Camp
Tom Fairfield's Pluck and Luck
Tom Fairfield's Hunting Trip

TOM SLADE SERIES, Percy Keese Fitzhugh, ca. 1910 – 20, Grosset, advertised as "endorsed by the Boy Scouts of America." $15.00
Tom Slade, Boy Scout
Tom Slade at Temple Camp
Tom Slade on the River
Tom Slade with the Colors
Tom Slade with a Transport
Tom Slade with the Boys Over There
Tom Slade, Motor Cycle Dispatch Bearer
Tom Slade with the Flying Corps
Tom Slade at Black Lake
Tom Slade on Mystery Trail
Tom Slade's Double Dare
Tom Slade on Overlook Mountain
Tom Slade Picks a Winner
Tom Slade on Bear Mountain
Tom Slade, Forest Ranger
Tom Slade in the North Woods

TOM SWIFT, Victor Appleton, ca. 1930s, Grosset. $35.00, later edition $10.00
Tom Swift and His Ocean Airport, 1934
Tom Swift and His Motor Cycle
Tom Swift and His Motor Boat
Tom Swift and His Airship
Tom Swift and His Submarine Boat
Tom Swift and His Electric Runabout

TRAILER STORIES SERIES, Mildred Wirt, 1937, Cupples. $15.00
Crimson Cruiser
Runaway Caravan
Timbered Treasure
Phantom Trailer

TRIPLETS SERIES, Bertha Moore, 1938 – 48, Eerdmans. $15.00
Three Baers
Baers' Christmas
Triplets in Business
Triplets Go South, 1940
Triplets Over J.O.Y.
Triplets Go Places
Triplets Sign Up

Triplets Become Good Neighbors

TRUDY AND TIMOTHY SERIES, Bertha Porter, 1917 – 33, Penn. $10.00

TUCKER TWINS SERIES, Emma Sampson. $15.00

TUCK-ME-IN TALES SERIES, Arthur Scott Bailey, ca. 1917, Grosset, small size, printed illustration on cover, 4 color plate illustrations by Harry Smith, advertised as "unusual series of bird and insect stories for boys and girls from three to eight years old, or thereabouts." $15.00
Tale of Solomon Owl
Tale of Jolly Robin
Old Mr. Crow
Jasper Jay
Rusty Wren
Daddy Longlegs
Kiddie Katydid
Buster Bumble Bee
Freddy Firefly
Betsy Butterfly
Bobby Bobolink
Chirpy Cricket
Mrs. Ladybug

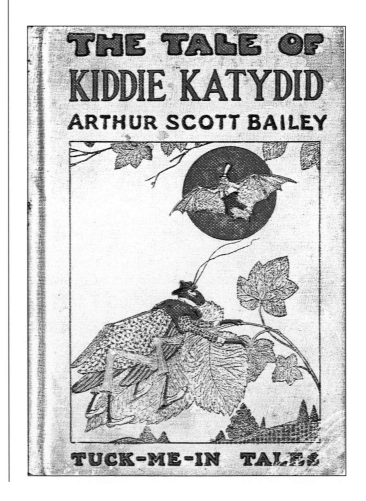

TWILIGHT ANIMAL STORIES SERIES, George Walsh,10 volumes, ca. 1917. $15.00

TWINS OF THE WORLD, Lucie Fitch Perkins, 1911-35, Houghton, 25 books, educational series for schools. $25.00
Belgian Twins, 1917
Eskimo Twins, 1914
Italian Twins, 1920
Japanese Twins, 1912
Spartan Twins, 1918

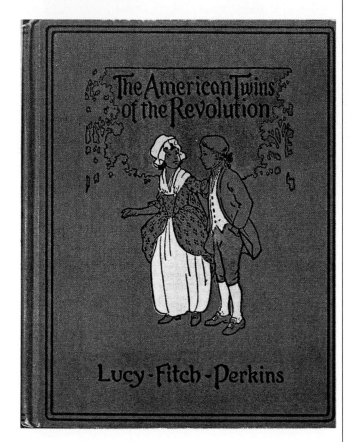

TWINS SERIES, Dorothy Whitehall, 1920 – 32, Barse, 13 books. $10.00

TWO WILD CHERRIES SERIES, Howard Garis, 1924, Milton Bradley, 4 books. $25.00

U

UNCLE JIM'S BIBLE STORIES SERIES, Frank Patchen, 1923, 3 books. $5.00

UNCLE REMUS, Joel Chandler Harris
Uncle Remus, 1881, Appleton, illustrations by E. W. Kemble. $350.00
Uncle Remus, His Songs and Sayings, 1881, NY, 1st edition. $400.00
Tar-Baby and Other Rhymes of Uncle Remus, 1904, Appleton, illustrations by A. B. Frost and Kemple. $75.00
Told by Uncle Remus, 1905, NY. $75.00
Uncle Remus and Brer Rabbit, 1907, NY. $75.00
Uncle Remus and the Little Boy, 1910, Boston. $65.00
Uncle Remus Returns, 1918, NY and Boston. $65.00
Tales from Uncle Remus, 1935 edition, Houghton, 62 pages, 12 color plates by Milo Winter. $40.00
Favorite Uncle Remus, 1948 edition, Houghton, story collection, 309 pages, b/w illustrations by A. B. Frost. $10.00

UNCLE WIGGILY STORIES, Howard R. Garis, copyright R. F. Fenno Publishers, Newark. Many of these stories first appeared in daily newspaper features and on a read-aloud radio show, before being compiled into individual books and series of books.

UNCLE WIGGILY BEDTIME STORIES SERIES, 8 color plate illustrations and 31 stories per book (a bedtime story per night for a month), ca. 1910-15, A. L. Burt Publishers. $55.00
Uncle Wiggily's Adventures, 1913
Uncle Wiggily's Travels
Uncle Wiggily's Fortune
Uncle Wiggily's Automobile, 1913
Uncle Wiggily at the Seashore
Uncle Wiggily in the Country
Uncle Wiggily in the Woods
Uncle Wiggily on the Farm
Uncle Wiggily's Journey
Uncle Wiggily's Rheumatism
Uncle Wiggily and Baby Bunty
Uncle Wiggily in Wonderland
Uncle Wiggily in Fairyland
Uncle Wiggily's Airship, 1915

UNCLE WIGGILY BEDTIME STORIES SERIES, reprinted without the series designation, ca. 1940s, Platt Munk, illustrations by Elmer Rache. $25.00
Uncle Wiggily's Adventures, 1940
Uncle Wiggily's Travels
Uncle Wiggily's Fortune
Uncle Wiggily's Automobile, 1939
Uncle Wiggily at the Seashore
Uncle Wiggily in the Country
Uncle Wiggily in the Woods
Uncle Wiggily on the Farm
Uncle Wiggily's Journey
Uncle Wiggily's Rheumatism

Uncle Wiggily and Baby Bunty
Uncle Wiggily in Wonderland
Uncle Wiggily in Fairyland
Uncle Wiggily's Airship, 1939

UNCLE WIGGILY, Howard Garis, other editions
Uncle Wiggily and the Littletails, 1942, Platt Munk, color plate illustrations by Elmer Rache. $35.00
Uncle Wiggily's Happy Days, 1947, Platt Munk, color plate illustrations by Elmer Rache. $45.00
Uncle Wiggily and Alice in Wonderland, 1918, Donohue, Chicago, color plate illustrations by Edward Bloomfield. $55.00
Uncle Wiggily at the Beach, (1919) 1936 edition, Whitman, illustrations by Lang Campbell. $35.00
Uncle Wiggily and his Flying Rug, (1919) 1940 edition, Whitman, illustrations by Lang Campbell $25.00
Uncle Wiggily and the Cowbird, 1943, Mary Perks, illustrations by Mary and Wallace Stover. $30.00

UNCLE WIGGILY Whitman Series, Howard Garis, ca. 1930s – 1940s, Whitman, small size, numbered books, 34 pages, 3 stories in each book, color illustrated paper-covered boards, color illustrations throughout by Lang Campbell. $20.00

Uncle Wiggily at the Beach
Uncle Wiggily's Auto Sled
Uncle Wiggily's Holidays
Uncle Wiggily's June Bug Friends
Uncle Wiggily's Visit to the Farm
Uncle Wiggily's Woodland Games
Uncle Wiggily and His Flying Rug
Uncle Wiggily and the Pirates
Uncle Wiggily and His Funny Auto
Uncle Wiggily Plays Indian Hunter
Uncle Wiggily Goes Camping
Uncle Wiggily on Roller Skates

VICKI BARR SERIES, Helen Wells, ca. 1930s Grosset, advertised as the Flight Stewardess Series, "fly to adventure with Vicki Barr." $15.00
Silver Wings Over Vicki
Vicki Finds the Answer
Hidden Valley Mystery
Secret of Magnolia Manor
Peril Over the Airport
Mystery of the Vanishing Lady
Search for the Missing Twin
Ghost at the Waterfall

VICTORY BOY SCOUTS SERIES, ca. 1920, Donohue, advertised as "stories by a writer who possesses a thorough knowledge of this

subject," but with no author identification.
$15.00
Campfires of the Wolf Patrol
Woodcraft
Pathfinder
Great Hike
Endurance Test
Under Canvas
Storm-bound
Afloat
Tenderfoot Squad
Boy Scouts in an Airship
Boy Scout Electricians
Boy Scouts on Open Plains

WEBSTER SERIES, Frank V. Webster, ca. 1920s, Cupples & Leon. $15.00
Airship Andy
Pen Hardy's Flying Machine
Bob Chester's Grit
Bob the Castaway
Boy from the Ranch
Boy Pilot of the Lakes
Boy Scouts of Lenox
Boys of Bellwood School
Boys of the Wireless
Comrades of the Saddle
Cowboy Dave
Darry the Life Saver
Dick the Bank Boy
Harry Watson's High School Days
High School Rivals
Jack of the Pony Express

Jack the Runaway
Newsboy Partner
Only a Farm Boy
Tom Taylor at West Point
Tom the Telephone Boy
Two Boy Gold Miners
Two Boys of the Battleship
Young Firemen of Lakeville
Young Treasure Hunter

WESTY MARTIN SERIES, Percy Fitzhugh, ca. 1910, Grosset. $10.00.
Westy Martin
Westy Martin in Yellowstone
Westy Martin in the Rockies
Westy Martin on the Santa Fe Trail
Westy Martin on the Old Indian Trail

WHITMAN AUTHORIZED EDITIONS SERIES, ca. 1940s, Whitman, standard size, b/w illustrations. $15.00
Ann Sheridan and the Sign of the Sphinx
Betty Grable and the House with Iron Shutters
Blondie and Dagwood's Adventure with Magic
Blondie and Dagwood's Snapshot Clue
Blondie and Dagwood's Secret Service
Bonita Granville and the Mystery of Star Island
Boots and the Mystery of the Unlucky Vase, Edgar Martin, 1943
Brenda Starr, Reporter
Dick Tracy, Ace Detective
Dick Tracy Meets the Night Crawler
Don Winslow and the FBI
Gene Autry and the Thief River Outlaws
Ginger Rogers and the Riddle of the Scarlet Cloak
Invisible Scarlet O'Neil

Jane Withers and the Hidden Room, Eleanor Packer, 1942

Jane Withers and the Phantom Violin

Jane Withers and the Swamp Wizard

John Payne and the Menace at Hawk's Nest

Judy Garland and the Hoo-doo Costume, Kathryn Heisenfelt, 1945

King of the Royal Mounted

Little Orphan Annie and the Gila Monster Gang

Lone Rider and the Treasure of the Vanished Men

Patty O'Neal on the Airways

Red Ryder and the Adventure of Chimney Rock

Red Ryder and the Mystery of the Whispering Walls

Red Ryder and the Secret of Wolf Canyon

Roy Rogers and the Gopher Creek Gunman

Shirley Temple and the Spirit of Dragonwood

Son of the Phantom

Sylvia Sanders and the Tangled Web

Winnie Winkle and the Diamond Heirlooms

Tillie the Toiler and the Masquerading Duchess

WHITMAN CLASSICS SERIES, ca. 1930s, 1940s reprints using earlier editions and illustrations, and some new illustrations. $10.00

Robinson Crusoe

Treasure Island

Kidnapped

Tom Sawyer

Heidi

Hans Brinker

Swiss Family Robinson

Eight Cousins

Little Women

Little Men

Gulliver's Travels

Robin Hood

Black Beauty

Dickens' Christmas Stories

Huckleberry Finn

Bible Stories

Alice in Wonderland

Three Musketeers

Fifty Famous Fairy Tales

Fifty Famous Americans

WINDEMERE SERIES, Rand McNally, reprints of classics, ca. 1910 – 1930, paste-on pictorial cover, full-page color illustrations. $45.00, later printings. $20.00

Adventures of Perrine, Hector Malot, illustrations by Milo Winter

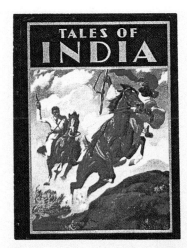
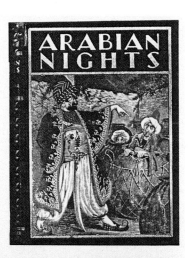
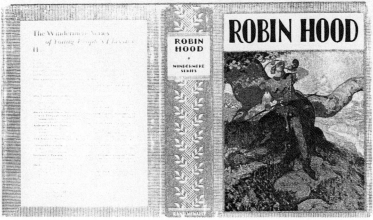

Adventures of Remi, Hector Malot, illustrations by Mead Schaeffer

Alice's Adventures in Wonderland, Lewis Carroll, illustrations by Milo Winter

Andersen's Fairy Tales, Hans Christian Andersen, illustrations by Milo Winter

Arabian Nights, illustrations by Milo Winter

Grimm's Fairy Tales, illustrations by Hope Dunlap

Gulliver's Travels, Jonathan Swift, 1912, illustrations by Milo Winter

Hans Brinker, Mary Mapes Dodge, illustrations by Milo Winter

Heidi, Johanna Spyri, 1921, illustrations by Maginal Wright Barney

Ivanhoe, Sir Walter Scott, illustrations by Milo Winter

Jungle Babies, Edyth Kaigh-Eustace, illustrations by Paul Bransom

Kidnapped, Robert Louis Stevenson, illustrations by Winter

King Arthur and His Knights, edited by Philip Allen, illustrations by Mead Schaeffer

Pinocchio, Carlo Collodi, illustrations by Esther Friend

Robin Hood, Edith Heal, illustrations by Dan Content

Robinson Crusoe, Daniel Defoe, illustrations by Milo Winter

Swiss Family Robinson, Johann Rudolf Wyss, 1916, illustrations by Milo Winter

Tales of India, Rudyard Kipling, illustrations by Paul Strayer

Tanglewood Tales, Nathaniel Hawthorne, 1913, illustrations by Milo Winter

Three Musketeers, Alexandre Dumas, illustrations by Milo Winter

Treasure Island, R. L. Stevenson, illustrations by Milo Winter

Twenty-Thousand Leagues Under the Sea, Jules Verne, illustrations by Milo Winter

A Wonder Book, Nathaniel Hawthorne, 1913, illustrations by Milo Winter

WINWOOD CLIFF SERIES, Daniel Wise, ca. late 1800s.

WISHING STONE SERIES, Thornton Burgess, 1920s, illustrated by Harrison Cady. $25.00
Tommy and the Wishing Stone, 1921
Tommy's Wishes Come True
Tommy's Change of Heart

"WOHELO" CAMP FIRE GIRLS SERIES, Margaret Widdemer, 1915 – 23, Lippincott, 6 books. $15.00

WORK-PLAY BOOKS SERIES, Miriam Blanton

Huber, 12 volumes, 1930. $15.00

✦⇒ X ⇐✦

X BAR X BOYS SERIES, Victor Appleton (see Stratemeyer), ca. 1910 – 20, Grosset, advertised as "These thrilling tales of the Great West concern the Manley boys, Roy and Teddy. They know how to ride, how to shoot, and how to take care of themselves." $10.00
X Bar X Boys on the Ranch
X Bar X Boys in Thunder Canyon
X Bar X Boys on Whirlpool River
X Bar X Boys on Big Bison Trail
X Bar X Boys at the Round Up

✦⇒ Y ⇐✦

YANKEE GIRL CIVIL WAR STORIES SERIES, Alice Curtis, 1920 – 30, Penn, 10 books. $10.00

YOUNG AMERICAN SERIES, 1898, Laird.
Rex Wayland's Fortune, H. A. Stanley, impressed cover, b/w illustrations. $40.00

YOUNG FOLKS TREASURY SERIES, 12 volumes, edited Hamilton Wright Mabie and Edward Everett Hale, ca. 1910 – 20, University Society, NY, cloth hardcover, color plate illustrations. $35.00

YOUNG PURITAN SERIES, Mary Wells Smith, 1897 – 1900, Little, 4 books. $15.00

YOUNG WIRELESS OPERATOR SERIES, Lewis Theiss, ca. 1920, 5 books. $10.00

✦⇒ Z ⇐✦

ZIG-ZAG JOURNEYS SERIES, Hezekiah Butterworth, written for *Youth's Companion* periodical, 1880 – 1895, 17 books. $35.00

ILLUSTRATORS

Can a picture be worth a thousand words? It can certainly add to the value of a children's book. In some cases, a book illustrated by a certain artist can be worth dramatically more than other editions. Consider the tales of Hans Christian Andersen. While there have been numerous editions of his fairy tales published, it is the editions illustrated by Arthur Rackham, Edmund Dulac, or Kay Nielsen that command the highest prices. The Maxfield Parrish edition of Hawthorne's *Wonder Book* commands a higher price than earlier, plainer versions.

An avid group of collectors seeks children's books published during the "golden age" of illustration, roughly dating from 1900 to 1920. The advent of new printing technology at the turn of the century dramatically lowered the cost of four-color printing, and children's books were the primary beneficiaries. Publishers prepared Christmas books, lavishly illustrated volumes of fairy tales or other children's stories. These books were meant to appeal to adults as well as children.

These books might boast eight to sixteen color plates. These color plates (see Glossary) were printed on a separate, higher quality glossy paper and then "tipped" into the book. In some books, the plate might be mounted on a separate sheet of heavier paper. Color plates are printed on only one side of the page, with the back left blank or perhaps printed with a line of text explaining the picture. Sometimes a sheet of tissue paper would be inserted between the color plate and the regular page to further protect the artwork.

Because color plates were tipped into the book separately, they could become loose and fall out. Usually such books will have a list of illustrations as well as a table of contents. Count the illustration titles and then count the color plates to quickly ascertain if all plates are intact.

Collectors who concentrate on illustrations are usually looking for early editions of books. Many of the fine illustrated volumes were kept in print for decades, or reprinted by other publishers at a later date. However, publishers might choose to cut down the number of color plates to save costs or the printing quality may decrease as the printing plates became damaged with repeated use.

We have tried to identify major artists whose work is collected or can make a difference to the price of the work. We have also given short biographies of other children's artists, whose work may make little difference to the price, but may help you date your books. Many times, publishers would forget to date or change the copyright of a popular work. Sometimes, the easiest way to determine the age of your book is to check the illustrator. For example, Gordon Browne was a popular Victorian illustrator of adventure stories, while H.J. Ford did all the first editions of Lang's fairy tale series.

Adams, Frank (d. 1944)

British illustrator Frank Adams used pen-and-ink or brightly colored pictures in his work for children. He did a number of titles for Blackie (often undated) until his death. Some books were also released under his name with no author credited. See also Adams in the author section.

Carroll, Lewis. *Alice's Adventures in Wonderland,* 1912, Blackie.

THE · STORY
OF
THE · FROG
who · would
a-wooing · go

ILLUSTRATED
BY
FRANK · ADAMS

NEW · YORK
DODGE PUBLISHING COMPANY
214-220 EAST TWENTY-THIRD STREET

Adams, Frank

Aldin, Cecil (1870 – 1935)

Cecil Charles Windsor Aldin specialized in horses, dogs, and the English countryside. He was extremely well-known in England for both book illustrations and several popular print advertisements. His obituary in *The Times,* London, read "there never yet has been a painter of dogs fit to hold a candle to him..."

Sewell, A. *Black Beauty*, 1912, Jarrold.

Artzybasheff, Boris (b. 1899)

Artzybasheff's life reads like an adventure novel. Son of a Russian writer, he fought in the Russian Revolution and then worked as a merchant seaman. When his ship docked in New York, he left the sea trade with 14 Turkish cents in his pocket. After his release from Ellis Island, Artzybasheff worked as an engraver. A newspaper story about his adventures led to newspaper work as well as commissions for fables and picture books. The influence of Russian folk art can be seen in many of Artzybasheff's books. See also Artzybasheff in author's section.

Allingham, W. *Fairy Shoemaker*, 1928.

Colum, P. *Forge in the Forest*, 1925, Macmillan.

Colum, P. *Orpheus: Myths of the World*, 1930 Macmillan.

Ardizzone, Edward (1900 – 1979)

Ardizzone began his free-lance career in England in 1927. He illustrated more than 170 books for adults and children as well as producing almost all of the *Strand* magazine covers in 1946 and 1947. For children's collectors, he is known primarily as the author/illustrator of a series of books about Little Tim and

Lucy Brown. These stories, like the works of Hugh Lofting, were originally written to amuse his own children. *Little Tim and the Brave Sea Captain* was the first children's picture book to be produced with offset lithography. Due to problems with the press and the humid New York summer of 1935, the printer could not get the sheets to dry properly. As a result, they redid the job, printing on only one side of the sheet. The resulting books have blank pages (the back of the sheet) appearing at regular intervals. See author section for books written and illustrated by Ardizzone.

Attwell, Mabel Lucie (1879 – 1964)

Attwell's pictures of chubby-cheeked children, like the American Campbell Kids, became very popular in the 1930s and 1940s in Great Britain. Her work appeared on cards, posters, bathroom plaques, and other decorative items. In 1943, she even began a comic strip called "Wot A Life" for the *London Opinion*. Attwell began illustrating gift books for the Raphael Tuck company in 1910. Attwell's publishers also used her pictures in "birthday books", annuals, and illustrated diaries, a practice that continued after her death.

Carroll, Lewis. *Alice In Wonderland*, 1910, Tuck.
Anderson, H.C. *Fairy Tales*, 1914, Tuck.
Kingsley, C. *The Water-Babies*, 1916, Tuck.
Barrie, J. *Peter Pan and Wendy,* 1923, Scribner.

Austen, John (1886 – 1948)

Influenced by Art Deco artist Aubrey Beardsley, Austen was labeled by contemporaries as more of a book decorator than an illustrator of the story's action. He did the majority of his work in the 1920s and illustrated primarily adult novels and poetry. His work should appeal to collectors of Art Deco.

Perrault, Charles. *Tales of Passed Time*, 1922, Selwyn & Blount.

Bannon, Laura

Chicago artist Laura Bannon exhibited her work at the Art Institute and ran the junior department of their school in the 1930s. She illustrated a few books during this period. In the 1940s, she left the Art Institute to concentrate on writing and illustrating children's books.

Bowman, J. *Pecos Bill,* 1937.
Wood, E. *Pepper Moon,* 1940.

Baynes, Pauline (b.1922)

Baynes, an English artist, is primarily known as the first illustrator of the Narnia chronicles written by C.S. Lewis. She began her career in the 1940s and new work continued to appear into the 1980s.

Tolkien, J.R.R. *Farmer Giles of Ham*, 1949, Allen & Unwin.

Bemelmans, Ludwig (b. 1898)

This Austrian born artist emigrated to the United States to escape the problems of pre-WWII Europe. He was so homesick that he painted a screen filled with Austrian mountain scenes to hide his view of the fire escape. This artwork so impressed a visiting editor that she commissioned him to illustrate children's books. Eventually, Bemelmans matched his loose, colorful style with humorous poetry, and a little girl named Madeline debuted in 1939. She was an outstanding success and her adventures continued through a series of picture books. Early editions of the Madeline titles are becoming highly collectible, and Bemelmans' other artwork will probably appeal to Madeline collectors also.

Berry, Erick (b. 1892)

Although her real name was Evangel Allena, this American artist picked up the nickname "Erick" in art school. She did her earliest published work for Volland in titles like *Pinky Pup* and *Empty Elephant*. By the late 1920s, she was illustrating books for Harper and Doubleday. In 1928, she and husband, diplomat Herbert Best, began collaborating on children's books based on their experiences living in Africa.

Alcott, Louisa May, *Little Men*, 1933, Blue Ribbon.

Beskow, Elsa (b. 1874)

This Swedish artist wrote and illustrated many books based on her own life. Her works were translated into English beginning in the 1920s. The best known of her works is probably *Aunt Green, Aunt Brown, and Aunt Lavender* (1928, Harper). See the author section for a list of her titles.

Bestall, A.E. (b. 1892)

English illustrator Bestall began by doing humorous pictures for various magazines including *Punch*. He illustrated many of *The Literary and Dramatic Reading* series (Schofield & Sons) used in the London schools. In 1936, he took over the *Rupert the Bear* comic strip from originator Mary Tourtel. He retired from drawing the strip in 1965, but continued to do annuals for the series until 1973. He illustrated a variety of children's books from the late 1920s through 1950.

Betts, Ethel Franklin

One of the many American artists who studied with Howard Pyle, Betts primarily illustrated children's stories for *St. Nicholas, McClures,* and *Collier's Weekly*. The bulk of her work was published between 1900 and 1920.

Burnett, F. *Little Princess,* 1905.
Chapin, A. *True Story of Humpty Dumpty,* 1905.
MacDonough, G. *Babes in Toyland,* 1924.
Riley, *Riley Child Verse,* 1906.

Bianco, Pamela (b. 1906)

Bianco first saw her artwork appear in print when she was only 13. An exhibition of her paintings inspired English poet Walter De La Mare, and her paintings were used to illustrate the poems when they were published under the title *Flora* (1919, Lippincott, American edition). Bianco also illustrated two stories by her mother, Margery Williams Bianco. By the late 1930s, Bianco was an established author-illustrator and her career continued for several decades.

Bianco, M.W. *The Little Wooden Doll*, 1925, Macmillan.
Bianco, M.W. *The Skin Horse*, 1927, Macmillan.
Wilde O. *The Birthday of the Infanta*, 1929, Macmillan.
Ewing, J. *Three Christmas Trees,* 1930.

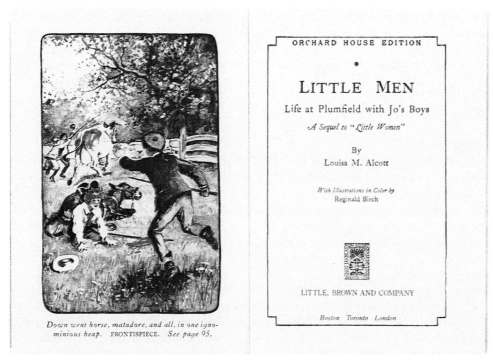

Birch, Reginald Bathurst

Birch, Reginald Bathurst (1856 – 1943)

Birch earned the nickname "the Children's Gibson" for the numerous drawings he did for *St. Nicholas*. Like his contemporary, Charles Dana Gibson, Birch's precise pen-and-ink drawings showed great detail and atmosphere. He was also responsible for the misery of an entire generation of little boys for his appealing drawings of Little Lord Fauntleroy in his velvet suit, lace collar, and long curls. His pictures for Fauntleroy were so popular that Scribner commissioned additional drawings and color plates for later editions.

Alcott, L. *Little Men*, 1901, Little.
Baldwin, J. *Story of Roland*, 1883, Scribner.
Burnett, F. *Little Lord Fauntleroy*, 1886, Scribner.
Burnett, F. *Little Lord Fauntleroy*, 1911, Scribner (with extra illustrations).
Burnett, F. *Little Princess*, 1938, Scribner.
Burnett, F. *Sara Crewe*, 1888, Scribner.

Bock, Vera

Bock's earliest children's book appeared at the end of the 1920s. The daughter of an American father and Russian mother, she grew up in St. Petersburg. When the family fortunes disappeared in the Russian Revolution, her father took the family out via Siberia and Japan. After several years in Europe as an art student, Bock returned to the United States as a commercial artist. Strong lines and block print work in books like Ella Young's *The Tangle Coated Horse* (1929, Longmans) reflect a definite Slavic influence.

Johansen, M. *Secret of the Circle*, 1937.
Gibson, K. *Bow Bells,* 1943.

Bransom, Paul (b. 1885)

A prolific wildlife illustrator, Bransom began his career drawing a comic strip called "The News From Bugville" (originated by Gus Dirks). His work most often appears in adventure stories and nature novels such as *Biggest Bear on Earth* (1943). He had a long career with his first books appearing in the teens and continuing into the 1940s.

Grahame, K. *Wind in the Willows*, 1913, Scribner.

Brock, Charles Edmund (1870 – 1938)

Three Brock brothers illustrated children's and adult novels during the late Victorian and Edwardian age. C.E. (as he signed himself) was considered the best of the three, and his delicate watercolor work compares favorably with Edwardian artists such as Rackham and Dulac. There was also another Charles Edmond Brock illustrating children's books in the 1920s who appears to be no relation to the Cambridge brothers (*Magic Ink-Pot,* 1928).

Burnett, F. *Little Lord Fauntleroy*. 1925, Warne.
Dickens, C. *Christmas Carol*. 1905, Dent.

Brock, Emma Lillian (b.1886)

This American illustrator is no relation to the Edwardian English brothers. Brock listed her influences as a summer in a Slovak settlement in Minneapolis, the pushcart vendors of New York, and the farm markets of Italy. Her work often emphasizes strong, peasant characters and ethnic dress. She wrote and illustrated a variety of picture books as well as doing illustrations for other works. See author section for books by Brock.

Owen, R. *Picture Tales from Scandinavia,* 1939.

Brock, Henry Matthew (1875 – 1960)

This Brock brother (see also C.E. and Richard) was the most prolific of the brothers. While his style lacked some of C.E.'s sensitive brushwork, his vigorous pictures worked well in school stories and boys' adventure books. Besides novels, he also illustrated magazines and annuals. Henry greatly enjoyed the works of Gilbert and Sullivan, and produced a variety of posters for the D'Oyly Carte Company.

Milne, A. A. *Once on a Time,* 1922.
Stevenson, R.L. *Treasure Island,* 1928, Macmillan.
Dickens, C. *Christmas Carol,* 1935, Dodd.

Brock, Richard Henry

In the 1930s, the third Brock brother, Richard, did some illustration work. One biographer listed Richard's work as the least skilled of the three.

Brooke, Leonard Leslie (1862 – 1940)

A contemporary of Beatrix Potter, Brooke's humorous animals and delicate use of line and color made his works extremely popular. Brooke, who was credited as "L. Leslie Brooke" in his books, began illustrating children's books in the 1880s, and became a regular illustrator for the works of Mrs. Molesworth. In 1897, he illustrated a nursery rhyme book for Frederick Warne & Company (the publishers of Potter's Peter Rabbit and other books). He continued to illustrate and write exclusively for Warne for the next 30 years. For a list of titles written and illustrated by Brooke, see the author's section.

Brooke, Leonard Leslie

Browne, Gordon (1858 – 1932)

Browne's work for children relied on adventure and realism, rather than fantasy. He worked mostly in pen-and-ink, illustrating numerous G.A. Henty stories as well as the adventures of the Bastable children in E. Nesbit's novels. He wrote and illustrated his own nonsense tales under the name "A. Nobody" (1895 – 1900). Browne was painstakingly attentive to detail, often reading manuscripts twice to match the pictures to the words, and using his own large collection of antique weapons for reference.

Lang, A. *Prince Prigio,* 1889.
Lang, A. *Prince Ricardo of Pantouflia,* 1893.

Burgess, Frank Gelett (1866 – 1951)

Gelett Burgess wrote "Purple Cow", a poem that made him famous as an American humorist. He also worked as a civil engineer, a drawing instructor, and the publisher of a literary magazine, *Lark*. While with *Lark*, Burgess began doing a series of grotesque cartoons that became the Goops. For a list of the Goop books written and illustrated by Burgess, see the author section.

Cady, Walter Harrison (b. 1877)

In 1913, Cady replaced George Kerr as Thornton Burgess' principal illustrator. Burgess loved Cady's interpretation of his animal tales, and their collaboration lasted more than 50 years. Cady contributed almost 15,000 drawings for Burgess' newspaper columns, and his work proved so popular that the publisher released early Burgess works with new Cady illustrations. Cady's style of huggable animals neatly dressed in Edwardian costumes remains popular with collectors today. See Series," Mother West Wind."

Burnett, F. *Racketty-Packetty House,* 1906.

Caldecott, Randolph (1846 – 1886)

When Walter Crane (see below) left the field of "toy books," as the English called the small books produced for the nursery trade, his publisher selected a young artist and bank clerk as Crane's successor. Caldecott produced approximately two toy books a year from 1878 to 1885. Each book measured 9" x 8" with nine colored illustrations as well as black and white drawings. Soon Caldecott's work became as popular with his Victorian audience as the works of Crane and Kate Greenaway. While his first titles were printed in first editions of 10,000, later books had an initial run of 100,000. See author section for his own titles.

Ewing, J. *Jackanapes,* 1884.

Caldecott, Randolph

Cameron, Kathrine (1874 – 1965)

A prolific illustrator, this Scottish artist began her career in the late 1890s. She illustrated adult novels, works of poetry, and children's books. Her most popular children's titles were *In Fairyland,* Kingsley's *The Water-Babies*, and *Iain the Happy Puppy.*

Chisholm, L. *Enchanted Land.*

Cox, Palmer (1840 – 1924)

Cox's stories and illustrations of his Brownies first appeared in the children's magazine, *St. Nicholas.* The characters were extremely popular with Victorian children. The Dude, the Dutchman, and the Policeman became familiar figures in various American advertising campaigns. For a list of Cox titles, see the author section.

Crane, Walter (1845 – 1916)

Crane was one of the first Victorian illustrators who could sell books on the strength of his name alone.

Because the majority of his work were fragile "toy books", early editions are rare. It is estimated that Crane produced approximately 40 toy books in two different "shilling series" between 1865 and 1876. By the 1880s, Crane worked on more elaborate books, such as a collection of the Brothers Grimm fairy stories (250 copies, first edition, 1882). Crane was a contemporary of the artist William Morris and also produced a variety of decorative items ranging from wallpaper to ceramic tiles. His final work reflects many Art Noveau motifs. For a listing of books credited to Crane, see the author section.

Hawthorne, Nathaniel, *A Wonder Book for Girls & Boys*, 1851, Houghton Mifflin.

Moleworth, Mrs., *A Christmas Child,* 1880, Macmillan.

Wise, J. *New Forest,* 1895.

Cruikshank, George (1792 – 1878)

The best of Cruikshank's work appeared prior to 1850. He started his career as a political caricaturist, and the majority of his books and illustrations were intended for adults. In particular, his dandies, villains and street urchins uniquely complimented the works of Charles Dickens. He first illustrated *Oliver Twist* in 1838. The posthumous edition (see below) included colored illustrations. His works continue to increase in value, and he has even been called "the best of English illustrators" by modern critics. Under authors, see Cruikshank's *Fairy Library*.

Dickens, Charles. *Oliver Twist*, 1894.

Dalziel Brothers

George, Edward, and John Dalziel were known as the best wood engravers in Victorian England. Their younger brother, Thomas (1823 – 1906), made his career in painting and drawing, but he often worked with his brothers on various projects. Starting in the 1850s, the Dalziels began producing a series of fine art books. Taking the pictures of popular artists such as W.H. Hunt, Dante Rossetti, and others, the brothers would prepare wood engravings of the paintings to illustrate everything from the poems of Tennyson to the Bible. One of their most popular works was a version of the Arabian Nights which included illustrations by John Tenniel (*Alice In Wonderland* illustrator) among others. The Dalziels were usually credited on the title page as "Engraved by the Brothers Dalziel" or their family name would appear in the title of the book.

Rossetti, C. *Sing-Song, a Nursery Rhyme Book*, 1872.

Daugherty, James (b. 1889)

American artist Daugherty generally illustrated adventure stories or historical tales with strong, vigorous line drawings or the imaginative use of two- or three-color printing. He also worked as a muralist, creating a series of murals for the Loew movie theaters in New York. He started working in illustration at the end of the 1920s and continued through the 1950s.

Doyle, A.C. *White Company*, 1928, Harper

Sandburg, C. *Abe Lincoln Grows Up*, 1929, Harcourt.

White, S. *Daniel Boone, Wilderness Scout*, 1926, Doubleday.

D'Aulaire, Edgar Parin (b. 1898)
D'Aulaire, Ingri Mortenson (b. 1904)

Edgar and Ingri D'Aulaire, a husband and wife team, wrote and illustrated several books of folktales and children's stories of Norway. Their work is becoming more collectible, especially the earlier picture books such as *Ola* or *Abraham Lincoln*. Edgar P. D'Aulaire also illustrated other children's novels in the early 1930s. See D'Aulaire in the author section.

De Angeli, Marguerite (b. 1889)

De Angeli is primarily known as an author-illustrator of her own books, including *The Door In The Wall* (1950 Newbery Award). She did some work for *St. Nicholas* as well as illustrating various titles for the Macmillan Children's Classics (see Series). For her own books, see the author section.

Yonge, C. *Little Duke*, 1927.

Dennis, Wesley (b. 1903)

Although he started out working for a Boston newspaper and then tried fashion illustrations, Dennis quickly concluded that what he liked best was drawing horses. He illustrated several titles for Marguerite Henry including *King of the Wind* (1949 Newbery Medal). In the 1940s, he began writing and illustrating his own books, often based on animals living on his Virginia farm. See also Henry in the author section.

Robertson, K. *Ticktock and Jim*, 1948.

Denslow, W.W. 1856 – 1915

The first illustrator of the Oz books, Denslow actually held a joint copyright on the Scarecrow, Tin Man, and other characters from the first Oz book, *The Wonderful Wizard of Oz*. He produced some of his own Oz tales, many taken from his newspaper cartoon strip, which now command high prices due to their rarity. Although he began as a newspaper illustrator, Denslow also did postcards, theater posters and other advertising art. Denslow designed several books for the Roycroft Press and taught at Elbert Hubbard's

Roycroft studios. His work is sought by Oz enthusiasts as well as collectors of the Arts and Crafts movement. See Denslow in author section and Oz in Series section.

Baum, L. F. *Dot and Tot of Merryland,* 1901
West, P. *Pearl and the Pumpkin,* 1904.

Denslow, W.W.

Detmold, C.M. (Charles Maurice) (1883 – 1908)
Detmold, E.J. (Edward Julius) (1883 – 1957)

Edward Julius Detmold began his career by illustrating a portfolio of animal and bird studies with his twin brother, Charles Maurice. The two also collaborated on a 1908 edition of Rudyard Kipling's *Jungle Book.* C.M. committed suicide in 1908, but E.J. continued to illustrate books with the majority of his work appearing in the 1920s. E.J. was often cited as the best of the Edwardian animal illustrators.

Doyle, Richard (1824 – 1883)

"Dicky" Doyle was the uncle of Sir Arthur Conan Doyle, the creator of Sherlock Holmes. An early *Punch* illustrator, Doyle's best known work, Allingham's *In Fairyland* (1870), cemented the Victorian ideal of fairies as delicate little creatures hiding under mushrooms. He illustrated his friend Ruskin's *The King of the Golden River* when he was 27. Doyle often signed his magazine work as "Dick Kitcat."

Grimm, Brothers, *The Fairy Ring,* 1846, London.
Lang, Arthur. *Princess Nobody,* 1886, Longmans.

Dulac, Edmund (1882 – 1957)

The French artist Edmund Dulac was most influenced by the works of English artists William Morris and Aubery Beardsley. The early part of his career was devoted to book illustration, but he also designed costumes, furniture, and postage stamps. His best work has an Oriental flair and borrows from the motifs of Persian paintings. Like Kay Nielsen and Arthur Rackham, his work has been featured in several books on fine children's books, and prices have risen sharply over the last decade. See Dulac in the author section.

Andersen, H.C. *Stories from Hans Andersen*, 1912, Hodder.
Hawthorne, N. *Tanglewood Tales,* 1918.
Stevenson, R.L. *Treasure Island*, 1927, Doran.

Dunlap, Hope (b. 1880)
Dunlap taught children's classes at the Chicago Art Institute as well as illustrating various picture books for Chicago publishers. Most of her Chicago work seems to date from 1908 to 1915. She later moved to New York.

Browning, R. *Pied Piper of Hamelin,* 1910.
Garnett, L. *Muffin Shop,* 1910.
Mulock, D. M. *The Little Lame Prince,* 1909, Rand McNally.

Edwards, George Wharton (b. 1869)
American artist Edwards did a few book illustrations starting in 1880s. The bulk of his work was done for Scribners, Macmillan, and Houghton, but he appears to have been more interested in a career as a painter than as an illustrator.
Dodge, M. *Hans Brinker*, 1915, Scribner.
Hawthorne, N. *Tanglewood Tales for Girls and Boys*, 1887, Houghton.

Enright, Elizabeth (1909 – 1968)
The daughter of illustrator Maginel Wright (see Wright) and artist W.J. Enright, Elizabeth Enright began illustrating books in 1930. By 1935, she gave up most outside work to concentrate on writing and illustrating her own books. See Enright in author section.

Evans, Edmund (1826 – 1905)
Evans was an engraver who began experimenting with color printing as early as 1852. He revolutionized children's books with the design and printing of "toy books" for the London firm of Routledge and Warne. These paperbound books, measuring approximately 9" by 7", initially sold for a sixpence. Each book contained six pages of text and six pages of colored illustrations. Later the price of these phenomenally popular books rose to a shilling. To illustrate his toy books, Evans called on the talents of Crane, Caldecott, and Greenaway as well as others. He later designed *The Nursery Alice* with 20 colored enlargements from Tenniel's illustrations of 1890, as well as numerous art books for the Victorian trade.

E.V.B. (1825 – 1916)
Englishwoman Eleanor Vere Boyle illustrated several Victorian books for children and adults. Her

dreamy style complimented familiar verses in a small series of children's books. For titles credited to Boyle, see the author section.

Andersen, H.C., *Fairy Tales*, 1875, New York.

Falls, Charles (1874 – 1960)

Falls began his art career by designing vaudeville posters. Another poster, "Books Wanted" (1918), earned him instant fame as well as raising hundreds of book donations for the WWI American troops. He also designed an ABC book for his three-year-old daughter using colored woodcuts. The book earned critical approval from other illustrators and remains a striking example of woodcut art. See Falls in author section.

Field, Rachel (1894 – 1942)

Field said that her artistic style came from an excessive fondness for cutting out paper dolls. Her early picture books were illustrated with silhouettes cut from black paper. Later, using various techniques including pen-and-ink, she kept to the simple lines inspired by those early cut-outs. Her books are popular with collectors of 1930s art. For a list of books written and illustrated by Field, see the author section.

Ford, Henry Justice (1860 – 1941)

Ford was the first illustrator of the Lang fairy tale books from the *Blue Fairy Book* (1889) to the *Violet Fairy Book* (1910). First or early editions of these books contain his rather stiff pen-and-ink illustrations. Some of the first editions also contain illustrations by other artists as well. Ford illustrated many Victorian children's books as well as other books edited by Lang, including *The Red True Story Book* (1897) and *The Tales of King Arthur* (1905). While his stiff, fussy style doesn't appeal to many collectors, his illustrations mark the transition from the Victorian to the Edwardian age.

Fraser, Claude Lovat (1890 – 1921)

Artist, book illustrator and theater designer, Lovat was discharged from the British Army after being gassed in WWI. His most productive year was 1920, when he produced a series of illustrations as well as set designs for the *Beggar's Opera* and *As You Like It.* He died in 1921 as a result of his war injury, and several books appeared posthumously.

De La Mare, W. *Peacock Pie*, 1924, Constable.

Frost, Arthur B. (1851 – 1928)

Like his contemporary, Pyle, Frost began illustrating books for Harper & Brothers. He is best-known for his work on Joel Chandler Harris' Uncle Remus books, but he also wrote his own books including *Stuff And Nonsense* (1884). Frost was red-green colorblind, but he memorized the position of the paints on his palette to circumvent the problem.

Aldrich. *Story of a Bad Boy*, 1895, Houghton.

Twain, M. *Tom Sawyer Abroad: Tom Sawyer, Detective and Other Stories,* 1896, Webster.

Gag, Flavia (b. 1907)

Wanda Gag's sister began illustrating books in 1935. Her art work is generally in black and white, and never reached the popularity of her sister's work with collectors. These books now sell in the $5.00 to $15.00 range.

Gag, Wanda Hazel (1893 – 1946)

Author and illustrator of the children's classic, *Millions of Cats* (1928), Gag was influenced by the old German customs of her family in Minnesota. Orphaned while in high school, she used her artistic talents to complete school and help support her family. Later, in New York, she supported herself by painting lampshades and drawing fashion pages. Her work is becoming more collectible. See author section for books written and illustrated by Gag.

Grimm, Bros. *Tales From Grimm*, 1936, Coward.

Grimm, Bros. *Snow White,* 1938, Coward.

Grimm, Bros. *Three Gay Tales From Grimm*, 1943, Coward.

Gaskin, Arthur (1863 – 1926)

Gaskin is considered a representative of the Birmingham School of Art. The headmaster of the school, Edward Taylor, was a disciple of William Morris and encouraged his students to study crafts as well as painting. Gaskin designed jewelry and enamel as well as working with Morris on *The Shepherdess Calendar*. Like Morris, Gaskin used a Gothic style in his illustrations.

Andersen, H.C. *Stories and Fairy Tales* (2 volumes), 1893, George Allen.

Neale, Dr. *Good King Wenceslas* (with introduction by W. Morris), 1895, Cornish Brothers.

Geisel, Theodor Seuss (b. 1904)

Theodor Geisel began his career illustrating various advertising campaigns with the same strange creatures that populate his stories. He later applied his talent for the pithy jingle and amusing characters to the works of "Dr. Seuss", his pseudonym. His advertising pieces, including a paper jigsaw for Esso, have become highly prized by the lovers of his *And To Think I Saw It on Mulberry Street* and other books. See the author section for a list of his titles.

Goble, Warwick

Goble began his career as an illustrator for magazine stories. One of his first assignments was designing Martians in the serialized version of H.G. Wells' *War of the Worlds*. Although not considered as great as that of his peers Rackham and Dulac, Goble's work is beginning to be collected by those interested in Edwardian children's books. He illustrated numerous fairy tale books as well as Stevenson's books for Macmillan.

James, G. *Green Willow and Other Japanese Fairy Tales*, 1910, Macmillan.

Stevenson, R.L. *Kidnapped*, 1925, Macmillan.

Stevenson, R.L. *Treasure Island*, 1923, Macmillan.

Gramatky, Hardie (1907 – 1979)

Gramatky ghosted the comic strip "Ella Cinders" during his college years in California. He also worked as an animator for the Walt Disney Studio. His children's books, including the perennially popular *Little Toot,* won him almost instant critical success. See the author section.

Grant, Gordon (b. San Francisco, 1875)

Grant spent part of his childhood in Scotland. He did general illustrating for many years, but retired in the 1930s to devote his time to painting. His first love was ships. His painting of the U.S.S. Constitution was made into a print by the Navy to raise money for the reconstruction of Old Ironsides. He wrote and illustrated some maritime books in the 1930s.

Tarkington, B. *Penrod*, 1914, Doubleday.

Baldwin, A. *Sou'wester Goes North,* 1938.

Greenaway, Kate (1846 – 1901)

Greenaway's children, with their high-waisted dresses and big hats, belong to an earlier age than the artist. When asked why she favored the dress of the Regency period for her people, Greenaway wrote she preferred "old-fashioned things." Her delicate drawings have been reproduced on everything from dishes to clothing, and she remains as popular today as she was during the Victorian age. For a list of titles credited to Greenaway, see the author section.

Browning, Robert. *A Pied Piper of Hamelin*, 1888, Routledge.

Taylor, Jane and Anne. *Little Ann and Other Poems*, 1882, E. Evans.

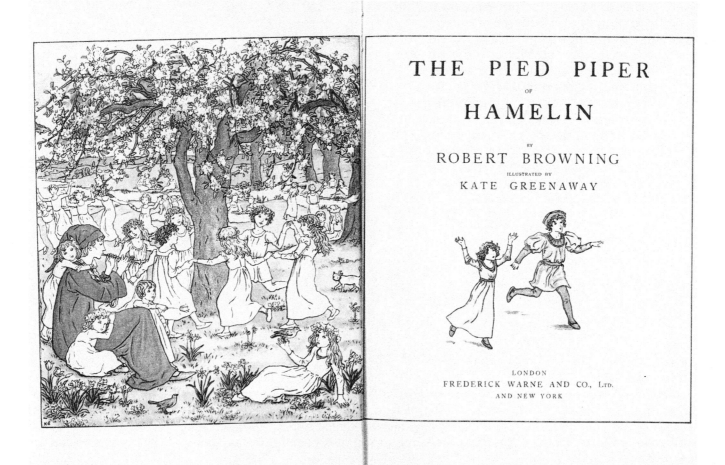

Greenaway, Kate

Gruelle, Johnny (1880 – 1938)

The creator of Raggedy Ann and Andy has been rediscovered by children's book collectors in the past few years. All of his work has become very collectible, with the Raggedy Ann titles being eagerly sought. The son of a professional artist, Gruelle began his career illustrating comic strips, including the popular *Mr. Twee Deedle,* while still in his 20s. His illustrations for the Volland Company's children's books are particularly fine, often with additional drawings for the endpapers and back covers that were dropped from later editions by other publishers. While working as a Volland illustrator, Gruelle designed and patented a "Raggedy Ann" doll. The whole close-knit Gruelle family pitched in to sew the prototypes. Raggedy Ann became the family's main business, allowing them to escape many of the hardships of the Depression. Gruelle's stories often appeared in magazines or newspapers, then were collected into books. To protect their rights to Gruelle's work, the family formed the Johnny Gruelle Publishing Company. After

Gruelle's death, his brother, Justin Gruelle, and Johnny's son, Worth Gruelle, continued to illustrate Johnny's stories. See Gruelle in the author section for a list of titles.

Grimm. *Grimm's Fairy Tales*. 1914, Cupples & Leon.

Hubbell, Rose S. *Quacky Doodles' and Danny Daddles' Book,* 1916, Volland.

Malot, Hector. *Nobody's Boy*, 1916, Cupples.

Lawrence, Josephine. *Gingerbread Man*, 1930, Whitman.

Housman, Laurence (1865 – 1959)

The younger brother of A.E. Housman, this Art Noveau artist wrote more than 80 books, including some fairy tales for children. He remains best known for his illustrations and decorative work. Early editions of his books often had elaborately designed bindings as well as highly detailed engravings. The whole look of his books probably appealed more to adults than children, but his work should be considered highly collectible in the Art Nouveau market.

Rossetti, Christina. *Goblin Market,* 1893, Macmillan.

Hughes, Arthur (1832 – 1915)

The primary English illustrator of George MacDonald, many of Hughes' pictures originally appeared in the magazine, *Good Words for the Young*, and were later collected into book form. One biographer reckoned that Hughes contributed more than 200 drawings to this magazine in its five years of existence in the late 1860s. Hughes' collaboration with MacDonald began in 1867. After MacDonald's death, Hughes continued illustrating the works of MacDonald's son, Greville, until 1913.

Hughes, Thomas. *Tom Brown's School Days*, 1869, Macmillan.

MacDonald, George. *At the Back of the North Wind*, 1871, Strahan.

MacDonald, George. *Dealings with the Fairies*, 1867, Strahan

MacDonald, George. *Princess and the Goblin,* 1872, Strahan.

MacDonald, George. *Ranald Bannerman's Boyhood*, 1871, Strahan.

Rossetti, Christina. *Sing-Song: A Nursery Rhyme Book,* 1872, George Routledge.

James, Will (1892 – 1942)

William James Dufault grew up in Montana. Orphaned at the age of 4, he was adopted by a fur trapper. When Will was 13, his adoptive father drowned, and Will started working as a cowboy and rodeo rider to support himself. Following a cattle drive to California, he was hired by Western artist, Harold Von Schmidt, to work as a model. Eventually, Will started doing his own drawings and sold a few pictures to *Sunset* magazine, then began writing and illustrating his own stories. His novel, *Smoky*, won the 1927 Newbery Award. His work appeals to Western collectors. See author section for a list of his books.

Kent, Rockwell (b. 1882)

New York state native Rockwell Kent identified himself as "a working man," interested in the goals of the labor movement of the 1940s. He wrote and illustrated several stories of his own travels through Newfoundland, Alaska, Ireland and Greenland. Other books concentrated on classic American folk heroes such as Paul Bunyan. His dramatic "wood block" style of illustrations was originally done in pen-and-ink. Kent also did advertising work for Rolls-Royce, and Marcus & Company Jewelers. Prices for his work have been slowly rising as collectors become more interested in the art of the 1930s and 1940s.

Shepard, Esther. *Paul Bunyan*, 1941, Harcourt.

Kipling, John Lockwood (1837 – 1911)

Rudyard Kipling's father, John Lockwood Kipling, taught art at the Bombay School of Art and later became curator of the Central Museum, Lahore, India, from 1875 to 1893. He illustrated a few books of Indian fables including his son's *Jungle Book*.

Steel, Flora. *Tales of the Punjab*, 1894, Macmillan.

Lathrop, Dorothy (b. 1891)

Dorothy Lathrop's favorite work involved animals, and she often used live models. Some of her color plate work echoes the Edwardian illustrators, and she had a long, prolific career. She won the first Caldecott medal ever presented for *Animals of the Bible* (1938). Her sister, Gertrude Lathrop, was a noted sculptor, and Lathrop shared a studio with her. See also Lathrop in author section.

De La Mare, W. *Crossings*. 1923, Knopf.
De La Mare. W. *Three Mulla-Mulgars*, 1919, Knopf.
MacDonald, G. *Princess and Curdie*. 1927, Macmillan.
Field, R. *Hitty*, 1929, Macmillan.

Lawson, Robert (1892 – 1957)

American artist Lawson began his career as an illustrator for *Vogue, Harper's Weekly* and several other New York magazines. In 1930, children's editor May Massee hired him to illustrate *The Wee Men of Ballywooden* (Viking), and his detailed, humorous style soon won other commissions as well as critical praise. In 1936, he illustrated *The Story of Ferdinand* for his friend, Munro Leaf. He did four more books with Leaf, and all of their collaborations remain highly collectible, with *Ferdinand* being the most popular. By the 1940s, Lawson had turned to writing and illustrating his own books. He is one of the few children's authors to win both a Caldecott and Newbery award. For a list of his novels, see the author's section.

Mason, A. *The Wee Men of Ballywooden*, 1930, Doran.
Young, E. *The Unicorn With Silver Shoes*, 1932, Longmans, Greene.
Leaf, M. *Wee Gillis*, 1938, Viking.
Atwater, R. & F. *Mr. Popper's Penguins*, 1938, Little, Brown.
Farjeon, E. *One Foot In Fairyland,* 1938, Stokes.
Gray, E. *Adam of the Road*, 1942, Viking.

Lawson, Robert

Leach, John (1817 – 1864)

A humorous English illustrator, Leach, along with his contemporary Cruikshank, was mostly known for his adult works. His drawings for Dickens' *Christmas Carol* (1843) won instant acclaim, and his work was picked up again for a collection of Dickens' Christmas stories published later. His illustrations for fairy tales, such as *Jack the Giant Killer*, first appeared in the 1840s.

Dickens, Charles. *Christmas Books*, 1854, Chapman.

Lear, Edward (1812 – 1888)

Lear called himself a "mad old Englishman" and sold the copyright of his *Book of Nonsense* (1846) for approximately $250, a decision he must have regretted since it went into 19 further editions in his lifetime. Lear was a professional landscape artist, but it was his illustrations for his own whimsical verse (he once dubbed it "Learical Lyrics") that earned everlasting fame and started the trend for brightly colored, funny children's books. Lear took unmitigated delight in poking fun at his friend, Victorian poet laureate Alfred Lord Tennyson, but he also illustrated one volume of Tennyson's verses. For a list of his titles, see the author section.

Lenski, Lois (1893 – 1974)

Lenski began illustrating and writing children's stories in the 1920s. She grew up in rural Ohio and she used those childhood experiences in her early works, including *Skipping Village* (1927) and *A Little Girl of Nineteen Hundred* (1928). She disliked illustrating other people's stories and accepted few commissions for such work. Her work is particularly sought by collectors of Depression era art. For a list of books authored and illustrated by Lenski, see the author's section.

Colum, Padraic. *The Peep Show Man,* 1924, Macmillan.

Hutchinson, V.S. *Chimney Corner Fairy Tales*, 1926, Minton Balch.

Lovelace, M. *Betsy Tacy*, 1940, Crowell.

Lofting, Hugh

Lofting, Hugh (1886 – 1947)

Lofting distracted himself from the horrors of World War I by writing letters to his children that included stories of a veterinarian who could "talk to the animals." He later illustrated these stories with crude pen-and-ink drawings that have an inherent charm. *Dr. Doolittle* was first published in New York in 1920, with the English edition appearing in 1922, a pattern that followed for most of the sequels despite the fact that Lofting lived in England. For a list of titles written and illustrated by Lofting, see Series, "Doctor Doolittle."

Marge (Majorie Henderson Buell)

In 1934, *The Saturday Evening Post* lost its popular cartoon, *Henry*, to the King Features Syndicate. The editors sketched out a little girl character to replace Henry and then turned over the idea to cartoonist Buell, who signed her artwork "Marge." Marge used the editor's suggested name of "Little Lulu" and designed a little girl with cork-screw curls and a determined air. "Little Lulu" was an overnight success and kept Marge busy. By 1944, Lulu was featured in animated cartoons, Kleenex advertisements, and several small books. Marge parted company with the *Saturday Evening Post,* but kept "Little Lulu" going in a variety of formats. Although Marge's name appears on *Little Lulu* comics published by Western, the writing was actually done by cartoonist John Stanley and the art by various Western employees. Marge also illustrated various children's stories and her funny artwork appeals to collectors of children's books and comic art.

Thompson, R. *King Kojo,* 1938.

McCay, Winsor (1871 – 1934)

McCay was primarily known as a comic strip artist. His "Little Nemo In Slumberland", a newspaper strip, chronicled the adventures of a little boy. He also created one of the first animated film characters, Gertie the Dinosaur, and was a strong influence on the works of early animators such as Walt Disney and Walter Lanz. Early printed collections of McCay's work are eagerly sought by animation and comic collectors. See author section.

McCloskey, Robert (b.1914)

During a recent television interview, author-illustrator McCloskey said that the hardest part of creating *Make Way For Ducklings* (1940) was to come up with appropriate "ducky" names for the little ones. Although born in Ohio, much of McCloskey's own work centers around his later life in Maine, including the small island where his family spent their summers (*Blueberries For Sal,* 1948). Much of his work has remained in print for over 50 years, creating generations of fans, and early editions continue to rise in value. See McCloskey in the author section.

Malcolmson, A. *Yankee Doodle's Cousin,* 1941.

Bishop, C. *Man Who Lost His Head,* 1942.

Mackenzie, Thomas B. (1887 – 1944)

Relatively unknown, this British artist did a few book illustrations during the Edwardian era. His work for Arthur Ransome's *Aladdin & His Wonderful Lamp* (1919) is similiar to Dulac.

Millar, Harold R. (d. 1935)

Millar's work began appearing in English children's books in the 1890s. He was a student of the Birmingham School. Millar liked to collect ancient weapons and Eastern art. His illustrations of Oriental stories won praise from contemporaries for their authenticity. He illustrated several children's adventure stories written by E. Nesbit (1900 – 1913).

Nesbit, E. *Book of Dragons,* 1900.

Nast, Thomas (1840 – 1902)

Nast began illustrating stories for newspapers at the age of 15. America's best-known political cartoonist in his time, he created the Tammany Tiger, the Republican Elephant, and the Democrat Donkey. His illustrations of battles during the Civil War led President Abraham Lincoln to credit him as the North's most influential recruiter. For children's book collectors, his most appealing title would be Clement Moore's *Visit from St. Nicholas* (1869). His work is also sought by collectors of Americana and Victorian era art.

Neill, John R. (1876 – 1943)

Born in Philadelphia, Neill was only 26 when he took on a lifetime commitment, illustrating the Oz books. A prolific magazine and book illustrator, Neill was tapped by Reilly & Britton to replace W.W. Denslow. Denslow and L. Frank Baum (the author of the series) had a creative falling out after the successful publication of *The Wonderful Wizard of Oz.* If Denslow was Arts & Crafts, then Neill was Art Nouveau. His ladies wore lovely, flowing gowns, reminiscent of Gibson's women, and even his most grotesque creatures had pretty touches. Dragons wore big silk bows, and the witches had lots of accessories. Neill illustrated the Oz series from 1904 to 1942, even writing three books toward the series' end. While doing the Oz series, Neill continued to do primarily pen-and-ink work for a variety of books and magazines stories.

He often reworked drawings to fit other assignments, so you might find some distinctly Oz characters in his other books. His work is primarily sought by Oz collectors, although art collectors of the Edwardian era are beginning to recognize his talent. See "Oz" in Series.

Grabo, C. *Peter and the Princess.*

Wright, H. *Uncrowned King,* 1910.

Newell, Peter (1862 – 1924)

American humorist Peter Newell was a favorite with turn-of-the-century art editors. His work appeared in several magazines including *Harper's Monthly*. He also produced a series of picture books (see Newell in the author section).

Carroll, Lewis. *Alice's Adventures In Wonderland*, 1901, Harper & Bros.

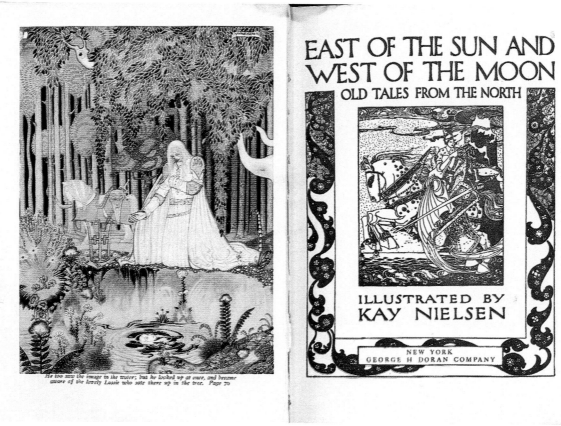

Nielsen, Kay

Nielsen, Kay (1886 – 1957)

Nielsen's first art exhibition was in London in 1912. The Danish artist quickly received commissions for fairy tale books intended for the Christmas trade. Like the work of contemporaries Rackham and Dulac, these books appeared in both deluxe editions and regular trade editions on both sides of the Atlantic. In 1926, Nielsen moved to the United States and worked in Hollywood as a set designer as well as an artist for the Walt Disney Studios. Although his highly stylized picture books fell out of favor by the end of the 1930s, his work was reproduced in several books about children's illustration in the 1980s and prices for his gift books soared.

Anderson, H.C. *Fairy Tales* ,1924, Doran.

Quiller-Couch, A. *Twelve Dancing Princess (Powder And Crinoline)*, 1923, Doran.

O'Neill, Rose (1875 – 1944)

A self-trained artist, O'Neill was nationally known as an illustrator by the age of 19. Her greatest invention was the Kewpies, who spawned an entire industry of dolls, books, and related items. She also illustrated and wrote magazine stories. Her illustrated stories appeared for several years as special sections in

Good Housekeeping and *The Ladies Home Journal*. Her work is also sought by doll collectors. For a list of her books, see author section.

Fillmore, P. *Hickory Limb.*

Pape, Eric (1870 – 1938)

An American illustrator, the majority of Pape's work for children seems to have been done for Macmillan. His illustrations for Hans Christian Andersen's *Fairy Tales And Stories* (1921, Macmillan) were based on Andersen's own silhouettes. Pape ran an art school in Boston, and he is listed as a major influence by many of the children's illustrators of the 1920s and 1930s.

Parrish, Maxfield

Parrish, Maxfield (1870 – 1966)

Arguably the most collectible illustrator in America during his lifetime, Parrish first editions continue to rise in value. Very rare works, such as *The Jack of Hearts,* can command prices in the thousands of dollars. Parrish was the son of a landscape painter, studied architecture in college, and then art at the Pennsylvania Academy of Fine Arts. Like many illustrators of his era, Parrish also attended classes taught by Howard Pyle. Although his permanent home was in New Hampshire, Parrish spent some time in Arizona for his health and also traveled to Italy on assignment to illustrate a garden book. His unique backgrounds are his own imaginary combination of New Hampshire oaks, Arizona mountains, and Italian cypress, bright skies and marble temples. His first book commission was *Mother Goose in Prose*, a book eagerly sought by serious collectors of both Baum and Parrish. Although he did full color artwork for Grahame's *Dream Days*, the publisher chose to reproduce the paintings in black and white. See also Parrish in author section.

Field, E. *Poems of Childhood*, 1904, Scribner.

Grahame, K. *Dream Days*, 1902, Lane.

Hawthorne, N. *Wonder Book*, 1910, Duffield.

Scudder, H. *Children's Book,* 1909, Boston.

Petersham, Maud Fuller (b. 1889)
Petersham, Miska (b. 1888)

Hungarian Miska emigrated to the United States in 1912. He met his wife, Maud Fuller, in New York while she was working at the International Art Service. One of their earliest works was *Poppy Seed Cakes* (1924). By 1929, they were writing and illustrating their own books. Prices are rising for their brilliantly colored works. See also Petersham in author section.

Clark, M. *Poppy Seed Cakes*, 1924, Doubleday.
Miller, E. *Young Trajan*, 1931, Doubleday.
Sandburg, C. *Rootabaga Stories*, 1923, Harcourt.

Pitz, Henry Clarence (1895 – 1976)

Pitz was a prolific American illustrator with more than 160 books to his credit. He also worked for St. *Nicholas* and *Saturday Evening Post*. Although he used every medium, the majority of his work was carefully done line drawings and somewhat similiar to Howard Pyle in style. Pitz wrote several books on illustration, including *Illustrating Children's Books*.

Bennett, John. *Master Skylark*, 1922, Century.
Riggs, Strafford. *Story of Beowulf*, 1933, Appleton.
Coblentz, Catherine. *Falcon of Eric the Red*, 1942, Longmans.

Pogany, Willy

Pogany, Willy (1882 – 1955)

A Hungarian artist who emigrated to the United States in 1915, Pogany's earliest work was done in England. His major influences were Oriental artists and illuminated books. Besides illustration, he designed theatrical productions and worked as an art director in Hollywood. Although not as well-known as his contemporaries, Pogany's color work appeals to collectors of Dulac and Rackham. See author section for a list of books released under his name.

Carroll, L. Alice's. *Adventures in Wonderland*, 1929, Dutton.
Colum, P. *Adventures of Odysseus*, 1918, Macmillan.

Colum, P. *Children of Odin*, 1920, Macmillan.
Colum, P. *Frenzied Prince*, 1943, McKay.

Potter, Beatrix (1866 – 1943)

Potter created her first story, *Peter Rabbit*, as a letter to a sick child. Encouraged by the response to this and to other illustrated stories, she sent her work to several London publishers including Frederick Warne. She was rejected by all of them, but decided to try a private printing of *Peter Rabbit* (1901). The 250 copies quickly sold out. The success of this and her second private printing, *The Tailor of Gloucester*, led Warne to reconsider their decision. It's hard to imagine now that anybody would manage to get through their childhood without encountering one of her tiny books designed to be held by children's hands. She carefully planned each book. The usual format was a colored picture on the front cover and dust jacket, illustrated end papers, and a color frontispiece. The color plates were printed on one side only in the color half-tone process perfected by Edmund Evans. Warne also experimented with releasing a few of her titles as folding panoramas in protective wallets. These proved very popular with children, and booksellers complained about large numbers of damaged and unsaleable copies left in their shops. Potter's work was enormously popular during her lifetime, and the Warne Company continues to print her books today as well as license dozens of uses of her characters. Peter Rabbit and friends appear on everything from plates to stuffed animals. Although she was a contemporary of Arthur Rackham, Potter's art is more similiar to the delicate watercolors of Kate Greenaway. Potter was an extremely careful wildlife artist, using pets and farm animals as her models. In 1905, Potter bought Hill Top farm in England's Lake District, which provided a background for many of her tales. In 1913, she married and began to concentrate on farm life, including the raising of Herdwick sheep. See also Potter in author section.

Pyle, Howard

Pyle, Howard (1853 – 1911)

This New England artist had an enormous influence on children's books in Victorian and Edwardian America. His classes for artists launched some of the best American illustrators including Maxfield Parrish, Jessie Willcox Smith, and N.C. Wyeth. They, and his other students, created a tradition of illustration and art known as the Brandywine School. Pyle's books are sought by collectors of fairy tales, fine line drawings, and decorative printing. His books are distinguished by their full-page drawings, illustrated capitals, and detailed border art. Pyle also wrote 19 titles, primarily for Harper and Scribner's. See author section for a list of titles written by Pyle.

Baldwin, J. *Story of Siegfried*, 1892, Scribner.

Baldwin, J. *Story of the Golden Age*, 1887, Scribner.

Rackham, Arthur

Rackham, Arthur (1867 – 1939)

By far the most proflic of the great Edwardian English illustrators, Rackham used silhouettes, pen-and-ink, and watercolor paintings in more than 50 books. For his color plate illustrations, Rackham used a strong tint of raw umber over the pen drawing to give his works an autumnal feeling. He understood the color half-tone process and worked with his publishers to insure exact reproductions of his art. Although he had done some magazine and novel illustration in the 1890s, his first real critical success in children's books was Charles and Mary Lamb's *Tales of Shakespeare* (1899). In 1905, Heinneman published the first deluxe edition of *Rip Van Winkle* that popularized the idea of fairy tale gift books. For *Peter Pan in Kensington Garden*, Hodder and Stoughton released a deluxe limited edition signed by Rackham, a trade edition, and American and French editions. This pattern was repeated for most of Rackham's larger fairy tale and fantasy works and also used for other popular Edwardian illustrators such as Dulac and Nielsen. Later in his career, Rackham's publishers would often have him go back and do more illustrations for an earlier title to bring a higher price for the gift market. Rackham's fairy tale books are highly prized by collectors, and first editions, especially deluxe editions, can command prices running from several hundred dollars to several thousand. His last illustrations for a deluxe edition of Grahame's *Wind in the Willows* were completed shortly before his death and published posthumously. Because of Rackham's immense popularity, his works have been picked up and reproduced in dozens of cheaper editions, many currently in print.

Andersen, H.C. *Fairy Tales*, 1932, Harrap.

Barrie, J.M. *Peter Pan in Kensington Gardens*, 1906, Hodder.

Carroll, L. *Alice's Adventures in Wonderland*, 1907, Heinemann.

Dickens, C. *Christmas Carol*, 1915, Heinemann.

Grahame, K. *Wind in the Willows*, 1940, Limited Editions.

Grimm, Bros. *Fairy Tales,* 1900.

Kipling, R. *Puck of Pook Hill,* 1906, Doubleday.
Moore, Clement. *Night Before Christmas*, 1931, Harrap.
Ruskin, J. *King of the Golden River*, 1932, Harrap.

Robinson, Charles (1870 – 1937)

Charles was the middle brother of a family of English illustrators. His father, Thomas (not to be confused with Thomas Heath, the oldest brother), was the chief staff artist for the *Penny Illustrated Paper*, London, while another uncle worked for the *Illustrated London News*. Charles worked with his brothers on one version of Andersen's fairy tales. His best work is considered to be the drawings done in the 1890s for books of verse by Field and Stevenson, although he continued to work into the 1930s.

Andersen, H.C. (translated by E. Lucas), *Fairy Tales From Hans Christian Andersen*, 1899, Dent (includes illustrations from Charles, Thomas and William).
Burnett, Frances Hodgson. *The Secret Garden,* 1911, Heinemann.
Field, Eugene. *Lullaby-Land*, 1897.
Stevenson, Robert Louis. *A Child's Garden of Verses*, 1896.
Wilde, Oscar. *The Happy Prince and Other Tales*, 1913.

Robinson, Thomas Heath (b. 1869)

Oldest brother of the Robinson family (see Charles above), Thomas did fewer children's books. His illustrations for adult novels include Hawthorne's *Scarlet Letter* (1897) and Thackeray's *History of Henry Esmond* (1896). By the 1920s, Thomas concentrated on illustrating stories in various boys' magazines.

Porter, Katherine. *Scottish Chiefs*, 1900, Dent.
Wyss, J. *Swiss Family Robinson*, 1913, Doran.

Robinson, William Heath (1872 – 1944)

The most collectible of the Robinson brothers (see Charles and Thomas above), William Heath's full color illustrations compare favorably with the other great Edwardian illustrators such as Rackham and Dulac. His work commands higher prices in Great Britain, where he is better known, than in the United States. His adult gift books include two lavishly illustrated versions of Rudyard Kipling's verse (*Collected Poems*, 1910, and *Song of the English*, 1909). In 1902, William Heath created Uncle Lubin, a naive but wise character, who uses a variety of wild contraptions and tricks to get himself out of absurd predicaments. To compliment the humorous stories, William Heath added more than 100 line drawings.

Andersen, H.C. *Danish Fairy Tales and Legends*, 1897, Bliss, Sands.
Andersen, H. C. *Fairy Tales*, 1924, Doran.
De La Mare, W. *Peacock Pie*, 1917, Constable.
Kingsley, C. *Water Babies*, 1915, Houghton

Rockwell, Norman (1894 – 1978)

For millions, Rockwell's images of America defined this country's style. He is best known for his magazine work including more than 300 covers for the *Saturday Evening Post*. Some of this artwork was picked up to illustrate the book form of stories, and he seems to have done some illustrations for various boys' series. Rockwell's pictures, especially early magazine covers, are eagerly sought by many types of collectors.

Twain, M. *Adventures of Huckleberry Finn,* 1940.
Barbour, R. *Purple Pennant,* 1916.

Sarg, Tony (1882 – 1942)

Sarg, an American illustrator, worked in early animated cartoons. He wrote and illustrated several books as well as designing toys and other household items. Sarg even designed some of the earliest giant balloons for the Macy's Thanksgiving Day parade.

Collodi, C. *Adventures of Pinocchio,* 1940.

Schaeffer, Mead (1898 – 1980)

Schaeffer's work appeals to collectors of N. C. Wyeth and other action/adventure artists. Some of his earliest work was illustrating "Captain Blood" stories of Rafael Sabatini. Schaeffer did a series of illustrated classics for the Dodd, Mead Company while still in his 20s. Like his friend, Norman Rockwell, Schaeffer painted numerous covers for the *Saturday Evening Post* including a famous WWII series depicting various branches of the military service.

Malot. *Adventures of Remi*, 1923, Rand (see Windemere Series).

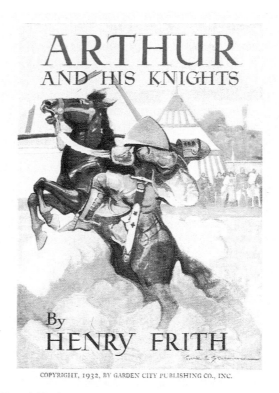

Schoonover, Frank Earle

Schoonover, Frank Earle (1877 – 1972)

Another American illustrator trained by Pyle, Schoonover did books and magazines, and designed stained glass windows. He followed Pyle's advice on immersing himself in his subject. When commissioned to do a series of stories about frontier life, he traveled by dog sled to the Hudson Bay territory. A second trip, done by canoe, helped him understand the challenges faced by early Indian tribes. His work is seen as typical of the Brandywine School.

Collier, V. *Roland the Warrior*, 1934, Harcourt.

Shepard, E. H. (b. 1879)

Because of his work on *Winnie the Pooh* and the other Milne children's books, Shepard became one of the most popular English illustrators of the 1920s. He began his career as an illustrator for *Punch* in 1907. His original illustrations for the Milne books were in black-and-white, and only later editions carried colored pictures. See Grahame and Milne in the author section.

Shepard, Mary Eleanor (b. 1909)

Ernest Shepard's daughter began her own career illustrating P.L. Travers' tales of Mary Poppins. While neither as popular nor prolific as her father, Shepard continued to illustrate children's books into the early 1980s.

Smith, Jessie Willcox (1863 – 1935)

Growing steadily in popularity, almost all of Smith's works command high prices, and her illustrations are eagerly sought by collectors. Like Wyeth and Parrish, fellow students of Pyle, Smith primarily did lush oil paintings of her subjects and enjoyed considerable popularity during her lifetime. She specialized in drawings of children. Besides her books, her work often appeared in *McClures* and *Good Housekeeping*.

Smith probably did more than 200 covers for *Good Housekeeping*. See also Smith under authors.
Alcott, L. *Little Women*, 1915, Little.
Alcott, L. *Old-Fashioned Girl*, 1920, Little.
Kingsley, C. *Water-babies*, 1916, Dodd.
MacDonald, G. *At the Back of the North Wind*, 1919, McKay.
Moore, C. *Twas the Night Before Christmas*, 1912, Houghton.
Spyri. *Heidi*, 1922, McKay.
Stevenson, R.L. *Child's Garden of Verses*, 1905, Scribner.

Tarrant, Margaret (1888 – 1959)

The daughter of Percy Tarrant (see below), Margaret enjoyed a long career producing popular postcards, greeting cards, birthday books, and a host of other printed material in Great Britain. Her first book commission was a version of Kingsley's *The Water-Babies* (1908, Dent). Her romantic watercolors of children, fairies, and animals appeared in a variety of gift books published by the Medici Society in the 1920s.

Tarrant, Percy (d. 1930)

The bulk of Tarrant's illustrations for children appeared in various English girls' and boys' adventure series published between 1900 and 1928. He also illustrated at least one of Mrs. Molesworth's books, *Greying Towers* (1898), as well as several stories by E.T. Meade.

Thackeray, William Makepeace (1811 – 1863)

Primarily known as the author of *Vanity Fair* and other Victorian novels, Thackeray also sketched the characters of most of his stories. Sometimes the sketches were published with the books, sometimes they were only meant as jokes for his friends. *The Rose and the Ring* was designed as a Christmas book for children. Thackeray originally drew the big-headed characters of Giglio and Bulbo to amuse children at a Christmas party, and later composed the story for the convalescent daughter of friends. See Thackeray under authors.

Tenniel, Sir John (1820 – 1914)

Almost exclusively known for his work on the "Alice" books by Lewis Carroll, Tenniel spent more than 50 years as one of *Punch's* chief political cartoonists. Various drawings by Tenniel appear in other works, primarily those engraved by the Dalziel brothers (see listing). Tenniel and Carroll quarreled over the drawings, but the story's fans have judged that Tenniel's version of Alice, right down to her hair band, suits the story best. Because Tenniel's drawings were engraved on wood, repeated printings of the books caused the very fine lines to blur and even disappear. The original wood blocks were recently discovered in a London bank vault. A fascimile edition published a few years ago by Wonder Books uses illustrations pulled from the original blocks with all the fine lines of the drawings restored.

Tourtel, Mary (1897 – 1940)

The wife of H.B. Tourtel, an editor of the *Daily Express* in London, Tourtel created a series of illustrated adventures for Rupert, a young bear in plaid trousers. Begun in 1920, Tourtel continued to draw the strip until 1935 when failing eyesight forced her to retire. The stories were then taken over by British artist, A.E. Bestall. Extremely popular in Great Britain, books continue to appear today. See "Rupert" in the Series section.

Tudor, Tasha (b. 1915)

Although Tasha Tudor continues to illustrate books today, her career began in the late 1930s. Her best-known work centered around the animals of her farm. Tudor's art reflects a sensibility of a Victorian America. She has numerous fans and her early work should be considered highly collectible. See Tudor in author section.

Webb, Clifford Cyril (1895 – 1972)

Webb mixed scrapboard, watercolor, and wood engravings in his book illustrations. In Great Britain, he was known for bringing about a revival of wood engraving in the 1920s and his engravings are considered highly collectible. Between 1933 and 1965, he did a series of picture books for the Warne company.
Ransome, A. *Swallows & Amazons*, 1931, Cape (2nd edition).

Wiese, Kurt (b. 1887)

German artist Kurt Wiese was working as a trader in China when WWI broke out. Captured by the Japanese armies and turned over to the British, he spent five years as a detainee. While waiting out his captivity in Australia, he began writing and drawing picture books for his own amusement. In 1919, he returned to Germany and sold his picture books to a German publisher. Deciding that there were greener pastures elsewhere, Wiese moved to Brazil where he worked for awhile in a children's publishing house. He finally emigrated to the United States at the end of the 1920s. Between 1928 and 1950, he illustrated or wrote well over 150 books for several New York publishers. His best known pictures were for the *Five Chinese Brothers* by Claire Huchet Bishop (1938), and a vast amount of his work is still readily available.

Flack, M. *Story About Ping*, 1933, Viking.

Kipling, R. *Jungle Book*, 1932, Doubleday.

Williams, Garth (b. 1912)

Although he was born in the United States, Williams spent his childhood in Canada and England. At the start of WWII, he returned to the States and began doing illustrations for the *New Yorker* magazine. In the 1950s, he began illustrating Margarey Sharpe's *Rescuers* series as well as a re-issue of the books of Laura Ingalls Wilder. He also authored and illustrated his own series of children's books. Williams' early books and artwork are becoming extremely popular with the baby boomer collectors.

White, E. B. *Stuart Little*, 1945, Harper.

Winter, Milo Kendall (1888 – 1956)

Midwestern artist Milo Winter trained at the Art Institute of Chicago. He illustrated numerous titles, ranging from the *Wonder Book* (1913) to *Twenty Thousand Leagues Under The Sea* (1922). He once noted that he preferred the whimsical to the real, and his drawings often portray humorous knaves and beautiful maidens. His books belong to the outpouring of fine illustrated volumes for children produced during the Edwardian age. Some books, like his *Arabian Nights*, were released under his name. Later editions of his illustrated books appeared in the Windemere series. See also Winter in the author section.

Wright, Maginel

Wright, Maginel (1881 – 1966)

Frank Lloyd Wright's baby sister began her career illustrating the stories of Laura Bancroft (an L. Frank Baum pseudonym). She had a long and prolific career illustrating children's books, school readers, and magazine stories and was one of Volland Publishing Company's regular illustrators. Her luminous use of color and elegant sense of line make her work as distinctive as her brother's. Wright signed her work "Maginel Wright Enright" (her first husband) and later used the name "Maginel Wright Barney."

Gordon, E. *Billy Bunny's Fortune*, 1919.

Willson, D. *Honey Bear,* 1923.

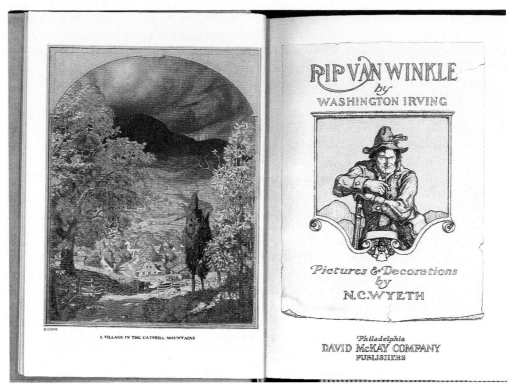

Wyeth, N.C.

Wyeth, N.C. (1881 – 1945)

Nobody did pirates, Mohawks, and battling heroes better than Wyeth. Throughout his long career and more than 3000 illustrations, Wyeth was known as the preeminent illustrator of adventure. He did more than 25 books for the Scribners Classic series, and his style was greatly influenced by his teacher, Howard Pyle. At the time of his death, Wyeth was considered one of the best of America's illustrators. Because of the often dark shades of his oil paints, many collectors prefer the "cleaner" color plates of early editions, which truly show the range of his palette. His work is sought by collectors of the Brandywine school, the Wyeth family (both his son and grandson are noted American painters), and children's books. Since his work was so popular during his lifetime, his books were issued in fairly large print runs and are still available at reasonable prices. Many of his works for Scribner and McKay were reprinted by Garden City Publishing.

Cooper, F. *Deerslayer*, 1925, Scribner.

Cooper, F. *Last of the Mohicans*, 1919, Scribner.

Creswick. *Robin Hood*, 1917, McKay.

Defoe, D. *Robinson Crusoe*, 1920, Cosmopolitan.

Irving. *Rip Van Winkle*, 1921, McKay.

Lanier. *The Boy's King Arthur*, 1917, Scribner.

Porter, K. *Scottish Chiefs*, 1921, Scribner.

Stevenson, R.L. *Black Arrow,* 1916, Scribner.

Stevenson, R.L. *David Balfour,* 1924, Scribner.

Stevenson, R.L. *Kidnapped*, 1913, Scribner.

Stevenson, R.L. *Treasure Island,* 1911, Scribner.

Verne, J. *Mysterious Island*, 1918, Scribner.

VOLLAND COMPANY

P. F. Volland Publishers, 58 East Washington Street, Chicago, in the Publishers Row district, was founded in 1908 by Paul Frederick Volland and later moved to Joliet, Illinois. The Volland company specialized in greeting cards and printed gift items, then moved into the children's book market, concentrating on fine quality printing, using expensive paper, full-color illustrated paper-over-hardboard covers, endpapers and numerous full-color illustrations throughout. They used free-lance writers and artists, buying material that fit the company image, picture books with cheerful stories that would please parents as well as children. Two of their most popular authors were Elizabeth Gordon and Johnny Gruelle, and illustrators included Gruelle, Gertrude Kay, Maginal Wright, and Lane Campbell.

Volland also produced toys or contracted with toy companies to have toys produced that matched story characters, their most famous book-and-toy combination being Johnny Gruelle's *Raggedy Ann.* Volland also created book series in which books were written by a variety of authors and illustrated by Volland artists or freelance artists over a period of time. The "series" designation was probably created for advertising purposes, as the books are otherwise unrelated. These series included *Sunny Books,* 12mo size books about 7 ½ " high by 6" wide, with about 40 pages, and *Happy Children Books* and *Nature Children Books* which were slightly narrower than standard size, about 9" high by 6" wide, and about 100 pages long. The 1912 printing of Elizabeth Gordon's *Bird Children* does not indicate that it is part of a series, but a 1920 1st edition of Gordon's *Turned In-To's* lists *Bird Children* on its advertising page as one of the *Nature Children* books. Again, these designations were apparently created for advertising purposes after some of the books had already been issued.

The Volland company ceased publication of most of their book lines in the early 1930s, selling off various rights and plates to other publishers, including Wise-Parslow, New York, who acquired many of the Elizabeth Gordon books. Wise-Parslow's reprint of Gordon's *Flower Children* is about a half inch higher and a half inch wider than the original Volland edition. Chicago-based Donohue purchased the Raggedy Ann book rights. In the late 1930s Gruelle's heirs formed their own company and acquired much of this material, including original plates of Gruelle's work, from Donohue.

Volland books were carefully crafted to be visually pleasing, and have become popular with collectors. The covers are illustrated paper-over-board, with illustrations on both front and back covers, and the cover theme often carried over to the colorful endpapers.

Listed below in their series designation are titles found in the advertising pages of the backs of the books. Many of these books are listed under the Author section of this book. Others are not, because we have not yet located a dealer familiar with the book and therefore could not give it a value. Front and back covers and endpapers of several Volland books are shown, to give an idea of the work typical of the Volland Publishing Company.

Sunny Books

These books were advertised as, "Your children are safe with Volland Books. It is the Volland ideal that books should make children happy and build character unconsciously and should contain nothing to cause fright, suggest fear, glorify mischief, excuse malice or condone cruelty."

Betty, Bobby and Bubbles, Edith Mitchell
Billy Bunny's Fortune, Elizabeth Gordon, illustrated by Maginel Wright
Come Play With Me, Olive Beaupre Miller
Daddy Dander, Maude Hankins, illustrated by Ve Elizabeth Cadie
Dinky Ducklings, written and illustrated by Lang Campbell
Eddie Elephant, written and illustrated by Johnny Gruelle
Funny Little Book, written and illustrated by Johnny Gruelle
Gigglequicks, Miriam Clark Potter
Grasshopper Green, John Rae
Happy Home Children, Elizabeth Gordon, illustrated by Marion Foster
Honey Bear, Dixie Willson, illustrated by Maginel Wright
How Sing Found the World was Round, Sydney Reid
Jolly Shadowman, Gertrude Kay

Just for You, Pauline Croll
Little Babs, George Mitchell
Little Brown Bear, written and illustrated by Johnny Gruelle
Little Red Balloon, Caroline Hofman
Little Sunny Stories, written and illustrated by Johnny Gruelle
Lovely Garden, Fairmont Snyder
Myself and I, Helen Van Valkenburgh
Over the Rainbow Bridge, Louise Marshall Haynes
Peeps, Nancy Cox-McCormack
Princess Finds a Playmate, Nancy Cox-McCormack
Remarkable Tale of a Whale, Isa L. Wright
Six Who Were Left in a Shoe, Padraic Colum
Sunny Bunny, Nina Wilcox, illustrated by Johnny Gruelle
Sunny Rhymes for Happy Children, Olive Beaupre Miller
Tale of Johnny Mouse, Elizabeth Gordon
Tales of Little Cats, Carrie Jacobs-Bond
Tales of Little Dogs, Carrie Jacobs-Bond, illustrated by Katharine Dodge
Three Little Frogs, John L. Mee
Tommy Tingle, Sarah Addington, illustrated by Gertrude Kay
Treasure Things, Annette Wynne
Tuffy Good Luck, Dixie Willson, Ilona de Kerekjarto
Wise Gray Cat, Caroline Hofman

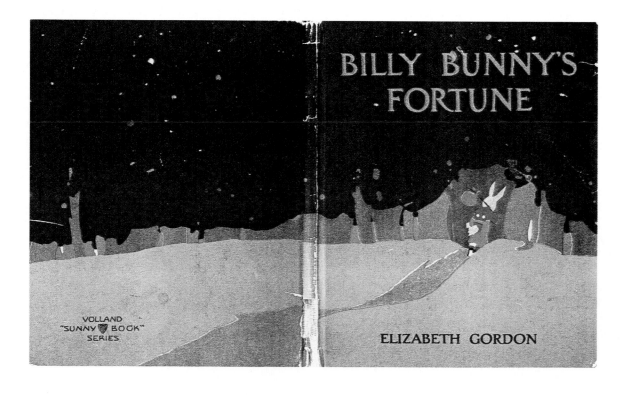

Happy Children Books

Advertised with the same slogan as the Sunny Books, but the added line, "That is why they are called Books for Good Children." This larger format included the early Raggedy Ann books.

Fairy Tales from France, W. T. Larned, illustrated by John Rae
Friendly Fairies, written and illustrated by Johnny Gruelle
Helping the Weatherman, written and illustrated by Gertrude Kay
Kernel Cob and Little Miss Sweetclover, George Mitchell, illustrated by Tony Sarg
My Very Own Fairy Stories, written and illustrated by Johnny Gruelle
Perhappsy Chaps, Ruth Plumly Thompson, illustrated by A. Henderson
Rhymes for Kindly Children, Fairmont Snyder, illustrated by J. Gruelle
Quacky Doodles' and Danny Daddles' Book, Rose S. Hubbell, illustrated by Johnny Gruelle
Winkle, Twinkle and Lollypop, Nina W. Smith, illustrated by Katherine Dodge

Nature Children Books

Animal Children, Edith Brown Kirkwood, illustrated by M. T. Ross
Bird Children, Elizabeth Gordon, illustrated by M. T. Ross
Fables in Rhyme, Wm. Trowbridge Larned, illustrated by John Rae
Flower Children, Elizabeth Gordon, illustrated by M. T. Ross
Mother Earth's Children, Elizabeth Gordon, illustrated by M. T. Ross
Turned-Intos, Elizabeth Gordon, illustrated by Janet Laura Scott
Whisk Away On a Sunbeam, Olive B. Miller, illustrated by Maginal Wright
Wild Flower Children, Elizabeth Gordon, illustrated by Janet Laura Scott

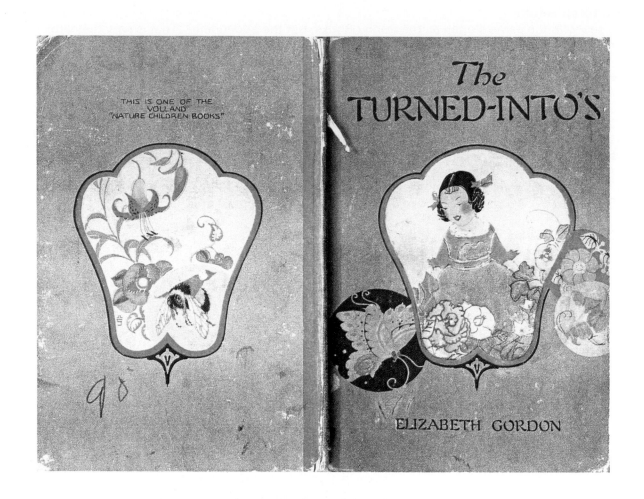

Wise-Parslow edition

PUBLISHERS

The following information on publishers is included to help collectors identify the age or a possible first edition. For price and information on specific titles, please look under the author or series sections.

Identifying first editions of books, especially children's books, can be difficult. In the early days, publishers might change how they marked their first editions to fit the artwork or the whims of a particular editor. British publishers rarely identified the date of publication or distinguished first editions from later editions prior to the adoption of the International Copyright Convention of 1957.

Children's books were often reproduced without crediting the earlier editions or, in some cases, the author. Both British and American writers of the Victorian age frequently complained about trans-Atlantic piracy. Later, publishers like Garden City or Donohue might buy the actual printing plates from the original publisher and not alter the copyright page.

During the Edwardian era, many fine illustrated books were brought out simultaneously in various editions including a signed, numbered, limited edition as well as a trade edition. For authors popular on both sides of the Atlantic, you might find an American and a British "first" edition issued at the same time. During WWII and the following years of paper shortages, you might also find some British authors whose American first editions predate their British first editions.

For series collectors, one simple way to identify first editions is to check the publisher's advertisements in the front or back of the book. First editions rarely carry advertisements for titles that follow that particular title in series. However, some series were carefully planned in advance by publishers, allowing future titles to appear on the advertising pages in first editions.

Finally, some collectors of first editions are seeking "first state" editions. These printings may include errors, incorrect text placement, changes in the binding colors or other "points" of identification. These points are usually listed in magazines such as *American Book Collector,* auction catalogs or other specialized reference material. Please see the bibliography at the back of this book for a further listing of resources.

Abingdon Press
First editions generally carry no additional printing dates on the copyright page.

Henry Altemus
First editions from this Philadelphia publisher show the first edition date with no additional printings indicated on the back of the title page.

Applewood Books
This American publisher recently began reprinting rare children's books such as *The Wizard of Oz Waddle Book* and early titles in the Nancy Drew series. These reissues are currently in print, clearly identified as Applewood Books on the title page, and should not cost more than the retail price in the secondary market.

D. Appleton
Prior to 1902, first editions carried only the first edition printing date on the copyright page. After 1902, first editions may be identified with the words "first edition" or a "1" appearing on the last page of the text.

Bobbs-Merrill Company
This Indianapolis publisher was founded in 1885 by two booksellers, Silas Bowen and Samual Merrill, and used the imprint, Bowen-Merrill Company. In 1903, the name was changed to Bobbs-Merrill. Early first editions may only show the month of publication on the copyright page. Starting in the 1920s, some books carried the words "first edition", and, in the 1930s, some first editions were identified with a bow-and-arrow symbol on the copyright page. For Oz collectors, Bobbs-Merrill is best known for buying the printer's plates of *The Wonderful Wizard of Oz* from the Geo. M. Hill Company. The Bobbs-Merrill edition published in 1903 carried the title of *The New Wizard of Oz* and new cover, title page and endpaper illustrations by W.W. Denslow. In 1913, Bobbs-Merrill leased these plates to the M.A. Donohue Company of Chicago. Various Bobbs-Merrill versions of *The New Wizard of Oz* continued to appear, including a 1939 MGM movie version.

Books of Wonder
Books of Wonder is the publishing imprint of a New York City children's bookstore with the same name. In the 1980s, they began printing reproductions of first editions of illustrated children's books, including the first six books in the Oz series. Most of their books are still in print. Like Applewood (see above), these books generally sell for retail price or less in the secondary market. They also use the imprint "Emerald City Press".

Bowen-Merrill Company
See Bobbs-Merrill.

Blackie & Sons

This British publisher began printing children's books during the 1800s. Early books usually do not have a printing date indicated.

Blue Ribbon Books

This subsidiary of the Doubleday, Doran company did specialty books including *The Wizard of Oz Waddle Book* in 1934.

Henry T. Coates

First editions may say "published" followed by the month and year or have only a single date on copyright page.

Copp, Clark Company, Ltd.

This Toronto publisher issued the Canadian editions of several children's books and series. Of particular interest to Oz collectors, the Copp, Clark's Oz books appear to be identical with the Reilly & Britton or Reilly & Lee books published between 1907 and 1931. These books command prices slightly higher than the comparable Reilly editions since far fewer copies were printed under the Copp, Clark name. In the 1940s, Copp, Clark reissued some of their Oz titles without color plates, and these are not considered collectible. Finally, in the 1960s, some Reilly & Lee reissues of the Oz series bear the Copp, Clark name on the title page due to a printer's error.

Coward-McCann

From 1928 to 1935, first editions would show a colophon with a torch on the copyright page or would have no additional publishing dates on the copyright page. For books first published outside the U.S., the back of the title page may say "First American Edition."

Thomas Y. Crowell

Early first editions varied, with the publisher using the words "first edition" or no additional printing dates on the copyright page. Starting in the 1940s, first editions were identified with a numerical code.

Cupples & Leon Company

A New York publishing house, Cupples & Leon specialized in series books and reprints of newspaper cartoons such as "Buster Brown." The company was started in 1902 by Victor Cupples and Arthur Leon. First editions were not designated from other printings.

Dean & Son

This London firm was one of the first English publishers to make extensive use of lithography and chromo-lithography for printing illustrations. Starting in the 1840s, they began making movable and flap books. (These books were often published under their own name such as Dean's New Book of Dissolving Pictures 1860). The firm adopted the name Dean & Son in 1846. Prior to that, they published under the name Thomas Dean or Dean & Munday.

J.M. Dent

This English publisher began printing children's books in the 19th century. Prior to the 1930s, Dent did not identify the date of printing. After 1929, books began appearing with the words "first published" followed by the year of publication.

M.A. Donohue & Co.

This Chicago publisher generally did not identify the dates of their publications. They bought or leased printing plates of books first published by other publishers, including P. F. Volland and Bobbs-Merrill. For example, the Donohue editions of the Raggedy Ann books lack Volland's elaborate endpapers and command lower prices than the earlier Volland editions.

George H. Doran

Early first editions show a GHD symbol on the title page or copyright page. After 1921, the GHD symbol appears on the copyright page under the copyright notice.

Doubleday, Doran

The words "first edition" usually appear on the copyright page with no additional printings indicated.

E.P. Dutton

Until 1928, Dutton first editions generally have a single date on the copyright page. After 1928, the words "first edition" or "first published" may appear on the copyright page.

Garden City Publishing Co.

This New Jersey publisher reprinted other publishers' originals. Many of their reprints appear to have been made from the original publisher's plates and may not show the actual date of printing. Other Garden City editions may carry the date in the artwork, on the frontispiece, or on the back of the title page.

Grosset & Dunlap

This American publisher reprinted other publishers' books and often did not designate the date of printing. On their own originals, the printing date may appear on the copyright page.

Johnny Gruelle Co.

This publishing company was formed in 1939 by Johnny Gruelle's widow and sons to print his works, especially the Raggedy Ann and Andy books. The family acquired many of the original printers' plates from the Donohue Company. Johnny Gruelle had also received rights to much of his work from Volland in the early 1930s when Volland ceased publishing children's books. The Johnny Gruelle Co. continued to build on Gruelle's legacy, using previously published stories and adding new artwork created by Justin Gruelle, Johnny's brother, and Worth Gruelle, Johnny's son. In the 1940s, the company sold licenses and authorizations to other publishers to continue the Gruelle books. Date of publication in Gruelle Co. books is not designated.

Harcourt Brace
Until 1926, no additional printing date would appear in first editions. Later first editions may show the month and year published or have a "1" on the copyright page. After 1935, the words "first edition" or "first American edition" begin to appear on the copyright page.

Harper & Brothers
Until 1911, this publisher used a single date on the back of the title page. From 1912 to 1922, they used an alphabetic code to identify the first editions. After 1922, the words "first edition" appeared on the copyright page.

George G. Harrap & Co.
No additional printing date may appear on a first edition copyright page. Original printing date may also not be designated in books.

Geo. M. Hill Co.
This Chicago publisher is best known for publishing the first edition of *The Wonderful Wizard of Oz* by L. Frank Baum in 1900. The first edition "points" of this book (which can command thousands of dollars in rare book auctions) have been extensively documented in *Bibliographia Oziana,* published by the International Wizard of Oz Club.

Henry Holt
First editions should have no additional printing date on copyright page or back of title page. After 1944, the words "first edition" or "first printing" may appear on copyright page.

Houghton Mifflin
This publisher's books date back to the late 19th century. First editions may have a single date on the title page.

The International Wizard of Oz Club
This club of Oz fans and collectors began printing various Oz books and related material starting in the 1970s. Sometimes, their books were facsimiles of rare books such as *The Oz Toy Book.* The quality of these books varies, and their resale value should be comparable to other modern reprints.

John Martin's Book
This publishing company was founded in 1912 by Morgan Shepard, who had previously written a newsletter for children and signed himself "John Martin." The hardcover publication was sold by subscription as a monthly publication for children and contained stories, puzzles, games, and various illustrations. Shepard hired a variety of freelance artists and writers for his books, and many later achieved fame in their own right. The value of the books varies according to the talent or later fame of the contributors.

Alfred A. Knopf
Until 1933, the first edition's copyright page or the back of the title page would have only a single date or no additional printing dates. After 1934, the words "first edition" may appear on the copyright page with no additional printing dates.

Lee & Shepard
The company was founded in 1861. See also Lothrop.

J.B. Lippincott
Until 1924, Lippincott used a single date on the copyright page or copyright date one year later than the title page date to designate their first editions. After 1925, the words "first edition" may appear, or a numerical code, or the words "published" followed by the month and year.

Little, Brown
Through 1929, first editions had only a single date on the back of the title page. Later first editions from this Boston publisher may be designated by the words "first edition" or "first printing".

Little Golden Books
First editions of these books generally had an "A" printed on the first, second or last page. Sometimes the "A" is hidden by the binding.

Longmans Green Co.
Established in 1724 in London, Longmans formed a New York branch in 1887. Until the 1920s, first editions generally had the same date on the back of the title page as the front. In the 1920s, the company switched to using the words "first edition" or "first published" to designate first editions.

Lothrop, Lee & Shepard Company, Inc.
Founded in Boston in 1850, the company incorporated in 1887 as D. Lothrop Co. By 1894, they used the name, Lothrop Publishing Company. In 1904, Lothrop consolidated with Lee & Shepard. In 1947, the company was purchased by Crown. First editions may be designated in a variety of ways including no additional publishing dates on the copyright page.

Macmillan (U.K.)
The British Macmillan generally gives no additional publishing date on the copyright page of first editions.

Macmillan (U.S.A.)

Through the 1930s, first editions of the American Macmillan generally stated the month and year of publication with a single date on the copyright page. After 1936, the words "first published" may appear on the copyright page.

McGraw-Hill

First editions have no additional printing dates on the back of the title page.

Medici Society

This English publisher issued a number of fine illustrated books, sometimes commissioning artists to provide new illustrations for well-known stories. First editions probably have no additional printing dates on the back of the title page.

Minton, Balch

For first editions, the date of printing appeared on the back of the title page with no additional printings indicated.

William Morrow

First editions generally have no additional printing dates indicated on the back of the title page. Occasionally, the words "first printing" may also appear, followed by the year, and with no additional dates indicated.

Ernest Nister, London

The English representative for the Nuremberg firm of Nister coordinated a variety of dissolving picture books and stand-up books for the Victorian children's market. The German craftsmen provided the fine printing, and the English agents carefully researched subjects intended to appeal to their market. The height of their art came with *Peeps Into Fairyland* (circa 1895), but they continued to produce books until WWI ended the trade.

Oxford University Press

This publisher had both a British and an American branch. First editions may have the words "first edition" on the back of the title page or may be designated by a single date on the copyright page with no additional dates.

L. C. Page & Company Publishers

This Boston company was founded in 1892. In 1914, they changed their name to Page Company, but by 1923 had resumed the L.C. Page name. They published many children's series including Anne of Green Gables, Glad Books, and Little Colonel.

Pickering & Inglis

The date of printing may appear on the title page. No additional dates appear in first editions.

G.P. Putnam's Sons

There is an American and a British Putnam's. The American publisher designated first editions by the words "first American edition" followed by the year or by showing no additional printing dates on the copyright page. In the 1920s and 1930s, some American books might also state "first edition" on the copyright page.

Rand McNally

Early first editions might have the letters "MA" on the copyright page or they would show no additional printing dates. After 1937, the words "first published" followed by the year or an alphabetical code might indicate a first edition.

Reilly & Britton or Reilly & Lee

This Chicago company published a variety of children's books and series. In 1919, they changed their name to Reilly & Lee. Under the Reilly & Lee name, they continued to publish children's books into the 1960s. First editions generally have no additional printing dates on the copyright page or, for a series, the publisher's advertisements generally end with or before that edition's title.

George Routledge & Sons

This British publisher began printing children's books in the 1800s. Their books were often designed by Edmund Evans (see Illustrators section). They are rarely dated.

Scribner's

Early first editions of Scribner's have a single date on the title page or no additional printings indicated on the back of the title page or copyright page. Starting in 1930, an "A" may be printed on the copyright page to designate the first edition.

Viking Press

First editions prior to 1937 usually had no additional printing dates on the back of the title page. Later, the words "first published" or "first edition" with no additional printing dates might be used.

P.F. Volland

See section Volland Company.

Frederick Warne & Co.

This English publishing company is best known for promoting Victorian author-illustrators, such as Beatrix Potter and Leslie Brooke. The London firm was started in 1865 with a New York branch established by 1881. Warne tended to keep their books in print for decades. Like many British publishers, first editions may not be clearly designated from later printings.

Whitman Publishing Co.

This Racine, Wisconsin, publisher issued the Big Little Books and the Better Little Books as well as a variety of series books based on comic strip characters or popular movie stars. They also reprinted various children's classics.

GLOSSARY

Annuals: Books issued once a year that collected the works published in a magazine. Since many children's writers and illustrators of the 19th and early 20th century also wrote for these children's magazines, annuals are sought by collectors for this additional material. In Great Britain, annuals of newspaper comic strips such as *Rupert* might contain strips published during the year and an additional new story.

Antiquarian Booksellers Association of America: The trade association of American antiquarian booksellers, founded in 1949. The British equivalent is the Antiquarian Bookseller's Association International founded in 1906.

Board: Material used to form the cover of a hard-bound book, usually paste-board. The boards were covered with cloth or leather, leading to terms such as "cloth bound" or "leather binding."

Cloth binding: The majority of hard bound children's books published in the 19th and 20th century were cloth bound. As opposed to leather bindings, cloth bindings were relatively inexpensive. The cloth was wrapped around a board (usually paste-board or another stiff base) and glued on the edges. Children's book publishers, such as Reilly & Britton, often used whatever cloth was available so that the color of binding may vary even when books are all from the same edition.

Cloth bound: See cloth binding.

Color plate: A color plate is a full-page illustration in color that is printed on paper that is a different weight or quality than the regular pages. Color plates may be bound directly into the text or mounted on a stiffer paper.

Copyright page: Generally, the back of the title page will have copyright information. Some publishers, such as Garden City, may put this information on the title page.

Dust jacket: In the 19th century, books were shipped to the bookseller in protective paper wrappings known as "dust jackets," "dust wrappings" or "wrappers." These were usually discarded by the buyer as soon as the book got home. Early dust jackets were often plainer than the book cover beneath. By the 1940s, the reverse was true, and the dust jackets were highly illustrated and the book covers left plain. Collectors usually pay more for a book with intact dust jacket (see also Explanation of Pricing in the front of the book).

Edition: See first edition.

Endpapers: The double leaves (pages) added at the front and back during the binding process. The outer leaf is pasted down to the inner surface of the cover, while the inner leaf forms the first or last page of the book. Endpapers can be plain or decorated, or contain a double-page illustration related to the text. Sometimes they are called endleaves.

Errata: Errors made in the printing or binding of the book. Sometimes, the errata can be used to identify first editions and first printings as such mistakes are usually corrected by the publisher as soon as possible.

Ex-library: This term applies to a book that has been removed from the collection of a public library. Ex-library editions are usually priced far less than originals because they have been altered or marked by the library. They might be rebound by the library, have cards pasted over the endpapers, or be stamped with the library's name throughout the text.

First edition: A first edition is generally defined to be the first time that a book appeared in print. For collectors and dealers of illustrated books, a first edition may be the first time that the text and pictures have appeared together. For example, although the Maxfield Parrish illustrated copy of Nathaniel Hawthorne's *Wonder Book* was printed many years after Hawthorne's work first appeared, it would be the "first edition" that appeared with Parrish's pictures. For books that are first privately printed by the author, such as Beatrix Potter's work, a "first" may be termed "first published edition" to designate the first edition published by a company, such as Warne. Collectors of first editions may also seek first states of books, first editions that contain certain features (usually errors) that do not appear in other copies.

Frontispiece: This illustration faces the title page of the book.

Gilt edges: Many finer editions of books had their pages trimmed and gilded along the outer edges. Sometimes, to save money, the publisher might only gild the top of the page.

Gilt lettering: When the letters are printed with gold-colored, metallic ink, the book has gilt lettering. Gilt lettering usually appears on the cover. In some cases, it may appear in the text as chapter headings. In some children's books, the picture on the front cover may also have gilt ink.

Half bound: A half bound book that has a leather spine while the rest of the cover is cloth or paper covered.

Half cloth: A half cloth book has a cloth spine while the rest of the cover is paper board sides. The title or cover illustration may be pasted on the paper board side.

Library binding: As books become worn by library patrons, they may be rebound. These library bindings replaced the original binding, and often required the page edges to be trimmed slightly from the original size. Library bindings are usually easy to spot as they are of a thicker, more durable material than regular book covers. They also considerably reduce the price of the book. See also ex-library.

Limited edition: A book issued in a stated number of copies. In the Edwardian era, fine illustrated books were often issued in a "limited edition" with leather bindings as well as a "trade edition" with a regular cover.

Marbled paper: Marbled paper is generally used for endpapers or covers, and has a colored pattern similiar to marble. Marbled paper is made by lowering the sheet of paper into a bath of dye where the colors have been swirled into a pattern by a stick or comb. Marbled papers first appeared in Europe in the 1600s. Starting in the 19th century, some publishers experimented with using marbled cloth for covers.

Mounted illustrations: Engravings or color plate illustrations which have been pasted down or attached to another type of paper have been "mounted" by the printer. For fine illustrated books, the illustration may be mounted on a much stronger sheet of paper and further protected by a tissue overlay to prevent the ink from rubbing off on the facing page.

Movables: Movables is a term most commonly used by British booksellers to describe pop-ups and other children's books that have illustrations that move.

No date: In this guide, "no date" or "undated" means a book that has no date of publication printed on the copyright or title page.

Paper boards: The paper boards are the stiff material that forms the outer cover of a book. Generally, these are made from pasted boards, layers of paper glued together layer on layer. When used by a dealer to describe the cover of a book, this generally means that the boards are plain and not covered by cloth, leather or marbled paper. See also half bound and half cloth.

Picture book: In this text, a picture book is a book that relies mostly on pictures to convey the story to very young readers.

Plate, plates: Generally, this term is used by booksellers to designate full-color illustrations printed on a different paper stock than the rest of the text. "Plate" may also refer to the actual printing plates used to produce the book, i.e., "The Johnny Gruelle Co. acquired the plates from Donohue to continue publishing Gruelle's work."

Points: Differences in printing or paper between one edition or state of a book and another are called "points". Dealers and collectors may use "points", such as a mis-spelled word, to distinguish a first edition or a rare edition of a book. Points are <u>not</u> marks, wear or tear, or other features picked up by a book during its normal shelf life.

Pop-up: These three-dimensional pictures have been cut and glued so that they "pop up" when the book has been opened. "Pop-ups" and other forms of movable books became a regular part of the children's book trade in the 19th century, but they date back to the 16th century. Early pop-ups and other movable books are fairly rare, since repeated use tended to destroy the pictures.

Privately printed: If an author pays for the printing of a book, then it is generally held to be "privately printed." Several 19th and 20th century authors, such as Beatrix Potter, Lewis Carroll, and L. Frank Baum, privately printed various works. Since authors rarely paid for more than a few hundred copies, these texts are considered either rare and valuable or an oddity, depending on the author's collectibility.

Provenance: The pedigree of a book's ownership rarely affects the price unless the book came from a famous person's library or bears an unusual autograph. If these features affect the price, the dealer may offer "provenance" to prove that these claims are true and justify the increased price.

Re-backed: A book that has had its spine or backstrip replaced has been re-backed. This, like any replacement in cover or pages, decreases the value of a book for the serious collector.

Series: This refers to a set of books with an on-going theme, a continuation of stories about specific characters, or an over-all series label put on the set by the publisher. A publisher series label is easy to classify. A continuation of stories about a set of characters is tricky. If a publisher, author, agent or syndicate creates a character or setting, then uses that subject in a number of books, everyone agrees that this is a series. But sometimes an author produces a successful novel and so decides to write a sequel. And sometimes that leads to another book or two over a period of time. Is that a series? This isn't always clear. Therefore, we've probably listed books by authors that some readers consider series, and occasionally put something in the series section that some might prefer listed by author. And sometimes we have only seen one book in a series and there is nothing about it to suggest that it is part of a series, and so we have erred. All we can say is that at no time have we based our call on the literary quality of the books listed. This is not a recommended reading list for children, but rather an identification guide for book collectors.

Sheet: Essentially, the sheet refers to the paper in the state that it is used by the printer. After printing, sheets are folded and cut by the printer to form two, four, or eight pages.

Size: Book size is defined in booksellers' catalogs by historical book printing terms. These terms referred to the original size of a sheet of printer's paper and then to the size obtained after a number of folds. Folio was the largest size, over thirteen inches tall, quarto or 4to meant between nine and twelve inches tall, octavo or 8vo meant standard size of about eight or nine inches tall, and duodecimo or 12mo meant under seven inches or small. As these terms can be confusing to collectors, we've tried to stay with *oversize, standard,* and *small* as designations. If the book size is well beyond these designations, we try to give precise inches of the cover height and width when available.

Spine: The spine is the part of the book which is visible when the book is closed and placed on a shelf.

Toy Books: Originally, this term refered to the 19th century small books designed by Edmund Evans (see Illustrators) that measured approximately 9" x 7". Each book contained six pages of text and six pages of colored illustrations. Many booksellers now use the term to refer to books with movable parts or other features that make them more of a toy than a book.

Tipped In: A separate piece of paper that has been inserted into the text and lightly attached with gum or paste on the inner edge has been tipped in. Color plates were often tipped in by publishers since they were printed separately from the rest of the text. Tipped in pages can come loose and fall out as the glue ages.

Tissue overlay: Printers often added a fine piece of tissue paper between a full-page illustration and the text page. This tissue overlay prevented the ink from rubbing off the text page and spoiling the picture.

Volume: This is another word for book. However, it can also mean a book that is one part of a larger whole, as a volume in a set of encyclopedias. We have tried to use the word volume in this context. In a series, where the stories may well be consecutive in the lives of characters but are nonetheless independent stories, we list the number of books in the series. But in a series that is of an encyclopedic nature, where each book deals with a section of the material, we list the number of volumes in the series. There are some very fine lines in this sort of judgment call, and so we've tried to make our choices in the direction of clarity of meaning for the reader.

Wood-block, Wood-cut: A wood-block illustration is done on a carved wooden block instead of a metal engraving. After the illustration is engraved on the wood, the impression may be made directly on the paper or, more commonly, on electrotype metal blocks which are then used during the printing process.

BIBLIOGRAPHY

American Authors and Books, W. J. Burke, 1962, Crown.

American Writers for Children, 1900 – 1960, edited by John Cech, 1983, Gale Research.

Arbuthnot Anthology of Children's Literature, May Hill Arbuthnot, 1961, Scott Foresman and Co., IL.

Authors of Books for Young People, Martha Eades Ward, 1971, Scarecrow Press, NJ.

Bibliographia Oziana, Douglas G. Greene and Peter E. Hanff, 1988, International Wizard of Oz Club.

Books, Nancy Wright, 1993, Avon, NY.

Collector's Book of Children's Books, Eric Quayle, 1971, Clarkson Potter, NY.

History of Children's Book Illustration, Joyce Irene and Tessa Rose Chester, 1988, John Murray Ltd., London.

Illustrators of Children's Books 1744 – 1945, Bertha E. Mahoney Miller, editor, 1947, Horn Book, Boston.

Johnny Gruelle, Creator of Raggedy Ann and Andy, Patricia Hall, 1993, Pelican Publishing, Los Angeles.

Kate Greenaway Treasury, 1967, World Publishing, Cleveland and New York.

L. Frank Baum: The Wonder Wizard of Oz, 1956 Columbia University Libraries (exhibit catalog).

List of Books Raphael and McLeish, 1981, Harmony Books, NY.

My Father Was Uncle Wiggily, Roger Garis, 1966, McGraw-Hill, NY.

Nancy Drew Scrapbook, Karen Plunkett-Powell, 1993, St. Martin's, NY.

Oz in Canada, C. J. Hinke, 1982, Hoffer, Vancouver, BC.

Pocket Guide to the Identification of First Editions, Bill McBride, 1995, West Hartford: McBride/Publisher.

Tomart's Price Guide to 20th Century Books, John Wade, 1994, Tomart Publications, OH.

To Please a Child, Frank Joslyn Baum and Russell P. MacFall, 1961, Reilly & Lee Co., Chicago.

Twentieth Century Children's Writers, 2nd edition, 1978, MacMillan, London.

Who's Who in Children's Books, Margery Fisher, 1975, Holt Rinehart Winston, NY.

INTERNET RESOURCES

For collectors online, there are a variety of Internet resources for finding antiquarian book dealers, chatting with other collectors, and even swapping want lists. If you are connected to a commercial service, such as America Online or Compuserve, check the members' bulletin boards for areas of interest to book collectors.

A recent search of the World Wide Web using the words "antiquarian bookseller" turned up more than 50 relevant sites, and we expect these resources to grow. If you have found a favorite newsgroup or Web site for children's books, we would like to hear from you. You can reach us at healingpgs@aol.com.

rec.arts.books.childrens

This Internet newsgroup discusses everything from new titles to collecting various series books. This seems an excellent place to describe that book you read as a child of which you can't remember the title or author. With even partial descriptions of plot or illustrations, somebody usually responds with title, author, date of publication, and related works. Some collectors and dealers do advertise books for sale or trade here, or make their lists available by e-mail. Like most Internet newsgroups, blatant advertising is not welcome, and you should read a few messages before posting any information on books for sale.

http://www.abaa-booknet.com/booknet1.html

The homepage of the Antiquarian Booksellers Association of America serves as a great launching place for a search of the World Wide Web. The ABAA site has links to their member booksellers with catalogs on the Web, information about book fairs throughout the country, a directory of member booksellers by region or specialty, and links to international organizations of booksellers. The address for this site has changed slightly over the past year. If you can't connect, use Web Crawler or another Web search program and the key words "antiquarian bookseller" to find their Web address. The organization's e-mail address is abaa@panix.com.

COLLECTOR BOOKS

Informing Today's Collector

For over two decades we have been keeping collectors informed on trends and values in all fields of antiques and collectibles.

DOLLS, FIGURES & TEDDY BEARS

4707	A Decade of **Barbie** Dolls & Collectibles, 1981–1991, Summers	$19.95
4631	**Barbie** Doll Boom, 1986–1995, Augustyniak	$18.95
2079	**Barbie** Doll Fashions, Volume I, Eames	$24.95
3957	**Barbie** Exclusives, Rana	$18.95
4632	**Barbie** Exclusives, Book II, Rana	$18.95
4557	**Barbie,** The First 30 Years, Deutsch	$24.95
4657	**Barbie** Years, 1959–1995, Olds	$16.95
3310	**Black Dolls,** 1820–1991, Perkins	$17.95
3873	**Black Dolls,** Book II, Perkins	$17.95
1529	Collector's Encyclopedia of **Barbie** Dolls, DeWein	$19.95
4506	Collector's Guide to **Dolls in Uniform,** Bourgeois	$18.95
3727	Collector's Guide to **Ideal Dolls,** Izen	$18.95
3728	Collector's Guide to Miniature **Teddy Bears,** Powell	$17.95
3967	Collector's Guide to **Trolls,** Peterson	$19.95
4571	**Liddle Kiddles,** Identification & Value Guide, Langford	$18.95
4645	**Madame Alexander** Dolls Price Guide #21, Smith	$9.95
3733	**Modern Collector's** Dolls, Sixth Series, Smith	$24.95
3991	**Modern Collector's** Dolls, Seventh Series, Smith	$24.95
4647	**Modern Collector's** Dolls, Eighth Series, Smith	$24.95
4640	Patricia Smith's **Doll Values,** Antique to Modern, 12th Edition	$12.95
3826	Story of **Barbie,** Westenhouser	$19.95
1513	**Teddy Bears & Steiff** Animals, Mandel	$9.95
1817	**Teddy Bears & Steiff** Animals, 2nd Series, Mandel	$19.95
2084	**Teddy Bears, Annalee's & Steiff** Animals, 3rd Series, Mandel	$19.95
1808	Wonder of **Barbie,** Manos	$9.95
1430	World of **Barbie** Dolls, Manos	$9.95

FURNITURE

1457	American **Oak** Furniture, McNerney	$9.95
3716	American **Oak** Furniture, Book II, McNerney	$12.95
1118	Antique **Oak** Furniture, Hill	$7.95
2132	Collector's Encyclopedia of **American** Furniture, Vol. I, Swedberg	$24.95
2271	Collector's Encyclopedia of **American** Furniture, Vol. II, Swedberg	$24.95
3720	Collector's Encyclopedia of **American** Furniture, Vol. III, Swedberg	$24.95
3878	Collector's Guide to **Oak** Furniture, George	$12.95
1755	Furniture of the **Depression Era,** Swedberg	$19.95
3906	**Heywood-Wakefield** Modern Furniture, Rouland	$18.95
1885	**Victorian** Furniture, Our American Heritage, McNerney	$9.95
3829	**Victorian** Furniture, Our American Heritage, Book II, McNerney	$9.95
3869	**Victorian** Furniture books, 2 volume set, McNerney	$19.90

JEWELRY, HATPINS, WATCHES & PURSES

1712	Antique & Collector's **Thimbles** & Accessories, Mathis	$19.95
1748	Antique **Purses,** Revised Second Ed., Holiner	$19.95
1278	Art Nouveau & Art Deco **Jewelry,** Baker	$9.95
4558	**Christmas Pins,** Past and Present, Gallina	$18.95
3875	Collecting Antique **Stickpins,** Kerins	$16.95
3722	Collector's Ency. of **Compacts, Carryalls & Face Powder Boxes,** Mueller	$24.95
4655	Complete Price Guide to **Watches,** #16, Shugart	$26.95
1716	Fifty Years of Collectible **Fashion Jewelry,** 1925-1975, Baker	$19.95
1424	**Hatpins** & Hatpin Holders, Baker	$9.95
4570	Ladies' **Compacts,** Gerson	$24.95
1181	100 Years of Collectible **Jewelry,** 1850-1950, Baker	$9.95
2348	20th Century Fashionable Plastic **Jewelry,** Baker	$19.95
3830	Vintage **Vanity Bags & Purses,** Gerson	$24.95

TOYS, MARBLES & CHRISTMAS COLLECTIBLES

3427	**Advertising Character** Collectibles, Dotz	$17.95
2333	Antique & Collector's **Marbles,** 3rd Ed., Grist	$9.95
3827	Antique & Collector's **Toys,** 1870–1950, Longest	$24.95
3956	Baby Boomer **Games,** Identification & Value Guide, Polizzi	$24.95
3717	**Christmas** Collectibles, 2nd Edition, Whitmyer	$24.95
1752	**Christmas** Ornaments, Lights & Decorations, Johnson	$19.95
4649	Classic Plastic **Model Kits,** Polizzi	$24.95

4559	Collectible **Action Figures,** 2nd Ed., Manos	$17.95
3874	Collectible Coca-Cola Toy **Trucks,** deCourtivron	$24.95
2338	Collector's Encyclopedia of **Disneyana,** Longest, Stern	$24.95
4639	Collector's Guide to **Diecast Toys & Scale Models,** Johnson	$19.95
4651	Collector's Guide to **Tinker Toys,** Strange	$18.95
4566	Collector's Guide to **Tootsietoys,** 2nd Ed., Richter	$19.95
3436	Grist's Big Book of **Marbles**	$19.95
3970	Grist's Machine-Made & Contemporary **Marbles,** 2nd Ed.	$9.95
4569	**Howdy Doody,** Collector's Reference and Trivia Guide, Koch	$16.95
4723	**Matchbox®** Toys, 1948 to 1993, Johnson, 2nd Ed	$18.95
3823	**Mego** Toys, An Illustrated Value Guide, Chrouch	15.95
1540	**Modern Toys** 1930–1980, Baker	$19.95
3888	**Motorcycle** Toys, Antique & Contemporary, Gentry/Downs	$18.95
4728	Schroeder's Collectible **Toys,** Antique to Modern Price Guide, 3rd Ed.	$17.95
1886	Stern's Guide to **Disney** Collectibles	$14.95
2139	Stern's Guide to **Disney** Collectibles, 2nd Series	$14.95
3975	Stern's Guide to **Disney** Collectibles, 3rd Series	$18.95
2028	**Toys,** Antique & Collectible, Longest	$14.95
3979	**Zany Characters** of the Ad World, Lamphier	$16.95

INDIANS, GUNS, KNIVES, TOOLS, PRIMITIVES

1868	Antique **Tools,** Our American Heritage, McNerney	$9.95
2015	Archaic **Indian** Points & Knives, Edler	$14.95
1426	**Arrowheads** & Projectile Points, Hothem	$7.95
4633	**Big Little Books,** Jacobs	$18.95
2279	**Indian** Artifacts of the Midwest, Hothem	$14.95
3885	**Indian** Artifacts of the Midwest, Book II, Hothem	$16.95
1964	**Indian** Axes & Related Stone Artifacts, Hothem	$14.95
2023	**Keen Kutter** Collectibles, Heuring	$14.95
4724	Modern **Guns,** Identification & Values, 11th Ed., Quertermous	$12.95
4505	Standard Guide to **Razors,** Ritchie & Stewart	$9.95
4730	Standard **Knife** Collector's Guide, 3rd Ed., Ritchie & Stewart	$12.95

PAPER COLLECTIBLES & BOOKS

4633	**Big Little Books,** Jacobs	$18.95
1441	Collector's Guide to **Post Cards,** Wood	$9.95
2081	Guide to Collecting **Cookbooks,** Allen	$14.95
4648	Huxford's **Old Book** Value Guide, 8th Ed.	$19.95
2080	Price Guide to **Cookbooks & Recipe Leaflets,** Dickinson	$9.95
2346	**Sheet Music** Reference & Price Guide, 2nd Ed., Pafik & Guiheen	$18.95
4654	**Victorian Trading Cards,** Historical Reference & Value Guide, Cheadle	$19.95

GLASSWARE

1006	**Cambridge Glass** Reprint 1930–1934	$14.95
1007	**Cambridge Glass** Reprint 1949–1953	$14.95
4561	Collectible **Drinking Glasses,** Chase & Kelly	$17.95
4642	Collectible **Glass Shoes,** Wheatley	$19.95
4553	Coll. **Glassware** from the 40's, 50's & 60's, 3rd Ed., Florence	$19.95
2352	Collector's Encyclopedia of **Akro Agate Glassware,** Florence	$14.95
1810	Collector's Encyclopedia of **American Art Glass,** Shuman	$29.95
3312	Collector's Encyclopedia of **Children's Dishes,** Whitmyer	$19.95
4552	Collector's Encyclopedia of **Depression Glass,** 12th Ed., Florence	$19.95
1664	Collector's Encyclopedia of **Heisey Glass,** 1925–1938, Bredehoft	$24.95
3905	Collector's Encyclopedia of **Milk Glass,** Newbound	$24.95
1523	Colors In **Cambridge Glass,** National Cambridge Society	$19.95
4564	**Crackle Glass,** Weitman	$19.95
2275	**Czechoslovakian Glass** and Collectibles, Barta/Rose	$16.95
4714	**Czechoslovakian Glass** and Collectibles, Book II, Barta/Rose	$16.95
4716	**Elegant Glassware** of the Depression Era, 7th Ed., Florence	$19.95
1380	Encyclopedia of **Pattern Glass,** McClain	$12.95
3981	Ever's Standard **Cut Glass** Value Guide	$12.95
4659	**Fenton** Art Glass, 1907–1939, Whitmyer	$24.95
3725	**Fostoria,** Pressed, Blown & Hand Molded Shapes, Kerr	$24.95
3883	**Fostoria Stemware,** The Crystal for America, Long & Seate	$24.95
3318	**Glass Animals** of the Depression Era, Garmon & Spencer	$19.95
4644	**Imperial Carnival Glass,** Burns	$18.95

COLLECTOR BOOKS
Informing Today's Collector

3886	**Kitchen Glassware** of the Depression Years, 5th Ed., Florence	$19.95
2394	**Oil Lamps II**, Glass Kerosene Lamps, Thuro	$24.95
4725	Pocket Guide to **Depression Glass**, 10th Ed., Florence	$9.95
4634	Standard Encyclopedia of **Carnival Glass**, 5th Ed., Edwards	$24.95
4635	Standard **Carnival Glass** Price Guide, 10th Ed.	$9.95
3974	Standard Encylopedia of **Opalescent Glass**, Edwards	$19.95
4731	**Stemware Identification**, Featuring Cordials with Values, Florence	$24.95
3326	**Very Rare Glassware** of the Depression Years, 3rd Series, Florence	$24.95
3909	**Very Rare Glassware** of the Depression Years, 4th Series, Florence	$24.95
4732	**Very Rare Glassware** of the Depression Years, 5th Series, Florence	$24.95
4656	**Westmoreland Glass**, Wilson	$24.95
2224	World of **Salt Shakers**, 2nd Ed., Lechner	$24.95

POTTERY

4630	**American Limoges**, Limoges	$24.95
1312	**Blue & White Stoneware**, McNerney	$9.95
1958	So. Potteries **Blue Ridge Dinnerware**, 3rd Ed., Newbound	$14.95
1959	**Blue Willow**, 2nd Ed., Gaston	$14.95
3816	Collectible **Vernon Kilns**, Nelson	$24.95
3311	Collecting **Yellow Ware** – Id. & Value Guide, McAllister	$16.95
1373	Collector's Encyclopedia of **American Dinnerware**, Cunningham	$24.95
3815	Collector's Encyclopedia of **Blue Ridge Dinnerware**, Newbound	$19.95
4658	Collector's Encyclopedia of **Brush-McCoy Pottery**, Huxford	$24.95
2272	Collector's Encyclopedia of **California Pottery**, Chipman	$24.95
3811	Collector's Encyclopedia of **Colorado Pottery**, Carlton	$24.95
2133	Collector's Encyclopedia of **Cookie Jars**, Roerig	$24.95
3723	Collector's Encyclopedia of **Cookie Jars**, Volume II, Roerig	$24.95
3429	Collector's Encyclopedia of **Cowan Pottery**, Saloff	$24.95
4638	Collector's Encyclopedia of **Dakota Potteries**, Dommel	$24.95
2209	Collector's Encyclopedia of **Fiesta**, 7th Ed., Huxford	$19.95
4718	Collector's Encyclopedia of **Figural Planters & Vases**, Newbound	$19.95
3961	Collector's Encyclopedia of **Early Noritake**, Alden	$24.95
1439	Collector's Encyclopedia of **Flow Blue China**, Gaston	$19.95
3812	Collector's Encyclopedia of **Flow Blue China**, 2nd Ed., Gaston	$24.95
3813	Collector's Encyclopedia of **Hall China**, 2nd Ed., Whitmyer	$24.95
3431	Collector's Encyclopedia of **Homer Laughlin China**, Jasper	$24.95
1276	Collector's Encyclopedia of **Hull Pottery**, Roberts	$19.95
4573	Collector's Encyclopedia of **Knowles, Taylor & Knowles**, Gaston	$24.95
3962	Collector's Encyclopedia of **Lefton China**, DeLozier	$19.95
2210	Collector's Encyclopedia of **Limoges Porcelain**, 2nd Ed., Gaston	$24.95
2334	Collector's Encyclopedia of **Majolica Pottery**, Katz-Marks	$19.95
1358	Collector's Encyclopedia of **McCoy Pottery**, Huxford	$19.95
3963	Collector's Encyclopedia of **Metlox Potteries**, Gibbs Jr.	$24.95
3313	Collector's Encyclopedia of **Niloak**, Gifford	$19.95
3837	Collector's Encyclopedia of **Nippon Porcelain I**, Van Patten	$24.95
2089	Collector's Ency. of **Nippon Porcelain**, 2nd Series, Van Patten	$24.95
1665	Collector's Ency. of **Nippon Porcelain**, 3rd Series, Van Patten	$24.95
3836	**Nippon Porcelain** Price Guide, Van Patten	$9.95
1447	Collector's Encyclopedia of **Noritake**, Van Patten	$19.95
3432	Collector's Encyclopedia of **Noritake**, Van Patten	$24.95
1037	Collector's Encyclopedia of **Occupied Japan**, Vol. I, Florence	$14.95
1038	Collector's Encyclopedia of **Occupied Japan**, Vol. II, Florence	$14.95
2088	Collector's Encyclopedia of **Occupied Japan**, Vol. III, Florence	$14.95
2019	Collector's Encyclopedia of **Occupied Japan**, Vol. IV, Florence	$14.95
2335	Collector's Encyclopedia of **Occupied Japan**, Vol. V, Florence	$14.95
3964	Collector's Encyclopedia of **Pickard China**, Reed	$24.95
1311	Collector's Encyclopedia of **R.S. Prussia**, 1st Series, Gaston	$24.95
1715	Collector's Encyclopedia of **R.S. Prussia**, 2nd Series, Gaston	$24.95
3726	Collector's Encyclopedia of **R.S. Prussia**, 3rd Series, Gaston	$24.95
3877	Collector's Encyclopedia of **R.S. Prussia**, 4th Series, Gaston	$24.95
1034	Collector's Encyclopedia of **Roseville Pottery**, Huxford	$19.95
1035	Collector's Encyclopedia of **Roseville Pottery**, 2nd Ed., Huxford	$19.95
3357	**Roseville** Price Guide No. 10	$9.95
3965	Collector's Encyclopedia of **Sascha Brastoff**, Conti, Bethany & Seay	$24.95
3314	Collector's Encyclopedia of **Van Briggle** Art Pottery, Sasicki	$24.95
4563	Collector's Encyclopedia of **Wall Pockets**, Newbound	$19.95
2111	Collector's Encyclopedia of **Weller Pottery**, Huxford	$29.95
3452	Coll. Guide to **Country Stoneware & Pottery**, Raycraft	$11.95
2077	Coll. Guide to **Country Stoneware & Pottery**, 2nd Series, Raycraft	$14.95
3434	Coll. Guide to **Hull Pottery**, The Dinnerware Line, Gick-Burke	$16.95

3876	Collector's Guide to **Lu-Ray Pastels**, Meehan	$18.95
3814	Collector's Guide to **Made in Japan** Ceramics, White	$18.95
4646	Collector's Guide to **Made in Japan** Ceramics, Book II, White	$18.95
4565	Collector's Guide to **Rockingham**, The Enduring Ware, Brewer	$14.95
2339	Collector's Guide to **Shawnee Pottery**, Vanderbilt	$19.95
1425	**Cookie Jars**, Westfall	$9.95
3440	**Cookie Jars**, Book II, Westfall	$19.95
3435	Debolt's Dictionary of **American Pottery Marks**	$17.95
2379	Lehner's Ency. of **U.S. Marks** on Pottery, Porcelain & China	$24.95
4722	**McCoy Pottery**, Collector's Reference & Value Guide, Hanson/Nissen	$19.95
3825	**Puritan Pottery**, Morris	$24.95
4726	**Red Wing Art Pottery**, 1920s–1960s, Dollen	$19.95
1670	**Red Wing Collectibles**, DePasquale	$9.95
1440	**Red Wing Stoneware**, DePasquale	$9.95
3738	**Shawnee Pottery**, Mangus	$24.95
4629	Turn of the Century **American Dinnerware**, 1880s–1920s, Jasper	$24.95
4572	**Wall Pockets** of the Past, Perkins	$17.95
3327	**Watt Pottery** – Identification & Value Guide, Morris	$19.95

OTHER COLLECTIBLES

4704	Antique & Collectible **Buttons**, Wisniewski	$19.95
2269	Antique **Brass & Copper** Collectibles, Gaston	$16.95
1880	Antique **Iron**, McNerney	$9.95
3872	Antique **Tins**, Dodge	$24.95
1714	**Black** Collectibles, Gibbs	$19.95
1128	**Bottle** Pricing Guide, 3rd Ed., Cleveland	$7.95
4636	**Celluloid Collectibles**, Dunn	$14.95
3959	**Cereal Box** Bonanza, The 1950's, Bruce	$19.95
3718	Collectible **Aluminum**, Grist	$16.95
3445	Collectible **Cats**, An Identification & Value Guide, Fyke	$18.95
4560	Collectible **Cats**, An Identification & Value Guide, Book II, Fyke	$19.95
1634	Collector's Ency. of Figural & Novelty **Salt & Pepper Shakers**, Davern	$19.95
2020	Collector's Ency. of Figural & Novelty **Salt & Pepper Shakers**, Vol. II, Davern	$19.95
2018	Collector's Encyclopedia of **Granite Ware**, Greguire	$24.95
3430	Collector's Encyclopedia of **Granite Ware**, Book II, Greguire	$24.95
4705	Collector's Guide to **Antique Radios**, 4th Ed., Bunis	$18.95
1916	Collector's Guide to **Art Deco**, Gaston	$14.95
3880	Collector's Guide to **Cigarette Lighters**, Flanagan	$17.95
4637	Collector's Guide to **Cigarette Lighters**, Book II, Flanagan	$17.95
1537	Collector's Guide to **Country Baskets**, Raycraft	$9.95
3966	Collector's Guide to **Inkwells**, Identification & Values, Badders	$18.95
3881	Collector's Guide to **Novelty Radios**, Bunis/Breed	$18.95
4652	Collector's Guide to **Transistor Radios**, 2nd Ed., Bunis	$16.95
4653	Collector's Guide to **TV Memorabilia**, 1960s–1970s, Davis/Morgan	$24.95
2276	**Decoys**, Kangas	$24.95
1629	**Doorstops**, Identification & Values, Bertoia	$9.95
4567	Figural **Napkin Rings**, Gottschalk & Whitson	$18.95
3968	**Fishing Lure** Collectibles, Murphy/Edmisten	$24.95
3817	**Flea Market Trader**, 10th Ed., Huxford	$12.95
3976	Foremost Guide to **Uncle Sam** Collectibles, Czulewicz	$24.95
4641	**Garage Sale & Flea Market Annual**, 4th Ed.	$19.95
3819	**General Store Collectibles**, Wilson	$24.95
4643	**Great American West** Collectibles, Wilson	$24.95
2215	Goldstein's **Coca-Cola** Collectibles	$16.95
3884	Huxford's Collectible **Advertising**, 2nd Ed.	$24.95
2216	**Kitchen Antiques**, 1790–1940, McNerney	$14.95
3321	Ornamental & Figural **Nutcrackers**, Rittenhouse	$16.95
2026	**Railroad** Collectibles, 4th Ed., Baker	$14.95
1632	**Salt & Pepper Shakers**, Guarnaccia	$9.95
1888	**Salt & Pepper Shakers** II, Identification & Value Guide, Book II, Guarnaccia	$14.95
2220	**Salt & Pepper Shakers** III, Guarnaccia	$14.95
3443	**Salt & Pepper Shakers** IV, Guarnaccia	$18.95
4555	**Schroeder's Antiques Price Guide**, 14th Ed., Huxford	$12.95
2096	**Silverplated Flatware**, Revised 4th Edition, Hagan	$14.95
1922	Standard **Old Bottle** Price Guide, Sellari	$14.95
4708	**Summers' Guide to Coca-Cola**	$19.95
3892	**Toy & Miniature Sewing Machines**, Thomas	$18.95
3828	Value Guide to **Advertising Memorabilia**, Summers	$18.95
3977	Value Guide to **Gas Station** Memorabilia, Summers & Priddy	$24.95
3444	**Wanted to Buy**, 5th Edition	$9.95

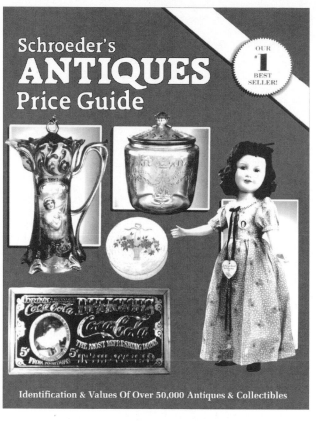